940.5318 WAL
Letters from the lost :
a memoir of discovery /
Waldstein Wilkes
897364

2011

MI 12/12
KD AUG 15
VE JUN 2016

Letters from the Lost

OUR LIVES: DIARY, MEMOIR, AND LETTERS
Series Editor: Janice Dickin

OUR LIVES aims at both student and general readership.
Today's students, living in a world of blogs, understand that there is much to be learned from the everyday lives of everyday people. *Our Lives* seeks to make available previously unheard voices from the past and present. Social history in general contests the construction of history as the story of elites and the act of making available the lives of everyday people, as seen by themselves, subverts even further the contentions of social historiography. At the same time, *Our Lives* aims to make available books that are good reads. General readers are guaranteed quality, provided with introductions that they can use to contextualize material and are given a glimpse of other works they might want to look at. It is not usual for university presses to provide this type of primary material. Athabasca University considers provision of this sort of material as important to its role as Canada's Open University.

SERIES TITLES

A Very Capable Life: The Autobiography of Zarah Petri
by John Leigh Walters

Letters from the Lost: A Memoir of Discovery
by Helen Waldstein Wilkes

Letters from the Lost

A Memoir of Discovery

HELEN WALDSTEIN WILKES

AU PRESS

© 2010 Helen Waldstein Wilkes
Fifth printing 2011

Published by AU Press, Athabasca University
1200, 10011 – 109 Street
Edmonton, AB T5J 3S8

Library and Archives Canada Cataloguing in Publication

Waldstein Wilkes, Helen, 1936-
    Letters from the lost : a memoir of discovery / Helen
Waldstein Wilkes.

(Our lives: diary, memoir, and letters, 1921-6653)
Includes bibliographical references.
Also available in electronic format (978-1-897425-54-1).
ISBN 978-1-897425-53-4

    1. Waldstein Wilkes, Helen, 1936-. 2. Waldstein
Wilkes, Helen, 1936- --Family. 3. Jews--Czech
Republic--Prague--Biography. 4. Holocaust, Jewish
(1939-1945)--Czech Republic--Personal narratives.
5. Jews--Czech Republic--Prague--Correspondence.
6. Jews--Canada--Biography. I. Title. II. Series: Our
lives: diary, memoir, and letters series (Edmonton, Alta.).

DS135.C97W35 2010   940.53'1809224371   C2009-906247-X

Cover design by Sergiy Kozakov.
Book design by Laura Brady.
Printed and bound in Canada by Marquis Book Printing.
All images unless otherwise credited are courtesy of Helen Waldstein Wilkes.

This project was funded in part by the
Alberta Foundation for the Arts.

This publication is licensed under a Creative Commons License, Attribution-Noncommer-
cial-No Derivative Works 2.5 Canada, see www.creativecommons.org. The text may be
reproduced for non-commercial purposes, provided that credit is given to the original
author.

Please contact AU Press, Athabasca University at aupress@athabascau.ca for permission
beyond the usage outlined in the Creative Commons license.

A volume in the *Our Lives: Diary, Memoir, and Letters* series:
ISSN 1921-6653 (Print)
ISSN 1921-6661 (Online)

Contents

Foreword

*M*OVING, SEARING, WRENCHING, INSPIRING—the adjectives that can apply to many memoirs of the Holocaust and the feelings they evoke certainly apply as well to *Letters from the Lost*. Each personal odyssey is individual, though, and this narrative is distinguished by the individuality of Helen Waldstein Wilkes' story and the insightful clarity with which she tells it. As she searches for her own history and for the family members who perished after she and her parents escaped Nazi-occupied Czechoslovakia, Wilkes' difficult return to that past illuminates the terrain of suppressed memory, as well as its costs. "Memories of our history hold us together as individuals," Wilkes writes, "as families and as communities. When we forget who we have been, we remain unaware of who we are." (p. vii) For some four decades Wilkes guarded but did not open the box of letters that held fragments and maps of her history. Not until she was past sixty was she ready to begin that journey of recovery. This memoir is the legacy of her search.

I read these pages as a historian, intrigued by the process of recovering lost memories and historical erasures, and as a Jew, familiar, in much-diluted form, with the process of self-protective selective forgetting. I was born shortly after World War II, nine months after my Dad was mustered out of the U.S. Army. As a child I learned that the Holocaust had happened, but also, my parents insisted, that it had not really touched our family. This childhood fiction was not an uncommon story for Jewish children born in post-war North America. Even for families like my own, who lost no immediate kin, it was rarely true. My father's family had emigrated to Canada and the United States by 1913; my mother's grandparents arrived even earlier. My great-grandfather fled the czar's army, not Hitler's. But ours was a large, extended family. Numerous cousins remained in Europe, and we may never know how many of them perished. Over three decades after the War ended, my Dad discovered a first cousin he had never known existed, living in Jerusalem, who had somehow survived, hiding in Prague throughout the war.

My story is not unusual. Nor is my parents' denial, or perhaps their attempt to shelter their children from a too-painful and too-recent past. The post-war years have, for the survivors, brought the gradual process of remembering, of painful reconstruction, and the inevitable questions about what might have been. This work of memory has generated a dense and varied literature of Holocaust memoirs: by survivors[I], by child survivors[II], by the children of survivors.[III] And there is a growing literature of reclamation, of the search for lost family members rarely mentioned, and then cryptically, or in whispers, those who might have been forgotten in time, to protect the next generations from painful memories. Daniel Mendelsohn opened *The Lost: A Search for Six of Six Million* with his childhood experience walking into rooms only to watch elderly relatives burst into tears at the very sight of him, as they remembered the great-uncle he resembled. When they spoke of the family they had lost, they switched to Yiddish, to protect the children.[IV]

Each person's journey into these suppressed pasts has been at once shared and intensely personal, as individual as each life taken, each story lost. *Letters from the Lost* impressively combines honest self-revelation, moral clarity, and compassion. It is unusual among survivors' memoirs because Wilkes' journey is almost without historical parallel. Born in

Sudetenland, that portion of Czechoslovakia the Allies ceded to Hitler in April 1938, her family was, according to her father, the last to receive an exit visa that enabled them to leave just days after German troops entered Prague. Even more remarkably, they were among the very few Jews who gained entry to Canada. "Someone was asleep at the switch," Wilkes surmises, when her aunt and uncle entered Canada through a Canadian Pacific Railway program to recruit farmers. Someone was asleep again when her aunt sponsored Edmund and Gretl Waldstein and little Helen. No one, apparently, realized that they were Jews.

Both the United States and Canada refused entry to most Jews in the immediate pre-war years. Both had admitted Jews through the early twentieth century. Canada, unlike the United States, had permitted Jewish agricultural colonies on the prairies. But neither welcomed Jewish immigrants during the 1930s. The United States severely restricted European immigration in 1924, and during the 1930s resisted appeals on behalf of European Jews. Canada separated Jews as a class from others who shared the same citizenship and then quietly restricted Jewish immigration.[V] Britain, too, closed its doors, and prevented Jewish immigration to Palestine as well.[VI] Although Germany allowed Jews to leave until 1941, few escaped the Holocaust not because they could not leave but because no country would take them. Canadian immigration policy was more generous after the War, and thus most Canadian Holocaust memoirs have been written by survivors who emigrated after years in hiding or in concentration camps.[VII]

Letters from the Lost differs from most narratives of the search for lost relatives because Helen Waldstein Wilkes was one of very few children to escape with her parents, and one of even fewer to enter Canada before the formal onset of the War. Her narrative speaks not only to the Holocaust, but also to her difficult transition to Canada as an immigrant Jewish child. The search for her roots, for those who were murdered and the few who survived, also helped unlock how her parents' experiences, and the memories they had hidden or forgotten, affected her own ability to connect— with people, with Canada, with Judaism. Although most children of survivors carried their parents' pasts in some ways, each response was particular. Some survivors adamantly held to Orthodox Judaism; others had not been particularly observant before the War and remained so afterward; some abandoned most religious practice in response to a faith that had not prevented the brutality they endured. Their children, like most, grappled in their own ways with Jewish and national identities.

The first steps toward healing from trauma and violence come with breaking silence. I had a colleague in the early 1980s, one of the first children born to Holocaust survivors, who told me how empowering it was for him to meet with other second-generation survivors, to find people who shared what he had thought were his own personal quirks. "Like what?" I asked him. "Well," he replied, "we are the only people I know who have all discussed with our spouses which city we will try to meet in if there is another Holocaust." Like my colleague, Wilkes planned ways to protect her children should another Holocaust separate them. Her personal journey, too, brought her to other second-generation survivors, and to new engagement with Judaism.[VIII]

Many who read this book will have no personal experience of the Holocaust. We all inherit its history, its unprobed silences. Breaking silence and recovering memory are essential steps for personal healing and for historical truth and reconciliation. The memoirs of Holocaust survivors record wrenching tales of loss and endurance. Because they mostly center on the concentration camps or years of hiding, they can seem far removed from Canada or any of the Allied nations that liberated the survivors. The Waldsteins' story, though, records the complex legacy of the nation that at once provided haven for them but which erected the immigration restrictions that kept them from saving the rest of their family.

Nations, like individuals, erase those memories too painful to confront. For Canada, the missing bits of memory are like missing tiles in a multicultural mosaic, the jagged empty spaces of "what might have been" if any of the countless lost had been welcomed. "When we forget who we have been, we remain unaware of who we are"—and of who we might yet become. Helen Waldstein Wilkes, to her enormous credit, embraces the complexity of a Canada that has done harm, but which promises "the best of a world still to be brought fully to fruition." (p. 234) To claim that complex promise, nations—like individuals who have survived deep trauma—require the courage to face their pasts. This book is one beginning.

Elizabeth Jameson
Calgary, December 2009

---

[1] For Canadian survivors' memoirs, see for instance Olga Barsony-Verrall, *Missing Pieces: My Life as a Child Survivor of the Holocaust* (Calgary: University of Calgary Press, 2007); Tommy Dick, *Getting Out Alive: A Memoir* (Toronto: Azrieli Foundation, 2007); John Freund, *Spring's End: A Memoir* (Toronto: Azrieli Foundation, 2007); Rachel Shtibel, *The Violin* (Toronto: Azrieli Foundation, 2007); Vera Kovesi, *Terror and Survival: A Family History* (Montreal: Concordia University Chair in Canadian Jewish Studies and The Montreal Institute for Genocide and Human Rights Studies, 2005); Jack Weiss, *Memories, Dreams, Nightmares: Memoirs of a Holocaust Survivor* (Calgary: University of Calgary Press, 2005); Leslie Vertes, *Can You Stop the Wind?: An Autobiography* (Montreal: Concordia Chair in Canadian Jewish Studies and The Montreal Institute for Genocide and Human Rights Studies, 2001); Helen Rodak-Izso, *The Last Chance to Remember* (Montreal: Concordia University Chair in Canadian Jewish History and The Montreal Institute for Genocide and Human Rights Studies, 2001); Paula Draper and Richard Menkis (Eds.), *New Perspectives on Canada, the Holocaust and Survivors: Nouvelles Perspectives sur le Canada, la Shoah et ses Survivants* (Montreal: Association for Canadian Jewish Studies, 2000); Perec Zylberberg, *This I Remember* (Montreal: Concordia University Chair in Canadian Jewish Studies and The Montreal Institute for Genocide and Human Rights Studies, 2000); Sam Smilovic, *Buchenwald 56466* (Montreal: Concordia University Chair in Canadian Jewish Studies and The Montreal Institute for Genocide and Human Rights Studies, 2000); David Jacobs, *Remember Your Heritage* (Montreal: Concordia University Chair in Canadian Jewish Studies and The Montreal Institute for Genocide and Human Rights Studies, 2000); Michel Melinicki, *Bialystok to Birkenau: The Holocaust Journey of Michel Mielnicki as Told to John Munro with Introduction by Sir Martin Gilbert* (Vancouver: Ronsdale Press, 2000); Rose Ickovits Weiss Svarts, *Forces of Darkness: Personal Diary of Rose Ickovits Weiss Svarts from 1938 to 1946* (Montreal: Concordia University Chair in Canadian Jewish Studies and The Montreal Institute for Genocide and Human Rights Studies, 2000); *Memoirs of Holocaust Survivors in Canada* (Montreal: Concordia University Chair in Canadian Jewish Studies and The Montreal Institute for Genocide and Human Rights Studies, 1999); Lisa Appignanesi, *Losing the Dead* (Toronto:

McArthur, 1999); Joil Alpern, *No One Awaiting Me: Two Brothers Defy Death during the Holocaust in Romania* (Calgary: University of Calgary Press, 2001). These represent a small sample of Canadian Holocaust survivors' memoirs, and much smaller sample of survivors' memoirs from all countries. For more on the genre, see Norman Ravvin, *A House of Words: Jewish Writing, Identity, and Memory* (Toronto: McGill-Queens University Press, 1997).

II See Andrew Shlomo, *Childhood in Times of War* (Montreal: Concordia University Chair in Canadian Jewish Studies and The Montreal Institute for Genocide and Holocaust Studies, 2001); Marian Finkielman, *Out of the Ghetto: A Jewish Orphan's Struggle for Survival* (Montreal: Concordia University Chair in Canadian Jewish Studies and The Montreal Institute for Genocide and Holocaust Studies, 2000).

III See for instance Bernice Eisenstein, *I Was a Child of Holocaust Survivors* (Toronto: McClelland and Stewart, 2006); Paula S. Fass, *Inheriting the Holocaust: A Second-Generation Memoir* (New Brunswick, NJ: Rutgers University Press, 2009).

IV Daniel Mendelsohn, *The Lost: A Search for Six of Six Million* (New York: Harper-Collins, 2006), 3–5.

V See Irving Abella and Harold Troper, *None is Too Many: Canada and the Jews of Europe, 1933–1948* (Toronto: Lester and Orpen Dennys, 1986); David Rome, *Clouds in the Thirties: On Antisemitism in Canada, 1929–1939: A Chapter on Canadian Jewish History, 13 vol.* (Montreal: National Archives, Canadian Jewish Congress, 1977–1981); Janine Stingel, *Social Discredit: Anti-Semitism, Social Credit and the Jewish Response* (Montreal: McGill-Queens University Press, 2000).

VI Unlike the United States and Canada, Britian did make room for 7,500 Jewish children from 1938 to 1940.

VII See Abella and Troper, *None Is Too Many*; Irving Abella, *A Coat of Many Colours: Two Centuries of Jewish Life in Canada* (Toronto: Lester and Orpen Dennys, 1990).

VIII The congregation that Helen Wilkes mentions in her text, Congregation Or Shalom in Vancouver, is affiliated with Jewish Renewal, a non-denominational movement that has provided a point of reconnection for many Jews of the post-war generations. See http://www.aleph.org and http://www.orshalom.ca.

Preface

Hᴉꜱᴛᴏʀʏ ɪꜱ ʙᴏᴛʜ ᴘᴏᴛᴇɴᴛ ᴀɴᴅ ᴘᴇʀꜱᴏɴᴀʟ. Memories of our history hold us together as individuals, as families and as communities. When we forget who we have been, we remain unaware of who we are.

My memory had huge gaps. I had erased much from my consciousness, especially my early years. Forgetting is rarely intentional, but the avoidance of pain is a basic tool of human survival.

My parents had also done a lot of forgetting. It was their way of coping. The details of their trauma had always been a shadowy presence in my life. As I celebrated my 60th birthday, I knew it was time to unravel the mysteries in order to be present in my own life.

We underestimate the storehouse of memory. It holds far more than we imagine, and reading the letters brought to life people I had known and lost. These absent family and friends occupy my thoughts. Occasionally, I have paraphrased or shortened their letters, but otherwise, they are reproduced, translated by me, as they were written, by very real people.

With the exception of one family, I have used the real names of those whose lives intersected with mine. These people matter greatly to me, and I hope they will see themselves reflected in a positive light with all the high regard in which I hold them. If my memory of events has allowed some details to fall away and others to stand in sharp relief, I beg forgiveness for any unintentional slights or oversights.

I have attempted to share with the reader my own journey into a past of which I knew more than many, yet understood very little. Because we are not and cannot be separate from our history, to learn from it is our only chance of moving beyond it.

I invite you to share in my journey and, in so doing, perhaps to cast light upon your own shadows, explore your own history, and come home to yourself.

Acknowledgements

To THANK ALL WHO HELPED with this project is a daunting task. I begin with Mary Ungerleider who saw potential in the letters and applied her skill as a film director to shaping the manuscript. Her unflagging support encouraged me to bring this project to fruition. Next, I owe thanks to Margaret Berger who deciphered the seemingly illegible and solved the thorniest of translation problems. To Allison Sullings who reviewed the manuscript through the discriminating lens of a lover of English literature, I extend my gratitude.

I am indebted to Athabasca University Press and especially to Senior Editor Erna Dominey who saw merit in the letters and made them accessible to a broad range of readers. I am indebted also to Adele Ritch for doing the structural editing with consummate skill and intelligence.

For their invaluable suggestions and unhesitating support, I sincerely thank Professor Christopher Friedrichs, Kit Krieger, Dodie Katzenstein, and Herbert Langshur. There are many others whose ideas have strengthened my work and whose help has been invaluable.

Finally, to family and friends whose steadfast support has buoyed me in moments of self-doubt, my gratitude is boundless.

Central Europe, March 15, 1939

···· From Strobnitz to Antwerp:
Edi, Gretl, and Helen cross
Nazi Germany in search of safety

Family Tree

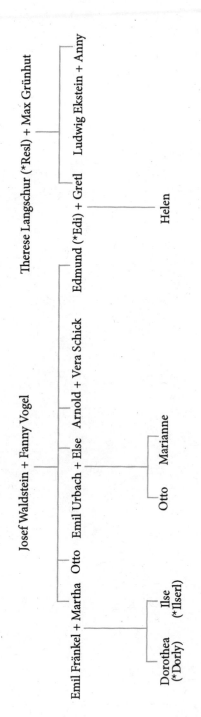

Josef Waldstein + Fanny Vogel

Therese Langschur (*Resl) + Max Grünhut

Emil Fränkel + Martha   Otto   Emil Urbach + Else   Arnold + Vera Schick   Edmund (*Edi) + Gretl   Ludwig Ekstein + Anny

Dorothea
(*Dorly)

Ilse
(*Ilserl)

Otto   Marianne

Helen

* nickname

"I cannot remember a time before the box.
My father's box. ... The plain cardboard bottom
has a cheerful red lid."

Opening the Box

I CANNOT REMEMBER A TIME before the box. My father's box. I think it came from Eaton's Department Store. The plain cardboard bottom has a cheerful red lid. Across its rectangular surface, glide pairs of skaters, children on toboggans, and a father pulling a sled with a Christmas tree. Scattered among the smiling people in bright scarves and mittens are little sprigs of holly, each with its own cluster of red berries.

Why did my father choose this particular box with its playful scenes to house the letters? Did the box represent for him the Canadian ideal of a jingle-bell family dashing through the snow and laughing all the way? Perhaps it reminded him of a childhood happiness forever left behind.

I was barely twenty-two in 1959 when he died. I had just left home for the first time to follow my dreams. For months, I had been immersed in travel, in books, in studies at the Sorbonne. One night in Paris, the telegram arrived. *Father ill. Return immediately.* I did, the next day, but it was too late.

Despite the shock of his death, my one thought was to rescue the box. I do not know what my mother did with my father's other possessions. Perhaps she buried him in his one good suit and gave his shirts to a needy neighbour. Perhaps she threw away his small collection of German books, thinking no one would ever read them. She did save the box.

My mother also saved the album. Real memories sometimes fade, but photos have a life of their own. The photo album contains pictures of people in a world that I do not remember. When I was a child, my mother would place the album on a clean tablecloth and leaf through the pages. Sometimes she seemed lost in a world of her own. At other times, speaking in that comfortable German dialect that was then our only language, she would identify the faces and tell me stories.

This is your father's brother Arnold and his wife Vera on their wedding day. Such a beautiful woman! And so intelligent, just like your uncle Arnold. He was an engineer, but she studied medicine. Imagine how hard it was for a woman in those days to become a doctor!

This is Aunt Martha, your father's younger sister. Look at those dark curls. Such a beauty! She was still so young when she married Emil Fränkel. And this is their daughter, your cousin Ilserl. You two spent hours playing together. Too bad that we have no pictures of her baby sister Dorly. She was born just before we left Europe.

This is your father's older sister Else. Your cousin Ilserl was named "Ilse" to honour Else who had been like a second mother to Martha. Here is Else on her wedding day. She married Emil Urbach, a renowned doctor whom people from all over Europe came to consult. Until the Nazis came. Here are the Urbach children, Marianne and Otto. They were a bit older, but they loved to play with you.

As an only child on an isolated farm, I was so lonely that I drank up these words. Living on a farm meant no nearby playmates and my parents had neither a car nor a telephone to bridge the distance. As soon as I turned five, I was finally allowed to go to school to learn my first English words. Until then, the photo album was the thread that linked me to others.

Sometimes even now, I listen enviously as my friends make plans for the holidays. *"What's important is that the whole family be together,"* they explain. *"Last year we were twenty-four,"* says one. *"My son is bringing his new girlfriend so we'll be thirty-two at the table,"* says another. *"Do you seat all the cousins together or do you separate them into age groups?"* asks a third.

Wedding, Vera Schick and Arnold Waldstein

Martha Waldstein

Brothers, sisters, aunts, uncles, cousins, grandparents. I often wondered what it would be like to know your relatives. My known family was always three. For a while, it was five. That was on the farm when my mother's only sister, Anny, and her husband Ludwig lived with us.

Anny and Ludwig never had children. It was rumoured that she couldn't because she had worked as an X-ray technician in the early days when the effects of X-ray were not fully understood. I used to urge my parents to have another child. Their response never varied: *"At first we were too scared. You were still a baby when we fled and became strangers in a strange land. We had no money, no skills, and no English. We were afraid. Now it's too late."*

Wedding, Else Waldstein and Emil Urbach

Why were we so few? Where were all those relatives in the album? My father was one of five children. Four of the siblings married. They danced at each other's weddings, rejoiced in each other's triumphs, and lent support when needed. Three of the siblings—Else, Martha, and my father—had children of their own, and had settled near the family home so that their own parents, Fanny and Josef, could enjoy the laughter of grandchildren.

There are no portraits of my father's parents. I know my grandmother Fanny only as a black and white snapshot. She is an elderly woman in a lawn chair who gazes fondly at a young child playing in the garden, my cousin Ilse. The only photo of my grandfather Josef shows him in uniform.

It is World War I and he is serving in the army with all three of his sons, Arnold, Otto, and Edmund.

I often hear stories about the strong impact of grandparents. A grandparent who loved nature and revealed its secrets to a wide-eyed youngster. A grandfather who taught a little boy to love tools and take pride in the work of his hands. A grandmother who provided unconditional love along with the smell of fresh baking.

What is it like to have a grandparent? I do not remember having one. The words *grandmother* and *grandfather* have no reality for me beyond the pictures in the album. The stiff figure in a three-piece suit is my mother's father Max. He has bushy eyebrows and a waxed handlebar moustache above unsmiling lips. The rather plain woman wearing a small, heart-shaped gold locket is my grandmother Resl.

Still, I collected stories about my grandparents as carefully as I collected thin bits of silver paper from cigarette packages to bring to school for the war effort. No teacher ever explained to me how the cigarette paper would help "our boys overseas." I used to imagine huge stacks of silver paper being hammered together to make wings for airplanes.

So much was never spelled out. At some level, even as a child, I knew the photo album and the letters that my father kept in the cheerful red box were connected. Whenever a letter came, the postman would leave it in the tin box on a wooden post where our long driveway intersected with the highway. The letters were always written on blue airmail paper. Each letter meant that a firm hand on my backside would push me out the door, and that an adult voice would tell me to go and play.

In solitude, I would wander through the overgrown garden behind the henhouse, wondering about secrets discussed behind closed doors. If it had rained recently, I would float sticks in puddles in the driveway that snaked past the house. I would give each stick a push, pretending it was a ship on the ocean. Some ships reached shore safely, others did not.

The letters kept coming, even after the war began. Later, I learned that my father's cousin in New York had forwarded them. When the Japanese attack on Pearl Harbour propelled the Americans into the war, the letters stopped. By war's end, I was almost nine, old enough to remember the

Josef Waldstein and his sons in their World War I uniforms
From left to right: Arnold, Edi, Otto, Josef

impatience with which my parents waited for news.

When that longed-for letter arrived, my banishment from the house was lengthy. Did I hear, or do I only imagine I heard a wail whose memory still turns my guts to water?

Eventually my parents emerged and took up their chores, for cows must be fed and milked and mucked out twice daily no matter what. I watched my parents as if they were fish in a tank. Their shapes were somehow distorted, and an eerie silence encased them in a world I could not reach.

In a way, that silence was never broken. Although my parents gradually resumed their routine tasks, something was clearly different. I could not give it a name, but that letter marked a turning point in what could be spoken. I never asked about its contents, and I was never told.

———

I AM NOT SURE WHEN I FIRST knew that my father kept all the letters, and that he had saved them in the red box. I am not even sure when I made the connection between the letters and his family. It was probably during the spring of 1946, when I was in Grade 6 and we moved to the city.

As soon as the war was over, my parents were free to leave the farm. Having proudly repaid what they saw as their debt to Canada, they were eager for some semblance of the circle of friends that had enriched their life in Europe. For them, moving to the city was a return to civilization, and they sold the farm to the first buyer who came their way. With the proceeds, they bought an old house in Hamilton. It meant living in a working class neighbourhood and sharing the house with another family in order to make mortgage payments, but anything was better than milking cows, slaughtering chickens, and the isolation of farm life.

My father went to work as a shipper in a warehouse, manually unloading heavy boxes and, a few days later, reloading them onto different trucks. My mother found employment as a pieceworker in a garment factory. I saw this as my father's greatest source of anguish. In those post-war years, he never ceased to bemoan the fact that his wife had to work. Sometimes he spoke longingly of wanting to buy a little corner grocery store, a Mom and

Pop operation that would let them get an economic toehold, but this never happened.

Were they afraid to risk what little they had? Would their small nest egg not have stretched to even the most rundown of stores? For whatever reason, my parents never made the move to independence. To the very end, they remained under the thumb of bosses who knew that those with limited English and no special skills had little choice about pay or working conditions.

The warehouse where my father shuffled cartons was downtown, but my mother had farther to travel. Each morning, in summer light and in winter darkness, my father accompanied her to the bus stop where he waited until she had safely boarded. Then he would come back to finish his coffee while I gathered up my schoolbooks.

There was only an hour lag between my return from school and my mother's arrival from work, but that hour was the longest of my day. It seemed to stretch endlessly. Sometimes I used it to poke about the house. One day I opened the drawer in my father's night table and found his stash of pamphlets on lovemaking techniques. I read those pamphlets incessantly, trying to make the connection between the diagrams and the puzzling bits of what my parents called *Aufklärung—enlightenment*—a single embarrassing talk that constituted my only sex education.

It was probably during a late afternoon of poking about in my father's night table that I first saw the box. I remember how my hands trembled when I untied the string and how I feared that my clumsy fingers would be unable to retie the bow. I also remember seeing the letters. Dozens of letters. And although I had read the sex manuals despite knowing that I shouldn't, I did not read the letters. I knew instinctively that they were different. Very carefully, I retied the string and put the box back where I had found it.

I do not think I gave the box another thought until my father died. Then, with unsettled years ahead in makeshift accommodations as a graduate student, I asked my mother to keep it for me. I remember her saying that she had put it next to my old high school notes and team badges stored in the basement. In 1967, I moved to Vancouver. Here too, there were unsettled years of moving from one apartment to another before I finally purchased a permanent home. When my mother brought the box on one of her visits, I saw it as her way of acknowledging that I was now an adult, and that her house in Hamilton was no longer my real home. I recall mumbling my thanks and placing it on the top shelf of the bedroom closet. There the box remained, year after year, deliberately ignored and largely forgotten.

It was not until 1996, the year of my sixtieth birthday, that I felt a need to open the box. That birthday told me that it was time to start a new chapter of my life. For years, I had been opening one door and closing another. My life felt very compartmentalized. Before graduation and after. Before marriage and after. Before children and after they left home. I longed to open all the doors at the same time, to move freely through the past as well as the present. That summer, I went to my cabin alone and brought the box with me. For the first time, I brought no books.

For a long time, I stared at the red lid. My hands were unsteady and my fingers fumbled with the old piece of string. Even after the bow yielded, I hesitated. The minutes ticked by as I sat in total stillness. Sunshine streamed through the window but my hands were frozen. Finally, I lifted the lid.

I saw carefully folded sheets of airmail paper. Some were in envelopes with red, white, and blue edges; others were pre-folded airmail letters with space for the address on the reverse side. The paper was so thin that I could see the handwriting right through it. Some sheets had writing on both sides; tiny German script that filled every inch of the page.

I picked up the top letter and felt the thinness of the transparent paper. Moments passed. Finally, I unfolded the sheet and looked for a signature. *Emil.* Right away, I knew that it was Emil Fränkel, husband of my father's younger sister Martha and the man who had become my father's best friend. I sat for a long time, remembering regular Sunday morning walks with my father after we moved to the city. I was lonely, but I think that my father was even lonelier. Together we would walk through the neighbourhood, just the two of us. Sometimes my father said how much he missed Emil and how lucky he had been to have a brother-in-law who became his

Emil Fränkel

best friend. Sometimes, he would gaze into space and say, "If only Emil had come to Canada…"

Emil had insisted that we go to Canada. It had never occurred to my parents to emigrate. Why would anyone with a close-knit family, dear friends, and a modest but comfortable way of life want to cross an ocean? And why Canada, of all places? My parents often said that they had expected to be battling bears all summer long, then to be hunkering down in an igloo over an endless winter.

My parents were simple folk. Like his four siblings, my father Edmund had been born at home in the family bed in Strobnitz. In 1900, the year of his birth, Strobnitz was just a tiny village in a remote corner of the Austro-Hungarian Empire. The village offered only primary schooling, so Edmund had gone off to study bookkeeping at the *Handelsakademie* in the nearby town of Gmünd before coming home to help his parents run the store that was their livelihood. He was introduced to my mother at a New Year's Eve dance to which she wore the midnight blue ball gown she brought to Canada and that I still have. Both my mother and father claimed that it was love at first sight. The following June, they married, and a year later, in the summer of 1936, I was born.

Hitler had come to power in January 1933 when Hindenberg, president of the German Republic, asked him to be chancellor of a coalition government. Like others outside of Germany, my father's family were not terribly concerned. Politics was for others to worry about, and their hometown of Strobnitz was a backwater in a democratic republic, a safe place in a safe country. My father's family had lived there since the area was Bohemia and formed part of the Austro-Hungarian Empire. Seeking to ensure that World War I had been "the war to end all wars," the Allies had redrawn the borders in 1918, stripping Bohemia and other strategic areas from Germany and Austria to create the new country called Czechoslovakia. Because it was a democratic nation established by the Allies and had treaties to guarantee its independence, there was nothing to fear.

According to my father, it was in the spring of 1938 that Emil Fränkel had come alone to Strobnitz for a serious talk. I imagine that their conversation went something like this:

—Canada! Emil, are you crazy?

—But Edi, we talked about it before.

—And I said "no."

—No, Edi. You said you would think about it.

—Well I have, and the answer is "no." I am just an ordinary fellow. I like it here, and I don't want to be alone in a strange country.

—Edi, listen to me! You must do this. For all our sakes.

—It's for all our sakes that I am refusing to go.

—Edi, you just don't understand how important it is.

—What's important is that I look after my family. My wife and child first, and then my parents.

—Looking after your family won't be possible if Hitler crosses the border.

—But Emil, only last week, Hitler said that he has no interest in any other country.

—And you believe him? This week he says one thing, next week another. The Sudetenland is rich, it's German speaking, and people here are no different from the Austrians. Last month, the citizens of my dear country voted 99.73% in favour of the Anschluss and annexation. Just like my fellow Austrians, voters in the Sudetenland will choose to join Germany.

—Emil, I know the newspapers are depressing. Bad news makes good headlines, but that is no reason to believe what they say. Reading the newspapers can make anybody crazy.

—Edi, I am not crazy. The reality is that Hitler is going to come to the Sudetenland. You must leave.

—But even if you're right, I can't leave. Who would run the store? Papa isn't getting any younger. What would we live on? You are a businessperson, and a successful one at that. You started with nothing, yet you have done really well.

—Yes, I did well, but now, I may have lost everything. Jews have been warned to leave Austria, but I have nowhere to go. The world doesn't want Jews, and I have no relatives elsewhere to sponsor me. Besides, we are expecting a baby, and the doctor has advised

Martha against travel.

—*You could at least go to my brother Arnold in Prague. He'll help you get established until this blows over.*

—*Blows over? Edi, Hitler's just getting started. And much as I love your brother and his wife, I'm no longer so sure that Prague is a safe place.*

—*Prague not safe? The capital of Czechoslovakia? The Allies have guaranteed its independence.*

—*I fear that Hitler will come first to the Sudetenland, then to the rest of Czechoslovakia.*

—*But what will I do? I've invested every cent into the store. They can't just take it away from me.*

—*They can and they will. Look at Gretl's parents. They've come here with only the clothes on their backs. Do you think Hitler will pay them for their house or their store in Germany?*

—*But I have no savings. What will we live on?*

—*But that is why you must leave. Leave everything here, and just get out.*

—*What about my wife? Can you imagine Gretl in Canada? It's wilderness. What about Helen? She is still a baby. I cannot leave them.*

—*No, of course not. You must all three go at once.*

—*Impossible. Gretl will not leave her parents. They are already upset because their other daughter is going to Canada. But Anny has always been the rebel.*

—*Gretl must go. I'll look after her parents and send them to Canada on the next available ship. They'll be right behind you. You must make Gretl see reason.*

—*See reason? I'm not sure that I do. Just because her sister Anny is crazy enough to leave...*

—*Not crazy. Smart. Anny and Ludwig are smart to leave.*

—*It's easier to be smart if you have some skills. Ludwig is getting into Canada because he's a country boy and Canada needs farmers.*

With father in front of the store bearing the family name

—*Then go as a farmer. You are young and Ludwig will teach you.*
—*Why don't you go if you think it's so easy?*
—*Edi, you know I'd go tomorrow if I could. You are the only one with a chance to get out. Because Gretl is Anny's only sister, Anny may be able to sponsor the three of you as first-degree relatives. There's no other way to get into Canada. They aren't taking Jews. Once you get there, you must find a way to sponsor us. Don't you see, Edi? You are our only hope. We are all depending on you. The future of the entire Waldstein family rests on your shoulders.*

Wedding, Gretl Grünhut and Edmund Waldstein, June 30, 1935

Edmund (Edi) Waldstein

Leaving Home

*H*OW HEAVILY THAT RESPONSIBILITY must have sat on my father's shoulders! I thought of him often as I continued reading the letters, always in small bits. Sometimes a single sentence was enough to reduce me to tears. Sometimes I would read a whole paragraph before experiencing the need to pace the floor. My thoughts were in turmoil, and no matter how many times a day I walked the nearby woodland paths, I could find no peace of mind.

Unasked questions haunted me. Childhood memories surfaced and mingled with stories I had heard fifty years ago. Why had my grandparents not been aboard the next ship? Why had they not followed us to Canada? What had happened to Emil and to the rest of the family? There were great gaps in my family story that I needed to bridge. Reading the letters broke the serenity of my adult life, making it seem as fragmented as an unassembled jigsaw puzzle.

Many a night, I walked the country road, trying to find the calmness that might lead to a few hours sleep. Longingly I gazed at the night sky, wishing I could name more than the big dipper. Stars have always fascinated me.

The very concept of a light year dazzles me. Despite its incredible speed, that light has taken countless years to reach me. There is even a good chance that the light of that star died long ago, and still, I see that star winking in the night sky.

So it seemed with those who had written the letters. Their words on paper were as real to me as the light reaching my eye from a distant star. Were any of these people still alive? Was even one of them alive? How could I not have seen what I now saw? Each of these people now existed through their letters as certainly as the stars fixed in the velvet sky.

Numbers do not have meaning for me. It is one reason the study of astronomy has remained a pipe dream. I am hopelessly humanist, and the struggle of a single individual has greater impact upon me than the most accurate of statistics. One parent's agony at the death of a child touches me. My eyes glaze over when children and parents are numbered in the thousands, tens of thousands, hundreds of thousands. Millions.

Particularly problematic for me has been the figure of six million, the number of Jews murdered in a deliberate, systematic, state-sanctioned effort to exterminate my family along with all the Jews of Europe. There is no reason why I should not have been among those murdered Jews. Why I am still alive is as accidental and as random as why six million others were caught in the net.

As a child, I had learned not to ask questions that would upset my parents. As an adult, although I questioned many socially accepted premises, I asked no questions about the war. Not until after I had read the letters did I realize the degree of my ignorance.

It was the first letter from my father's sister Martha in Prague that jolted my thinking. The letter was dated April 2, 1939. The handwriting was not hard to read and the German words easily yielded their meaning.

Today, Sunday, it hits us especially hard to be without you. When you left us on Saturday, the house brimmed with sadness.

I had never given thought to the exact date of our departure from Europe. My parents had always been vague. I only remember them saying, *"We left before Hitler."* The letter gave me a date. Quickly I counted backwards the eight days that Martha was referring to, first on my fingers, then on paper. If there are 31 days in March and April 2 is a Sunday, then April 1 was Saturday and the previous Saturday was March 25. That must be the day we left Prague.

Why was seeing this date so unsettling? Something was troubling me, and I needed time to process the new information. I headed for the local library. The history section had a whole shelf of books about the war. I checked for dates. Hitler and his armies marched into Prague on March 15, 1939. That was a full ten days before we left.

But why would my parents have been in the capital of Czechoslovakia? It was miles from our home in Strobnitz, and my mother had often denied seeing Prague. Whenever friends spoke of it, she would say with a sigh, *"Everyone claims it is a beautiful city. Too bad that I never saw it."*

My mind whirled. I had never connected the dots. To me, the war had always started in September 1939, months after we got to England where we boarded a ship to Canada. I had never thought about events prior to September. Vaguely I remembered something about Neville Chamberlain, the British Prime Minister who tried to buy "peace in our time" at the expense of Czechoslovakia. Now I looked up the details.

Czechoslovakia had been stitched together after World War I by clumping disparate ethnic groups including Czechs, Slovaks, Ruthenians, Poles, Hungarians, and speakers of German into a country with artificially defined borders. The German-speakers lived mostly in areas adjacent to Germany and Austria that were called "the Sudetenland." From the moment that Hitler was elected chancellor in 1933, he sought to bring the Sudetenland under his wing.

How did the Jews know what Hitler would do and that it was time for them to leave the Sudetenland? From a public telephone booth just outside the library, I called my mother's friend Mimi. She was twenty-six in 1938 and clearly remembered the pre-packed suitcases waiting in the hallway as her family gathered around the radio. In the early hours of September 30, the major powers of Europe announced the result of their negotiations. Without inviting Czechoslovakia to the table, Britain, France, Germany, and Italy had signed the Munich Agreement that allowed Germany to occupy the Sudetenland. As Neville Chamberlain, the Prime Minister of Britain stepped from the plane in London, proud to have averted the danger of another war by dealing diplomatically with Herr Hitler, the German army stirred and Chamberlain's name became forever linked with the term "appeasement." Knowing full well what had happened in Germany where Jews had been stripped of citizenship and publicly vilified, the Jews of the Sudetenland boarded early morning trains to safety. That afternoon, German troops crossed the border.

It must have been on that same morning, October 1, 1938, that my parents sought refuge in Prague. Six months later, on March 15, they were still there as Hitler stood on the balcony of Hradcany Castle, accepting Nazi salutes from the courtyard. To the world, he announced that not just the Sudetenland, but the entire country of Czechoslovakia had ceased to exist.

Why had my parents stayed in Prague so long? Had they been hiding, afraid to venture to the highly guarded railway station? Had it been dangerous to be seen on the streets, suitcase in hand and ready to flee? Had they stayed because they had no exit visa and nowhere to go? Was it not until March 15 that my father finally got an exit visa?

He told me the story only once, on one of our Sunday morning walks, but it left a deep impression:

> *I went to the bank early that day. Some intuition told me to be the first in line. The moment the doors opened, I rushed to the nearest teller and pushed the documents under the grille. The teller sighed and picked up his stamp. Just as he was inking the stamp on the pad, the voice of another employee called out. Automatically, the teller pressed the freshly inked stamp onto the blue card as he turned his head.*

> TELLER: *"What did you say?"*
> VOICE: *"I said 'no more exit stamps.' Orders from above. No more stamps to be issued. We're closing up."*

*The teller slammed shut his grille, but not before I had snatched
back my papers.*

Now I understood why the discovery of the dates was so strangely upset-
ting. Not only had my parents fled twice in less than a year, my father had
also received the very last exit stamp to be issued.

How did it feel to be a Jew in 1938 and 1939, waiting to escape the net?
These are the days, weeks, and months that my parents never spoke about.
I now believe that my mother had totally erased them from her memory.

I found more evidence that we had indeed spent months in Prague. The
strongest clue was a postcard addressed to us there. Its message indicates
that we fled from the Sudetenland in September of 1938. Six months later,
when the card was postmarked, we were still in Prague, hunkered down
and waiting for the other shoe to drop.

When I returned from the cabin, I asked my mother about Prague. Once
again, she denied ever having been there. I tried to push further, but my
mother would not remember. She allowed one concession that shielded her
from what she had experienced during those months of uncertainty: *"It is
possible that we were there, but only for a few hours. Just in the railway station
on our way to Antwerp."*

Compulsively I checked the dates again. If we left Prague on March 25,
1939, then we were clearly still there when Hitler marched into the city.
What experience had made my mother draw the curtain on that part of
her life?

I cannot imagine her terror. Had she and my father sat trembling by the
radio, listening to Hitler's raucous voice? Did they analyze his every word,
or were they too frightened to think? Who was there? Were we alone, my
parents and I? Was it too dangerous to venture forth? Was even the short
distance between houses too far? Had the madness in the streets and the
wild jubilation that greeted Hitler's arrival cautioned them to stay hidden
indoors, drapes drawn?

Every Jew in Prague would have felt the ground give way. *Kristallnacht*,
the Night of Broken Glass, a coordinated attack on Jewish people in towns
and cities all over Germany, Austria, and the Sudetenland, had already

A studio photo of Helen, dated and stamped *Prague, 1939* —
proof positive that my family did more than merely pass
through the railway station

happened. On November 9 and 10, 1938, synagogues were torched, businesses and homes looted, and Jews beaten in the streets as onlookers spat and jeered at their plight.

Did my parents not have the documentation they needed? Is that why we were still in Prague? With incomplete paperwork, they would have feared for their lives.

Fearful thoughts must have churned about in my father, literally turning his guts to water. My mother often said that he suffered from "dysentery" on the trip to Antwerp and that he'd "picked up a bug" on the train. How much came from an outside bacterial source and how much came from raw fear?

"Nobody took the train in those days," asserts Mimi when I call her again. *"The planes were rickety, but people flew anyway. Taking the train was too dangerous. You would have had to go through Nazi Germany."* The letters confirm my mother's story. We took the train from Prague to Antwerp. The only route was through Nazi Germany.

I try to imagine my parents, heads bowed, determined not to attract attention. Somehow, my toddler energy had been reined in and my inquisitive voice silenced. Although the actual scenes did not stay in my memory, the sense of fear is still with me.

In the film *Julia*, Jane Fonda plays the role of an American crossing Nazi Germany by train. Many times, I have rented the video. Heart pounding, I watch as the Nazis board the train. I wait for the scene where the inspector demands her passport, and hesitates for just a fraction of a moment. Mesmerized, I see my father in the same scene, not daring to breathe as the Nazi inspector scrutinizes his documents.

———

AMONG THE LETTERS IN THE box is a starkly plain postcard addressed to us in Antwerp. There is no scenic photo, and both the address and message are typed. The only personal touch is the signature: *Emil.* Was the signature of his brother-in-law Emil Fränkel enough to make my father keep that humble postcard and bring it to Canada?

The address reeks of temporary asylum with its amateur abbreviation of *Monsieur* to the understandable but not quite correct *Mons.* This is followed by my father's full Germanic name: *Edmund Waldstein.* The location is a similar mixture of languages: *Hotel Maison Max.* The street address, *Rue de la Station 40-42-44,* indicates that my parents had chosen a hotel close to the railway, the lifeline of those in flight. Then the French veneer slips off totally as both city and country take on their Teutonic form: *Antwerpen, Belgien.*

Emil acknowledges receipt of a telegram and three letters from us, suggesting that we spent a considerable time in Antwerp. What had kept my parents from boarding the next ship to Canada?

I scrutinize Emil's words in search of clues.

> *I went to the Canadian Pacific Company today and Mr. Steiner told me that I don't have to make a deposit, but that the boat tickets must be sent from Canada. Because the regulations are changing so frequently, he said to come back in a few days. When I asked him today, he said nothing about a permit, so I must leave all that for you to inquire about the moment you get to Canada. Especially about whether I can emigrate without a deposit of capital and whether I need both the permit and the boat tickets to be sent from over there.*

That must be why we stayed in Antwerp. We must have been waiting for Anny and Ludwig to send our entry permit, our boat tickets, and to make a monetary deposit of $1000 to the Canadian government on our behalf. Mimi told me that because money could not be taken out of Europe, we had arrived in Canada with the equivalent of one dollar.

Letters to Antwerp

Beginnings are always bitter, and there is much that you will find hard and even painful. Good intentions, however, along with necessity, that hard taskmaster, will build a bridge over all the difficulties.

THESE WORDS PENNED BY my father's older brother Arnold have stayed with me. Their imagery takes me by surprise, as does so much in that first letter dated April 2, 1939. The only description of Arnold that I recall my father using is *vernünftig—sensible*.

That terminology sat well with my own longing for an elder brother to smooth my path and with my concept of people drawn, as was Arnold, to the profession of engineering. Now, I discover the three-dimensional Arnold whose tenacious optimism is an outgrowth of a deep family connection.

Today marks the eighth day since we took leave of each other, and still I have this terrible sadness in me that for the first time has grabbed me so deeply. You can imagine how happy we were when we learned of your safe arrival in Antwerp and how much lighter we all felt. In our thoughts, we accompany you every single day on your big journey and we talk about you constantly.

I am writing to you on my very first free day so that you will get my lines right after you arrive in Antwerp. I hope that greetings from the homeland will bring you some consolation in your new and unaccustomed surroundings. Gretl's sister Anny and her dear husband Ludwig will certainly do all they can to make the transition bearable for you, soften the circumstances, and spare you many an unpleasant encounter that they themselves were forced to undergo. For us, it is very reassuring and our strongest spiritual support to know that you are in an assured existence, for we are also building our future upon you.

In this connection, I beg you to write immediately to Bella regarding her promise of sending us an affidavit. It would certainly comfort Vera and me if we had any prospect of emigrating to America.

Yesterday afternoon we were at Elsa's. We were the only guests, so it was really quiet in contrast to last week. We talked a lot about you, and Emil reported on your letter. For your efforts regarding Tovona, please accept many thanks, dear Edi. Unfortunately, in the meantime we have had a negative answer because the regulations there will not allow the immigration of Jews.

———

A NEW HANDWRITING FOLLOWS, that of Arnold's wife Vera. As a doctor, Vera has eyes like a camera, and she captures the moment of our departure

I still see you in front of my eyes as you looked out of the train window, especially the curly blond head of little Helen who was so

joyful and so cute and who laughed as if there were no such word as "farewell." I hope that the child with her unconscious optimism will be all right in the end.

With gentle humour, Vera acknowledges that far from being an elegant cruise, our Atlantic crossing will be a time of seasickness and misery.

We think and speak of you often, and will continue to do so during your days on the high seas. We will think of you with special empathy every time we see food.

———

WHERE ARNOLD AND VERA leave off, the elegant penmanship of my father's sister Else fills the page.

My dear ones, it has been a week already since we said farewell to you and in the meantime, you have gone a considerable distance from us. We think of you every hour and our soul follows you every step of your journey. It is now Sunday afternoon, the first one without you. Any moment, I expect the door to open and you to come in. I will hear Helly say "Aunty Elsa, I want a piece of bread and goose fat."

Aunty Elsa. *Tante* Else. I experimented in both English and German, rolling the words about on my tongue, but the words had no familiar feel. I found it difficult to imagine that I used to burst through the door regularly, calling out to this beloved aunt.

What was less surprising is that my insatiable appetite dates back even further than I had known. My mother had often told me the story of our Atlantic crossing. As she and my father lay below deck, retching in airless cabins crammed with bunk beds, I wandered the ship telling complete strangers that I was hungry. Even today, it is difficult for me not to head for the kitchen the moment I walk through my front door.

If my hunger has not changed, at least the food that calms it is different. Rendered goose fat is no longer a staple in my diet. In my mother's world, the hierarchy of treats was goose fat, duck fat, and chicken fat, in descending order. My mother loved to reach in with her hand to pull out the thick creamy white layer nestled beneath the skin of the bird. She'd render it slowly in a pan, perhaps adding a bit of onion for extra flavour. Only when it had cooled and resolidified was I allowed to spread it on a thick slab of rye bread.

> It has still not sunk into my consciousness that you really are gone. Still, we must all count our blessings that things went so quickly and so favourably because now it would be much harder and maybe impossible because they've stopped issuing exit visas.
>
> Our Marianne has suddenly been seized by a great urge to go to England. However, I doubt if it will be possible for her because there is such a crowd wanting to go. My dear Emil had to spend several hours in line this week for her even to get a number and she won't hear anything further for at least two weeks. I cannot get used to the thought of letting her go abroad already, yet the sooner it were to happen, the better for her.
>
> Sadly, this is now the lot of so many parents. I just keep hoping that we can all stay together for a few more years. Fate seems to be determining otherwise.

Although she tries to conceal it, Else's sadness at the prospect of sending Marianne to England looms large. I picture my own daughters as they were in their early teens, fiercely independent yet needing support in order to grow straight and tall. How reluctant I would have been to entrust their care to others at that crucial stage of development!

Having always imagined that I would have the ferocity of a tiger when it came to defending my children, I have often wondered how bad things would have to be before I would send my children to another country to be parented by strangers. I have been unable to imagine it, that sending away of my children. Other horrors I can imagine easily, and these are seldom far from my thoughts. The fear of persecution is with me always.

With the birth of each child, I bought gold coins that I planned to sew into the hem of their clothing should we ever need to flee. If my children risked being separated from me, I wanted whoever found them to have the means to provide food and shelter. Even today, each new world crisis fans the flames of my paranoia. Old fears may lie buried, but they do not vanish.

I still have the gold.

————

THE NEXT FAMILY MEMBER who adds a few lines to the April 2 letter is Else's husband, Dr. Emil Urbach. He addresses his words only to my father, and they are a mixture of sensible advice and unvarnished facts.

> I was very pleased that things went relatively well en route, and I hope that you will also have good weather at sea. In your present situation, you need to consume a rich diet in order to build up strength for farming.

Emil gives no indication of wanting to come to Canada, but he is arranging to send his daughter to safety in England.

> For us, nothing has changed. We intend to send Marianne to a family in England, and we have had her registered for this. On Friday the 14th of this month, we will find out whether and under what circumstances it may come to pass.

It was Emil's wording that led me to think of *Kindertransport*, a word I vaguely remembered. Now, I looked up the specifics.

Between 1938 and 1940, Britain eased its immigration restrictions to allow at least 7500 Jewish children from Austria, Germany, and Czechoslovakia into the country. Although Britain's altruism was tempered by a hefty dose of practicality—private citizens or organizations had to guarantee to pay for not only the care and education of these children but also for their eventual emigration from Britain—Britain did reach out.

Canada and the U.S. opted instead to prevent such emigration to their shores. In 1940, the Canadian embassy in Washington informed the Prime Minister that the American government opposed the admission of Jewish children to Canada, fearing that these children might somehow slip across the border into the United States. However, even as it closed its doors to Jewish children, Canada granted both temporary and permanent residence to British-born children, and to children born in France, the Netherlands, Belgium, and Scandinavia.[1] It shocked me deeply to discover that anti-Semitism had put down such strong roots both in both Canada and in the United States.

It was with thoughts of the Urbach letter still freshly in my mind that I watched *Nicolas Winton: The Power of Good*, a documentary film in the CBC-TV *Witness* series. The program features reporter Joseph Schlesinger spotlighting "Nicky," a very modest Englishman who single-handedly saved over six hundred Czech children, including Joseph. On the off chance that he might have seen the program, I emailed my only Canadian relative, a cousin thrice removed on my mother's side.

Now in his eighties, Cousin Herbert had indeed seen the program. More remarkably, he had been among the tearful Czech children peering from the train windows, waving a last farewell to their parents. I have kept Herbert's email.

> *Schlesinger is excellent and the film is almost a fairy tale come true. At one point, I was moved to sobbing. And of course, the moments of parting from my parents at our small town railway station are etched into my memory. The things said and swallowed, the thoughts held in check. ...*

Once again, I was tongue-tied by another's pain. I could not ask Herbert to relive that departure from Prague. Seeking to know more, however, I attended a local workshop where "child survivors" told their story. Particularly moving was the saga of a man exactly my age. His parents had put him aboard a train to England, but the German invasion trapped that train in the Netherlands. A kind family opened its doors to a child from the train.

Just as I had forgotten ever knowing my relatives, he too quickly forgot the people of his earliest years. He never questioned the blond hair or blue eyes of his siblings. His memory of another family vanished. Shortly after war's end, there was a knock at the door. The young boy was greeted by a distraught stranger, a haggard, wild-eyed woman who claimed to be his mother. Decades later, his wounds are still fresh.

————

FOLLOWING CLOSELY UPON Emil Urbach's words is the handwriting of my father's sister Martha. Her words carry a noticeable whiff of fear, perhaps wondering if the goodbyes were forever.

> We miss you terribly, yet you are "the chosen" for blessed are those who can move far away. May God grant that you arrive safely and well at your destination. As you step onto the new earth, we wish you every imaginable good thing. May the air of your new homeland give you the strength to regain a good foothold and may you earn your daily bread in peaceful work.

There is an unexpected poetry and grandeur to Martha's words. Where did this village girl with minimum schooling acquire such language skills?

As if in counterbalance, Martha wraps herself in the love that binds the family together. She addresses us playfully, using terms of endearment. My mother is "Greterl," and my father is "Ederle." I am "Helly-child." To my surprise, I discover that I also had a name for Martha.

> I believe that little Helly-child will have it easiest. She will make herself at home and feel happy everywhere. Does she still remember Matie? I send her many thousands of kisses.

I linger over the word "Matie." The childish nickname tells me that Aunt Martha was a beloved fixture in my life. How can I have no memory of her? I am taken aback to learn that before we left Europe, I could speak and understand. I had never thought of myself as talking to this aunt, as running to embrace her, as smelling her perfume and feeling her arms around me. Through her letter, Martha moves from the abstract shadows to a concrete reality. For the first time, I realize that I was young but I was not unaware.

Matie. The word touches me deeply. Having no memory of Martha's presence, I am taken by surprise at the impact of her absence.

I am surprised too by the level of her anxiety. It is palpable. She makes no pretence of reassuring my father that all is well, and there is no escaping the directness of her words.

> *Unfortunately, the situation is getting more serious with each passing day. We rack our brains day and night, and if possible, we would leave tomorrow. If we survive this new test of nerves, more trials await us. And yet, if one has no choice, one must, that is, if one can.*
>
> *And going to Palestine? Well then, what happens to the children? You know the situation only too well! It's just that it's getting sadder by the day. It's totally impossible to get the blue cards now.*
>
> *Dearest Ederle, I don't need to repeat to you our urgent plea, but nevertheless, should the matter be totally hopeless, then write to us as soon as possible, even though it would pain us terribly. Perhaps fate will still grant us some nice hours together. After all, we spent our youth together. Perhaps there will also be time together for us as adults?*

There is much in Martha's letter that begins to haunt me. I begin with her question about going to Palestine. Why is this not an obvious solution, and why does she seem to imply that this would be without the children? Once again, I head for the library, trying to understand the circumstances in 1939.

I knew that the state of Israel had not been founded until 1948, and that its creation had been an effort by the nations of the world to make amends. I knew that Israel had not been founded without a struggle, but the details had blurred. I wondered why the Fränkels did not simply board the next ship heading across the Mediterranean to Palestine.

Now, I discovered that after World War I, the League of Nations had approved and signed the British Mandate giving Britain the power to rule Palestine. Between 1920 and 1948, Britain placed severe limits on Jewish emigration to Palestine. The greater the pressure from those seeking to escape the Nazis, the more strictly the British enforced the regulations.

To break the bottleneck, some Zionist groups organized illegal "transports," mostly of able-bodied adults who could work the land and fight for freedom. This knowledge provided the answer to a translation problem I was having with a later part of the letter, a part where Martha's husband uses the word *transport*, which is not a German word. The only time I ever heard my parents use the word was later, after the war, and only in reference to the trains that took Jews to the concentration camps. I was afraid that I had misunderstood.

I found my answer in the words of novelist Arthur Koestler who draws a parallel between the locked boxcars carrying Jews to their death and the ships headed for Palestine. He calls them "the little death ships."

> *The story of Palestine from May 1939 to the end of the war is essentially the story of Jews trying to save their skins, and of the effects of the Mandatory power to prevent this through an immigration blockade. ... It is essential... to bear in mind that the Jews in immediate danger of life were those in German-occupied territory; that precisely these people's escape had been declared "illegal". ...*
>
> *The practical consequences of this policy were... that in Palestine, over half a million Jews waited with open arms for their tormented kin... while over the Mediterranean and Black Sea, unclean and unseaworthy little cargo boats... tossed about in open waters, waiting in vain for permission to discharge their crowded human cargoes. Hunger, thirst, disease and unspeakable living conditions reigned on those floating coffins.*
>
> *In March and April 1939, three-refugee ships... packed with Jews reached Palestine and were refused permission to land.*
>
> *In the British House of Commons, Mr. Noel-Baker asked what*

would happen to these people. The Colonial Secretary, Mr Malcolm MacDonald said that they had been sent back to where they came from.

Mr. Noel-Baker: "Does that mean to concentration camps?"

Mr. MacDonald: "The responsibility rests with those responsible for organizing illegal immigration."[2]

I did not know that Dachau and other concentration camps had been established even before the outbreak of war, and that the Allies had been aware of the existence of these camps. I thought the horror stories had only become known after the liberation. Perhaps that is what I needed to believe.

———

WHEN I CLOSED THE HISTORY books and returned again to Martha's letter, the narrowness of my father's escape leapt out at me.

You know the situation only too well. It's just that it's getting worse by the day. It's totally impossible now to get the blue cards.

I telephoned Mimi with new questions. She confirmed what I suspected. The blue cards were exit visas requiring authorization stamps from both the bank and the Gestapo. It must have been a blue card that my father took to the bank, along with his other documents, on the morning that a sleepy teller gave him the last exit visa to be issued in Prague.

Small wonder that Martha is overwhelmed by their plight. In begging my father for help, I note that twice she has underlined the words "urgent plea." She switches to other topics, but her pretence of a normal life is quickly shattered.

Yesterday we visited our friend Wally. Wherever we go, people are talking about the same topic.

Only when Martha is talking about her children do the shadows lift. The baby provides flickering glimpses of happiness.

> *Our dear Dorothy is very cute, but for the last week, she has been getting up on her knees in the baby carriage. We have to strap her in so that she can't fall out. We are going to have to put up a little bed for her. Ilserl is very good.*

The bed seems symbolic. If they put up a bed for her, it means that they will not be leaving just yet. The bed also leads me to another question. How and where is this family of four living? They must have left everything behind in Nazi-controlled Austria and made their way from their home in Linz to Prague, where Arnold and Vera would have reached out. I scan carefully, but this first letter offers no clues.

My eyes are drawn to the very short sentence, *"Ilserl is very good."* It is another bond between me and my nine-year old cousin, for I too was a good child. Raised in a country where self-assertion and rebellion against parental control seemed to be the norm, I wrestled with being so different from my peers. As an adult, I have learned that "goodness" is an issue for every child whose family has stared death in the face. How does one imagine Anne Frank misbehaving? When life and death are at stake, children learn quickly to "be good."

MANY DAYS PASSED BEFORE I again picked up Martha's letter. I welcomed every excuse to procrastinate. She had touched a nerve, and I did not want to feel the intense emotions that her words evoked.

> *... should the matter be totally hopeless, then write to us as soon as possible, even though it would pain us terribly. Perhaps fate will still grant us some nice hours together. After all, we spent our youth together. Perhaps there will also be time together for us as adults?*

Written on the back of this photo:
To my dear Uncle Edi, a souvenir of my second birthday,
January 23, 1933. Ilserl.

How heavy Martha's heart must have been when she penned those words. From my own childhood, I have retained the perspective that a heavy heart is the norm. My parents always seemed to be walking under a cloud, and their conversation always focused on problems. Equipment that malfunctioned. People who disappointed. Expenses. *"Life is not easy,"* my mother would often say with a sigh.

But my mother and father tried to make me happy. Although they did without themselves, they managed to buy a special gift for each of my birthdays. My first watch. A ring with a small green chip marketed as my birthstone. I knew that the gift was an expression of their love, and was supposed to make me happy.

In return, I tried to make my parents happy. I was always a good girl. I succeeded in making them proud of my achievements. School was an easy route to that pride. I earned good grades while hiding my social struggles and the many ways in which I knew myself to be a major misfit. As a teenager lacking in Saturday night dates, this became a difficult challenge, but in the early years, my parents were easy to fool.

Their childhood in Europe had been so very different from my early years in Canada. My father had been part of a large, bustling family. My mother had lived with a sister almost her own age and a bevy of friends in a small town in Bavaria. I grew up as an only child on an isolated farm in Southern Ontario where I attended a one-room schoolhouse. My first years in school were so traumatic that I have almost completely erased them from conscious memory. My classmates made it clear that I would never attain social acceptance.

My first sin was that I spoke no English in a school where we were taught to sing "Rule Britannia! Britannia, rule the waves!" My second sin was that I spoke German, the language of the enemy. My third sin was that I was a Jew when that was still a dirty word.

For years, I blamed myself for being a social outcast. After we left the farm, I did try to make Jewish friends, but the relationships never gelled. In the late 1940s and early 1950s, the young Jews that I met seemed either materialistic or caught up in a pro-Israeli world of which I knew nothing. I was as baffled by those who sought to fight for a homeland far from Canadian shores as I was by those who thought only of what to wear to the next party.

For a while, I thought that if non-Jews got to know me first as a person, then the fact of my having been born Jewish would not matter. Life taught me otherwise. The girls in my high school formed a "sorority" from which I alone was excluded. The few boys who tried to date me backed out after their parents asked, "Helen who?" and heard my last name.

Slowly, I began to understand my parents a little, and to notice the deep scars left by a world that had totally rejected them. I spent much time trying to imagine what it had been like for them. How could they trust again, after their former classmates and the friends with whom they had once played soccer or hopscotch turned against them? What new meaning did they attach to the word "neighbour" after watching those who had always lived next door hide behind drawn curtains and avert their eyes on the street? For my part, I became both reluctant to trust and eager to trust, knowing well that a diet of suspicion corrodes the soul.

As I think back, not once during those years on the farm or even during our time in the city did my parents connect with what they called "real" Canadians. All the visitors to our home who sat down for tea or a meal spoke with that same Germanic accent that set them apart, no matter what their degree of fluency.

I do not believe that my parents ever lost that sense of alienation, of "otherness" imposed by the outside world. They often mentioned being "foreigners" or "greenhorns," and there were audible quotation marks around their use of these words. While my mother partly mastered the art of sour grapes, claiming not to want what she could not have, my father was more complex. It was difficult for me to grasp that he had once been a carefree soul who strummed the ukulele and played piano at family gatherings in Europe. I saw him as quiet, thoughtful, sensitive, and shadowed by loneliness.

Although he often thought aloud during our Sunday morning walks, seeming to forget that I was just a child, the concerns my father voiced were always about the present. About his adult years in Europe, he rarely spoke. Now, as I began reading the letters, I also began looking for the roots of that lingering sadness even my best efforts could not dissolve.

I found a clue to that sadness in Emil Fränkel's first letter. His handwriting follows closely that of his wife Martha's in that letter of April 2, 1939. Emil's words seem to leave the page and reverberate in the silence of my morning.

> *My dear ones,*
> *Longingly we awaited your first news about your trip and your arrival in Antwerp.*
> *I was just over visiting your parents at 11 o'clock in the morning when your letter arrived.*
> *I opened the letter and Papa read it to us.*
> *We were all overjoyed to have good news from you, and we all*

have only one wish: that the dear Lord continue to accompany you to your destination. Whenever I'm so lonely for you, I comfort myself with the thought that at last, after such a long time, in a matter of days you will have reached your place of rest.

I visit your parents twice a day and do all their errands. Your furniture is now at Bush's where it sits next to Anny's things. Both will be shipped together, but please do tell Anny that it is totally impossible to send the additional items she has requested.

As dear Martha has just written, we are waiting for your report in order to get a picture of what our chances are of getting there. At the moment there is absolutely no possibility of being allowed to emigrate.

Liebreich and his family were supposed to leave this week for Palestine, but the transport has been delayed indefinitely. Uncle Fritz thinks we should all report for the next transport. Arnold would join us. And so my thoughts are working day and night, and I just don't know what to do next.

Line by line, I pored over the letter, seeking to understand. Because Emil was the first to glimpse the shadows on the horizon and to encourage my father to go to Canada, I expected him to provide details that others had missed. Although many questions remain, his letter did not disappoint.

> *Longingly we awaited your first news about your trip and your arrival in Antwerp.*

Longingly. Sehnsüchtig. The poetically positioned adverb is as strikingly out of place in German as it is in English. I must remind myself that these words were penned not by a poet, but by a practical, down-to-earth businessman. I double-check Martha's part of the letter, and note that she has added a postscript that she underlines. *Emil is* VERY *lonely for you.*

How seldom in my world today do I hear a man acknowledge being lonely, let alone for his brother-in-law? Martha's words are a testimonial to the level of affection between these two men, and to the depth of my father's loss. Emil had been not just his brother-in-law, but also his confidant and best friend.

> *I was just over visiting your parents at 11 o'clock in the morning when your letter arrived.*

Morning finds Emil at his daily post: visiting my mother's parents, Max and Resl. I knew that it was Emil's promise to look after them that had finally convinced my mother to leave for Canada. There has never been, and there still is no doubt in my mind that my mother firmly expected her parents to follow. Realities and potential complications would not have prevented her from believing whatever she needed to believe. Because Emil had assured her that he would look after Max and Resl and book their immediate passage to Canada, my mother left Europe convinced that she and her parents would soon be reunited.

> *I visit Gretl's parents twice a day and do all their errands.*

I try to imagine the scene that greeted Emil every morning. My grandmother Resl would be sitting quietly in a chair, barely registering Emil's knock at the door. In a misguided attempt to cure my grandmother's menopausal symptoms, the medical experts of the early 1930s had destroyed her mind. Fearing the approach of her own menopausal symptoms, my mother had often told me the story. It had only been mid-day when my grandmother took off her apron for the last time. Bone-weary from cooking, cleaning, raising two children as well as daily bookkeeping and work in the shop that was my grandparents' livelihood, she had sunk into her chair and spoken the fatal words: "*I cannot. I am too tired. I just cannot do it anymore.*" They had sent her off to a sanatorium for electroshock treatment to regain her ability to work. Now she could barely function.

I try to picture my grandfather Max opening the door to admit Emil. Even on a weekday morning, Max would be formally attired in a three-piece suit befitting his self-image as *pater familias*. Although he would proffer

Emil a hearty welcome, there would not even be a cup of coffee waiting. If his wife could no longer serve him and his daughters had run off to foreign parts, then someone else would have to fill that breach.

Every detail leads me to another question. If my grandmother Resl was unable to function, who did the actual cooking? Surely not Emil, for men of his class and generation stayed out of the kitchen. Did Martha prepare extra food that Emil brought over? An unlikely scenario because my mother's father was among the very few observant German Jews who insisted on a strictly kosher diet. He would have refused food prepared in Martha's kitchen.

Beyond the family specifics, how did my grandfather and other observant Jews cope with having to violate dietary principles that had been among the very foundations of their life? Did such issues dwindle in importance compared to all else that was happening?

My grandparents Max and Resl were completely dependent on others. They had remained in Germany until 1937, when Anny had finally convinced them to come to Czechoslovakia. Their assets remained frozen in Germany, as did Emil's in Austria. How did Emil cope? In Prague only on a visitor's visa and denied gainful employment, he must have felt so superfluous. Not once but twice a day, he visits Max and Resl and does all their errands.

What were these errands and what was my grandfather doing while Emil did the errands? Max was only in his early fifties, and in the prime of life. Back home in Cham, Germany, he had been president of the town's Jewish congregation. For many years, he had also been a member of Cham's volunteer fire brigade, a responsibility that would only have been entrusted to a fit and healthy man.

When the Nazis first came to power in Germany in 1933, my mother had not yet married and was still living at home. As the new regulations came into effect, there had been a knock at the door. It was a neighbour, telling her father that a Jew could no longer be a fireman, not even as a volunteer. Silently, my grandmother had opened her sewing basket, taken out her best scissors, and cut the brass buttons from the jacket that Max would never wear again.

I opened the letter and Papa read it to us.

I note with interest that although Emil opens the letter, it is Papa Max who reads it aloud. The letter may be intended for the whole family, but Emil defers to the older man. Emil again stresses his personal loneliness.

> *We were all overjoyed to have good news from you, and we all have only one wish: that the dear Lord continue to accompany you all the way to your destination. Whenever I'm so lonely for you, I comfort myself with the thought that at last, after such a long time, in a matter of days you will have reached your place of rest.*

Emil's list of additional responsibilities was long. Already in charge of my grandparents, he was now also being asked to ship both our belongings and those of my mother's sister Anny.

> *Your furniture is packed up in a lift (a large shipping crate) next to Anny's things and the expediter will ship both lifts together. It is totally impossible to send Anny the extras she has requested.*

What were Emil's thoughts as such requests were made? With all his assets frozen in Austria, what was his source of food and rent? How did he make decisions when all about him the sands of reality were shifting?

> *As dear Martha has just written, we are waiting for your report in order to get a picture of what our chances are of getting there. At the moment, there is absolutely no possibility of being allowed to emigrate.*

For a very long time, I sat unseeing with this letter in my lap. "*At the moment there is absolutely no possibility of being allowed to emigrate.*" The words are so freezingly final. Only a week after our departure, the situation had become hopeless. How narrowly we had escaped!

Starting Over

*H*ow did we gain admission to Canada when others found all doors locked?

I fear that the one person who deserves credit for our entry, my Aunt Anny, has gone to her grave with nary a thank you. The day of her funeral, I went to the market and bought all the yellow roses I could find and threw them on her casket. A small cluster of mourners stood by the grave on that cold and rainy day. There were a few neighbours and acquaintances, but no one who knew her well. Her only sister did not attend.

Family histories are complex, and none more so than for those whose wounds have not healed. My Aunt Anny died childless, but for years she let people think that I was her daughter. She loved it when others would say, *"It's okay. We Canadians are modern. These days it's no shame to have had a child out of wedlock. We know that you only pretend Helen is your sister's child. Helen is so like you. And look, Ludwig now loves her just as much as you do."*

It would not have been a far stretch to imagine my aunt breaking that social taboo. My mother had always been the good girl in the family while

Anny, seated provocatively on the bonnet of a car

her sister played the role of the wild one. An early photo shows Anny astride a motorcycle. Although two years younger than my mother, it was always Anny who dared, Anny who defied authority, and Anny who ventured into forbidden territory.

Both Anny and my mother loved to tell tales of their childhood. I remember the story of Papa Max who enjoyed the occasional stein of beer, fresh from the barrel at the local pub. Because he preferred to sip it at home in the comfort of his armchair, he often sent the girls out to fetch him a beer in the evening. Anny always slurped off the white foam, never flinching when Max complained that the publican was becoming stingy with his liquid measurements.

Anny Grünhut, a beauty with her hair cut short

Later, there were more serious clashes with parental authority. On a holiday visit to relatives, Anny brazenly cut her long tresses and returned home sporting a flapper bob. Next, she demanded the right to move to Regensburg, where she apprenticed as a technician on Roentgen's new X-ray device. There, she fell in love with a doctor.

The affair was passionate, but it did not end happily. It was the early 1930s and Hitler was already chancellor of Germany. Anny was a Jew; the doctor was Aryan. He chose safety.

Heartbroken, Anny watched as her sister garnered all the accolades. Gretl, the blushing bride in virginal white splendour. Gretl, the mother-to-be, proudly patting her visible badge of womanhood. Gretl, the mother of a healthy child, little Helen born in 1936.

Anny was nobody's fool. Her sister and her parents might well be totally focused upon this new infant, but Anny saw what was happening in Germany. Anny knew that she had to do something. Getting herself and her parents out of Germany had to be the priority. She would make it *her* priority.

Czechoslovakia was the obvious place to go. Much of the country was German speaking, so it would be an easy transition in terms of language. It was a democracy created and backed by the League of Nations. Thanks to a midnight blue ball gown and a fortuitous invitation to a New Year's Eve dance, Gretl was already there, living in the tiny village of Strobnitz.

All Anny needed was a Czech husband. She whispered her request to a relative who whispered it to another woman and soon, the matchmaking was done. Ludwig Ekstein agreed to marry Anny Grünhut.

Ludwig was a slightly older man with the best of references and connections. He was a prosperous landowner with an excellent reputation as a cattle-dealer. This line of work attracted many a scoundrel, but Ludwig was the rare exception: a man who honoured his word.

Anny had tried the route of love and found it wanting. She agreed to follow the path of reason. Hastily, she and Ludwig were wed, Anny in a suit and matching hat and carrying a simple bouquet of yellow roses. She moved into his house in Bischofteinitz near Pilsen and promptly did what she had set out to do. She got her parents out of Germany. It was 1937.

By 1938, Czechoslovakia no longer seemed like such a safe place. When Hitler annexed Austria in March of that year, several of Ludwig's cousins said, "*We're next. Hitler will take Czechoslovakia.*"

In the face of hundreds of thousands of Jews clamouring to flee Germany, Austria, and Czechoslovakia, Canada closed its doors. A memorandum to Prime Minister Mackenzie King, prepared jointly by the Departments of External Affairs and Mines and Resources on November

Gretl as a new mother,
elegantly attired for her afternoon walk in Strobnitz

Wedding, Anny and Ludwig Ekstein

29, 1938, stated the blunt reality: *"We do not want to take in too many Jews, but in the present circumstances, we do not want to say so."*[3] In major centres like Prague, the only sources of information for would-be immigrants to Canada were agents from the Canadian National Railway and the Canadian Pacific Railway (CPR, known colloquially as "The Canadian") who were seeking to attract settlers to the lands granted to them by the Canadian government for having completed the Canadian railway.

Ludwig's cattle-dealer cousins invited a representative of the Canadian Pacific Railway to visit their rural holdings near Pilsen in Czechoslovakia. Impressed by their industriousness, the CPR representative agreed to put forward a special recommendation to the Canadian authorities. Shortly thereafter, Ludwig's cousins were granted permission to buy land in Canada and to immigrate as Czech farmers.

Did no one in Ottawa realize that Ludwig and Ludwig's cousins were Jews? Was F. C. Blair, Director of the Immigration Branch of the Department of Mines and Resources sick or on holidays when the application was sent to Ottawa?

I have directed my questions to numerous history professors whose specialty is Canada in the 1930s. They all say the same thing: *"Someone was asleep at the switch."* Immigration officials likely did not realize that the leader of the Czech group was a Jew. Ludwig's cousin Karl Abeles was far from the stereotypical Jew that Canadian newspapers of the day portrayed as dark, hunched, and hook-nosed. Karl Abeles was a big, blond man with a handlebar moustache. From his occasional visits to our farm, I remember him as robust and outgoing, with a jovial manner that would fit right into a contemporary beer commercial.

In November of 1938, Anny and Ludwig joined his cousins in Ontario at the Ridge Farm near what was then the small village of Mount Hope, south of Hamilton. Anny and Ludwig immediately sponsored my mother, father, and me to immigrate to Canada.

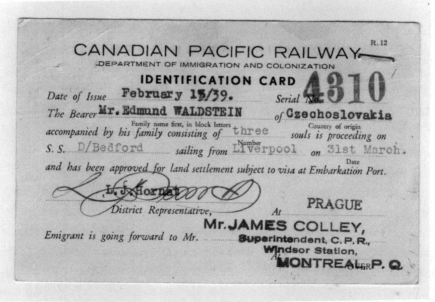

An ID card issued by the CPR to Edmund Waldstein

And so, on April 16, 1939, we stepped off the old S. S. Montcalm in Saint John, New Brunswick. From there we travelled by train to Montreal where Mimi greeted us. This dear friend, now in her nineties, was then a beautiful young woman whose parents had sent her to Canada with an aunt and uncle related by marriage to the Czech cousins that included my Uncle Ludwig.

Mimi was in Montreal to see Mr. James Colley of the CPR. She had been told that Mr. Colley held the candle of life and the sword of death over the head of each family member now trapped in Europe. Mimi hoped that by making a personal appeal, she could break through the wall of red tape and bring her parents to Canada.

When I asked how she recognized us, Mimi laughed. *"It was easy,"* she said. *"You were obviously foreigners. A skinny man in a too large suit, and an elegant woman in a heavy wool dress with matching cape and feathered hat who was holding the hand of a little girl in a beige velveteen coat with a brown collar. You looked so out of place, so* benebbicht.*"*

Although the Yiddish expression—an adjective for a person who has become an object of pity after failing so often and so miserably—is difficult to translate, I can easily picture the scene. Indeed, the feel of that scratchy collar, so drab and drearily brown, remains etched in my memory, as does the texture and drama of my mother's bottle-green ensemble.

Because their documents labelled them as Czech farmers, my parents put aside their fine clothes and prepared for a new way of life. They had promised the Canadian government that they would farm for a minimum of five years.

It was a big leap. My mother needed to go from being the belle of the village ball to plucking and disembowelling chickens, milking large, ungainly cows, and feeding slop to pigs that disgusted her. My father needed to say farewell to a life that was all he'd ever wanted, and step into a life that he hated. He was completely unsuited to farming. His thin body never filled out and his hands remained clumsy. Worse, he was ashamed. He lived in daily humiliation at what he had done. He had reduced to a life of drudgery his Gretl, the beautiful bride to whom he had promised the world.

At first, my parents and I lived communally on the Ridge farm, crowded together with the entire clan of Ludwig's cousins. As soon as possible, my father and Ludwig pooled their resources and purchased their own farm several miles south of Mount Hope. Their overriding hope was that someday my mother's parents and all the members of my father's family would join us there.

They chose the Wren farm because it was cheap, as were many farms in the 1930s. Canadians had fled to the cities in the wake of the Depression, preferring to seek well-paying work in the factories rather than till the land.

The Wren farm was doubly cheap because it consisted of 180 acres that no one wanted. The land was uneven and planting was difficult. Parts were swampy and never seemed to dry out. The fields contained more rocks than fertile soil. Where fences existed, their posts leaned at odd angles. The barn and outbuildings threatened to collapse in the next strong wind.

Still, a beginning was made. Ludwig and my father bought a neighbour's cow that was dead by morning. They bought another cow and my mother heated its milk on the wood-burning stove in the kitchen. To this day, the smell of warm milk lingers in my memory along with the skin it formed as it cooled in the cup. To this day, I drink my coffee black and the very smell of hot cocoa makes me gag.

More cows were added to the stable, and the barn became a favourite place for me. It was my mother's job to do the milking. I still picture her perched fearfully on the little milking stool, pulling the teats until the warm milk squirted into the tin pail. Whenever she got up to empty it into the big milk can in the cooling shed, she'd sigh as she tucked a stray lock of hair under the red bandanna she always wore in the barn.

Meanwhile Ludwig and my father cultivated the fields. They had purchased a workhorse to pull the rusty old plough, and they trudged along behind it. Ludwig gradually repaired a few farm implements, often tying them together with bits of binder twine. I spent many hours watching him patiently figure out how things worked. I also loved to walk with my father as he inserted single kernels of corn into the ground, rhythmically depressing the planter handle until it gave a satisfying click.

Aunt Anny took on the outside world. Armed with her dictionary, her ready smile, and her willingness to use gestures, Anny learned English. In

Helen wandering alone by the lift that became the henhouse

Europe, people had frowned upon her refusal to bow to convention. Now her traits were seen as entrepreneurial. She decided to raise chickens. Each week she stood on the highway to hitchhike her way into Hamilton where she trudged door to door with a basket of eggs.

There were many setbacks, but gradually the farm began to produce a better yield. Anny added fresh-killed chickens to her load, and I was allowed to help clean them. First, they had to be eyed for plumpness and caught. This involved much squawking and ruffling of feathers with chickens darting madly about the henhouse. Ludwig did the actual killing by inserting a very sharp knife into their open beak. He explained that this was faster and more humane than cutting off their heads, which often resulted in headless chickens running about in crazed circles.

Next, the chickens were dipped into very hot water. It needed to be just the right temperature to soften the feathers without burning the skin. Then the chickens were hung by their legs from a long pole, and I was allowed to help pluck them, taking great care to not tear the delicate skin in the process. When even the most stubborn of pinfeathers had been removed, my mother would take the chickens to the stove where the iron lid would be lifted and the last small, almost invisible hairs would be singed over the open flame. Finally, my mother would slice open the hen's bum and insert her hand deep into the cavity, pulling out guts, stomach, and liver all in a single quivering mass. Sometimes there would be eggs without a shell, and these would be scooped into a bowl for our meals as would stray bits of fat that could be scraped from the intestines. Any lumps of good fat along with the stomach, heart, and liver would be returned to the washed cavity as a treasure for the lucky purchaser.

The fields too began to produce increasingly respectable crops. Some fields grew wheat that had to be cut and bundled with twine into bunches that were propped against each other to form stooks, the little tent-like structures that many an artist has romanticized in paint. To me, the bundling and propping took forever, and I spent endless days sitting at the edge of the field under a tree that gave minimal shelter from the relentless sun. I watched as Anny and my mother, wearing high rubber boots to shield their legs from snakes as well as from the rough stubble, joined the men in this nerve-racking task. Rain at this point would ruin the harvest, and haste was of the essence.

Only when the wheat was dry could it be loaded upon a wagon and brought to the threshing machine, a gigantic contraption that needed to be

Ready for work in the fields,
mother in rubber boots to protect her legs from snakes

booked far in advance along with its owner-operator. This in itself was a problem. Book too early and the grain might not yet be dry; book too late and a sudden rain meant disaster. Moreover, not only the thresher but also all the neighbouring farmers had to be available on that date, for threshing was very much a communal activity.

There was always much excitement on threshing day. Once the neighbours had been recruited to help, it was time for the women to start planning the food. This invariably threw my mother and Anny into a state bordering on panic. In their first year of threshing, the two women had prepared European food for the big midday meal. It was the best meal they had to offer: *Kraut, Knödel, Schweinfleisch,* and *Kuchen.* The farmers had taken one look, pushed away their plates, and walked out. They expected roast beef, mashed potatoes with gravy, and two boiled vegetables. Worst of all for Gretl and Anny, they wanted pie for dessert.

Although they eventually learned to "cook Canadian," the art of pie making remained a mystery to both women. Their cookbooks were stuffed with loose bits of paper on which they had copied recipes from Robin Hood and Five Roses flour, from the backs of blocks of Crisco and lard, and even from bottles of cooking oil. Still their crusts remained rock hard. Neither woman ever succeeded in making the flaky mixture that seemed to be the innate gift of every Canadian farm wife. Finally, Mrs. Bates, our kindly neighbour took pity on them and offered to prepare the pies oven-ready for threshing day.

Mrs. Bates really was a dear, sweet woman. I spent many days tagging behind her as she worked her magic in the kitchen. Unlike my family, she never seemed too busy to let me watch, and my questions did not bother her. I don't know how we communicated, for in those days, I spoke no English.

So that I could learn English as soon as possible, my parents sent me to First Grade at the one-room schoolhouse at Glanford Station when I turned five rather than wait until I was six as was the norm.

Before I was allowed to attend school, my parents made me promise never to say that I was Jewish. If a teacher asked for my religion, I was to answer, "I am Czech." There had been several long debates at home about whether people would believe that there was a Czech church. In the end, my parents decided that Canadians knew so little about Czechoslovakia that no statement about the country and its people would sound too far-fetched.

I do not remember my first day of school. I suspect that I have blocked it from memory. Children who have not been taught kindness can be cruel. These children of Ontario farmers who had never encountered a non-English speaker must have viewed me as a rare bird indeed.

I do remember the years of being taunted at every opportunity. My very name gave rise to great hilarity, especially after my parents were overheard using its affectionate form. "Helly" works fine in German, but not in English. Put this together with Waldstein, so close in sound to Holstein (the black and white cows that many of my classmates milked before and after school as part of their daily chores), and you have the makings of endless mockery.

My lunches were another source of daily amusement. I dreaded opening the little red pail that my mother so proudly packed with leftover treats. While others removed crisp new waxed paper from their coveted lily-white sandwiches, I'd have meat on thick slices of rye. To make matters worse, my meat was not thinly sliced roast beef or ham, but slabs of tongue and other cheap cuts. I never got used to the fake barfing of my classmates as they watched me open the brown butcher-paper wrapping so carefully saved to last out the week.

Except in unusually warm weather, lunches were eaten at our desks. There was nowhere else in the school, except that one room and a little cloakroom where, in winter, we hung our sodden coats and lined up our boots. All winter long, our lessons were accompanied by the smell of drying woollens. The wood stove adjacent to the cloakroom always seemed to be lit. Many a morning, I welcomed its glow after ploughing my way through ever-shifting snowdrifts. How early those poor teachers must have arrived to ensure us of this cozy welcome!

The teacher I remember most fondly is Miss Martindale. I picture her as having glasses perched upon a small nose, fluffy brown hair, and a very warm smile. Somehow, despite the clamouring of a roomful of students of

Helen sets off for her first day at school, September 1941

all different grades and abilities, she managed to find time for me. Once I had learned to read, Miss Martindale just kept giving me more books and skipping me ahead until I was more than two years younger than were the others in my grade. While my interest in books has never waned, skipping two years unfortunately increased my social isolation even further.

After school, I would rush home in search of Ludwig. At least I did until my mother told me how much I hurt my father by not seeking him out first. Hurting my father was the last thing I intended.

Still, Ludwig was so much more fun. Ludwig took me by the hand and introduced me to each of the cows by name as he made the rounds, doling out the pre-measured quantity of food to each. Ludwig allowed me to scramble up the ladder and sit on a bale while he pitched straw through the chute. Sometimes he'd manage to catch one of the cats we kept in the barn and hold it gently while I buried my face in the soft fur. Some afternoons when he had harnessed old Dolly to the stone sledge to fetch the empty milk cans from the highway, he'd lift me way, way up, onto her broad white back and let me ride. But this only happened if my mother wasn't around because she'd start screaming, *"Careful, she's going to fall"* until he'd lift me off and deposit me far from the menacing horse.

In the evening, I loved to sit and watch Ludwig peel apples, the paper-thin peel curling unbroken in long spirals onto the plate. Neighbours with an orchard let us take all we wanted of the apples that had fallen to the ground, and we collected enough to last through the long winter evenings. Ludwig knew endless jokes and riddles and he never seemed too busy or too preoccupied to talk to me. Sometimes he'd teach me Czech tongue twisters: *"Strc prst skrz krk,"* the classic all-consonant line that means roughly, "Stick finger through neck," and my all-time favourite *"Trsta trstetz tria tribernek,"* which involves three thousand three hundred and thirty-three red fire engines. Ludwig would laugh and laugh until I joined him.

As he sat peeling, I'd often count freckles on the back of his hands until the dots blurred. To me, Ludwig was so handsome. A head of tight red curls framed large green eyes, and a huge dimple sat squarely in the middle of his chin.

Both Anny and Ludwig had more patience than my parents did. They also seemed to be more cheerful, and certainly, they knew how to cheer me up. I still remember the little ditty Anny used to sing whenever tears gathered in my eyes:

Doodle-oodle-ei,	*Doodle-oodle-life*
Sagt my Wei'	*Says my wife*
Das Heferl ist zerbrochen	*The bowl, it got broken*
Hab' kein Salz,	*I've got no salt*
Hab kein Schmalz	*I've got no fat*
Wie soll ich da kochen?	*How can I be cookin'?*

Neither of my parents could have coped without the help of these two amazing people. Ludwig the fixer was the real glue that held everything together. Whatever was broken, eventually he'd figure out how to repair it. To this day, I keep every bit of string that comes my way, partly as a frugal habit that does not die easily, partly in memory of the way Ludwig could tie things together. The same knack that he brought to broken machinery, he also brought to human relationships.

Ludwig and my father got along beautifully, but the friction between my mother and my aunt was constant. Old rivalries from their childhood surfaced repeatedly, and usually Ludwig poured soothing oil on troubled waters.

I often wonder at the source of Ludwig's inner calm. He was not a very learned man, yet he had a wisdom that I find all the more admirable as I struggle to find my own perspective. There were frequent rumours that Anny had flagrant affairs. Did she? Or were the rumours just envy on the part of straitlaced outsiders who secretly admired her uninhibited social interactions? New acquaintances, both women and men, instantly felt they were her best friend. Anny knew how to reach out.

Ludwig, in turn, knew how to hold his tongue. After his death, Anny complained that it was the one piece of his advice that she had failed to master. Ludwig also knew how to recognize and foster the good in others. Just as he had encouraged me to sit unafraid on the back of a huge horse, so he helped others in later years. Long before "Native rights" became prevalent in Canadian consciousness, Ludwig began hiring men from a nearby reserve. Frequently, there were accidents and problems, but Ludwig never lost sight of what was right. He continued to support the men, and their families, who often became his friends.

At Ludwig's funeral, there were all sorts of people. Absent were a handful of people that Ludwig had been unable to forgive, those who had turned their back when Jews had clamoured for entry to Canada. Some had been fellow Jewish immigrants more concerned with getting ahead in the new world than with reaching out to those stranded in Europe.

Anny had always been a woman of action, the one who grabbed life by the scruff of the neck and shook it until change happened. Just as she had taken the lead in learning English and in selling eggs, she had stepped forward in other ways. Ironically, the more Anny did, the more my mother's resentment of her grew. Petty complaints, all voiced behind closed doors. Although her food tasted great to me and largely came from the same cookbook that my mother used, I grew up hearing that Anny was a terrible cook. Today, I still make her red current cake. The tart berries are covered with a sugared meringue, the two extremes evocative of Anny's own sweet-topped turbulence.

Even though I knew my aunt as a lively, outgoing woman who talked to everyone and had many friends, my mother claimed that nobody liked Anny. My admiration of my aunt was another of those dark secrets I hid from my mother.

Sadly, the lifelong rivalry between the two sisters grew worse as they aged. After Ludwig died, Anny retreated into a shell from which she emerged only briefly. She threw up walls and rarely deviated from the rigid daily routine that became her life. It was her way of creating a semblance of control.

There was always a reason why Anny could not make the short trip to Hamilton. Monday was laundry, Tuesday was ironing, Wednesday was hairdresser, Thursday was banking, Friday was shopping, and weekends were unsuitable. Although my mother routinely smuggled her little white lap dog into stores, restaurants, and local buses, my mother claimed that because of the dog, she could not board the bus to Brantford.

Three days before she died, I visited Anny for the last time. She was lucid but ready to rejoin her beloved Ludwig in the next life. She had no desire to see her sister again. After Anny's death, the letters that Max and Resl had sent to both sisters before the war were nowhere to be found.

Letters to Canada

*J*UST A SINGLE SET OF LETTERS, dated April 2, 1939 and sent to us in Antwerp, had restored each aunt and uncle to me. I seemed to hear them speak and watch them act. In 1996, with those letters in my lap, the family I had not known began to take shape.

I trembled with my father's sister Martha as she contemplated an uncertain future for herself and her children. I agonized with her husband Emil Fränkel as he hesitated, not knowing which way to turn to escape the Nazi net. Stretching across the miles and through the years, their longing to be with us reached deep into my heart.

I shared my Aunt Else's hopes as she smiled in the face of adversity. Her efforts seemed to parallel my own struggle to smooth life's bumpy road with food and cheerful conversation. I felt comfortable with her husband Emil Urbach, and saw the parallel between his directness and the abruptness of which I often stand accused. Even Emil's unsolicited advice to my parents seemed to echo my misguided efforts to be helpful. All too often, without being asked, I propose solutions to the problems of others.

However, it was in my Uncle Arnold that I most clearly recognized myself: fundamentally optimistic but rooted in reality and alert to human possibility. It was with great eagerness, therefore, that I opened the next letter in his handwriting. The letter is dated June 25, 1939. Much had transpired since that first letter from all six of my aunts and uncles in Prague to my parents in an Antwerp hotel. As of April 16, 1939, my parents had become Canadian farmers. How eagerly my father would have seized the letter, seeking some reassurance that the sky was not falling upon his family.

Arnold's letter does not disappoint. Its tone is newsy and chipper. There are many comings and goings. My grandmother Fanny had been to Prague, to visit the family and to check on the progress of her youngest grandchild, the "uncommonly cute" Dorly. Arnold paints life as warm, familial, and comfortingly normal.

> As always, there were many visitors at Else's and the conversation was lively. Of course, we talked about everything under the sun, but the main topic of conversation was you. Repeatedly, we discussed your new living conditions and there were great debates ranging from coping with your lack of drinking water to what you should plant in the fields. Well, these days we who are "left-behinders" must become more multi-faceted than ever and learn to understand much that is new.

Still, if this was a normal family visit, why did my grandfather Josef not accompany Fanny? Did she go alone to start the search for accommodation? In March of 1939, Hitler had declared Bohemia to be a "protectorate" of Germany, and by August, Jews living in the provinces of the protectorate had been ordered to resettle in Prague within the year. Fanny and Josef would soon be forced to move.

Arnold avoids troubling my parents with matters they could not change. However, he points out that Emil Fränkel has resisted all pressure to sell his house and his business premises in Linz, despite the new laws in Austria that bar Jews from owning property. In desperation, the man who assumed interim control of Emil's business affairs had come all the way to Prague to persuade Emil to sign over the property to him.

In 1996, safely under my own roof, I began to rethink what my parents meant when they said, *"When we fled, we lost everything."* Because I have been both fortunate and frugal, I own my home and do not wake up wondering if someone will take it away from me. Yet in Germany, Austria, and Czechoslovakia, that is precisely what happened. The government simply changed the law. Jews could no longer own property. Whatever they owned was simply taken by the state, and the state signed over to Aryan citizens any property that it did not keep. That is how we "lost" our home and the store in Strobnitz, how my mother's parents "lost" their home and their store in Germany, and how the Fränkels "lost" everything in Austria.

Some Jews hastily sold their property for very little, but Emil Fränkel refused to give up. If the man who took over the business came from Linz to Prague to pressure Emil, is it not because that very same man expects to be the new owner?

Arnold describes his own work situation in a surprisingly open manner.

> *I need some rest and relaxation, and am actually overdue for holiday time, but I shall have to be patient until early August. Because several of our employees have now been given permanent vacation time, the weeks ahead promise to be sour and work-intensive. Of course, we have no holiday plans, since it's impossible to plan very far into the future. Still, I'd at least like to go to Taus for a week to get my teeth fixed.*

The German that Arnold uses is somewhat unusual, compelling me to read between the lines. I conclude that the "permanent vacation" granted to certain employees is a euphemism for Jews who have been fired in accordance with new regulations excluding them from medicine, the law, and other professions. I note too that conditions are so unstable that even a month ahead is considered "long-range" planning. Given the uncertain future, Arnold urges my parents to write more often.

> *I had counted on a letter this week from you, my dear Canadians,*
> *but on the other hand, we do understand that you are preoccupied*
> *with concerns beyond keeping up a correspondence, and that your*
> *hand is perhaps too tired at day's end to pick up pen and paper.*

Arnold adds one more paragraph to reassure my parents that the bonds of
family transcend distance.

> *Our thoughts are always with you and I visualize your situation*
> *with all its difficulties and shortages as if I really knew it. Vera is*
> *often caught up in her thoughts by your description of the natural*
> *surroundings. Every little creek that we come to, she wonders if it*
> *looks like yours. On the other hand, I often wonder if the weather*
> *there is as miserable as what we have been having here. Does it*
> *make you frantic and is there anyone who will help you if it*
> *suddenly starts to rain when the ripened hay is in the field?*

Arnold's letter is followed by a few paragraphs from his wife Vera who has
mailed us a book on naturopathic healing. She apologizes for having been
unsuccessful in finding the up-to-date health lexicon that my parents had
requested.

I wonder why Vera does not have access to recent books and publica-
tions. She does not spell out the answer, but her letter suggests that life is
changing for her and for all European Jews. Everyone is under stress.

> *I always read your letters with great pleasure and await them*
> *impatiently, but please do not be angry with me if I just attach*
> *good wishes or even nothing to Arnold's letters. We know each*
> *other well enough that surely you will not take it as indifference if*
> *I am sometimes simply not able to write. The inner unease and a*
> *certain restlessness that now characterize each day cause such an*
> *emptiness in my brain that I am sometimes incapable of putting*
> *two sentences together. It is a well-known fact that great stress usu-*
> *ally attacks the human organ that is by nature inclined to be the*

weakest. In some, that organ is the stomach, in some the intestines, and in my case, the brain.

Vera's struggle leads her to speak twice in a row of the need for God's help. Calamity and uncertainty are cruel reminders of our own limitations.

Perhaps God will not abandon His own. I hope that this will be true for you, my dear Canadians. We are very aware of all the hardships that you will have to endure. We know how all the harsh, demanding labour will sap your limited strength. God will really have to help.

———

UNLIKE HIS SISTER-IN-LAW Vera, Emil Urbach trusts his own powers of rational thought. Having spent hours poring over books, his typed letters are treasure-troves of information and well-intentioned advice.

We always read your letters with great interest, but unfortunately we have not so far been able to imagine clearly your present life and circumstances. Even the dominant climatic conditions there will be markedly different from ours.

It is hard to give you advice from a distance, because many things aren't clear to us. Given the proximity of a larger city (Hamilton), you have a good market for agricultural products, and you are in the best part of Canada. Soil there consists of sand mixed with clay; the terrain is level and can easily be worked. Unfortunately, you don't have coal, but you do have water power there. In the summer you won't be too hot but in the winter it will be rather cold. The temperature in Toronto, for example, ranges from -20 in January to +33 or higher in July. The Great Lakes don't freeze, but winter lasts 5 months.

It is perhaps also advisable to proceed from small to large, getting a smaller farm next and managing it well and then undertaking

something larger with the money earned and saved. For sure, a
small landowner can't do much; farming on a small scale isn't
worthwhile anywhere, and certainly not in Canada. Even before the
present crisis, farming was already unprofitable here in Czechoslo-
vakia. A small landowner was only able to survive by taking advan-
tage of by-products like pig manure or by raising bees alongside
profitable plants (poppies, mustard, sunflowers for oil, crops that
attract bees while also providing fodder for animals.)

Since you have a very real shortage of money, the best solution
would be to build (under very strict conditions) a collective with
people who have a stronger base of capital. You would get paid for
your labour and in this way, you could obtain some capital. Of
course this means slaving away. A large farm also involves greater
mangement demands, whereas your part in a collective would be
easier to manage.

Even on the topic of location, Emil has advice to offer. He points out that
land on the prairies is cheap in part because the weather is brutal, and that
tracts of land on the Gaspé Peninsula could lead to sudden riches if they
were to contain mineral deposits. The outraged voice of my father still
echoes in my head. "*Wie stellt er sich denn das vor?* How does he expect us
to follow these preposterous suggestions?"

Emil's well-meant words might have encouraged a more self-confident
man. My father's goal was modest: survival in this alien environment for
which he was so woefully unprepared. Emil must have known this to be
true, for the books that he sent are reminders of how little my father knew
about farming.

In the same mail, I'm sending you three books:
1. Introduction to Vegetable Gardening by Friederich Huck
2. The Practical Vegetable Gardener by Fr. Saftenberg
3. The Garden Book for Beginners by Johann Boettner.
Wishing you good results, we remain with best regards
Yours

I smile at the end of another letter that Emil Urbach does not sign. His letters are indeed so unique that he need not identify himself. Still, there was nothing in Emil's world to help him conceptualize the physical demands of life on the farm. He pictured my parents as sitting about on Sundays, eagerly reading horticultural books. The reality was that they worked from darkness to darkness, seven days a week. We ate our evening meal in the kitchen by the thin light of a coal oil lantern. Then, exhausted, my parents fell into bed.

———

BY JULY OF 1939, MY PARENTS had progressed from communal living in Mount Hope to farm ownership with Ludwig and Anny as partners. In a letter from Emil Urbach dated June 11, 1939, Emil sends *"a wish that, with God's help and your own diligence, you become mega-agriculturalists and millionaires."* Along with congratulations, Emil sends a myriad of new suggestions that might have merit in a modern context. For my overwhelmed parents, it was all too much. They were barely coping, and Emil kept sending suggestions that they could not imagine implementing.

> *Dear Gretel and dear Edi,*
> *Your letter really satisfied us this time because it was very descriptive and contained lots of details that we welcomed. We send you our sincerest congratulations on the advantageous acquisition of the new farm, and wish with God's help and your own diligence, that you become mega-agriculturalists and millionaires. Of course this is hard when you start small, but slowly but surely it happens, especially if one has the necessary luck in addition and clear-minded determination, with persevereance to last out the setbacks of all beginnings.*
> *Before the onset of the rainy season, it would be important to have the roof repaired so that the rain won't damage the foundations of the interior of the barn. Ask the local authorities whether you can have the water from your well definitively tested. I'm*

sending you (albeit for lack of a German translation) a copy of the Czech regulations regarding wells, so that you will have some points of reference as to how a well should be constituted. The water must not have any aftertaste. If it does, it contains abnormal ingredients (perhaps epsom salts or sulphate of magnesia.) This can easily be determined in an apothecary in Hamilton. You then might have "mineral water" to draw off in the house.

Perhaps you will succeed after all in planting cabbage in the good sandy soil near the little brook. Maybe a small attempt at planting rye in the incipient garden, so that you can find out whether and why it won't grow there. According to the data in the books on Canada available to me, almost all of our plants grow there, and even several kinds of some plants. Maybe rye too can thrive there, although it is not listed in the kinds of grains that were harvested there in the year 1891.

If the women do not have to work in the fields, they could occupy themselves with the raising of bees. Then you would have healthful honey in the house. The care and raising of poultry should also be their lot. Maybe you could connect with a veterinarian whose only job would be to supervise the fattening of poultry using kitchen waste. Just make sure to get varieties of poultry that lay lots and that lay early on, so that you can be the first to reach the market with fresh eggs. Whoever brings new or rare things can charge more for them and makes a greater profit on everything. It would be thus for early flowers in spring!

Unable to grasp the conditions under which we lived, Emil continued urging my parents to install both plumbing and electricity.

It would be a wonderful thing to get electric lights first, then some sort of reservoir in the top corner of the roof as plumbing for the house and rinsing for the toilet so that you could create some kind of bathroom facility.

His timing could not have been worse. During that first uncertain season of coaxing the soil to yield a viable harvest, during that long hot summer of scanning the skies for sun and rain in due measure, my penniless parents were not concerned with creature comforts. Although we did eventually install electricity, indoor plumbing was a luxury we never achieved on the farm.

———

MEANWHILE, A VERY DIFFERENT kind of letter had been sent by Martha and Emil Fränkel. They are desperate to join us on the farm my parents now owned with Anny and Ludwig as partners. Their eagerness is as palpable as their awareness of impending events.

Martha writes first, and seesaws between hope and despair.

> *How gladly we would already be helping you with everything. When we join you in Canada, there will be no lack of good will and love of work, but I suspect we are still far away from it.*

Martha does her best to make allowances for my father's predicament, but her desperation seeps through.

> *Because of your move to the farm and all the work you have now, you probably will not have much time left to speed up the matter of getting us into Canada. We know that things cannot be done in a day, but try to imagine yourself in our situation. We have been waiting just as long as you and we have not even the tiniest glimmer of light ahead.*
>
> *Dear Edi, your efforts do not seem to be falling on fertile soil. If your time permits, we would be happy to pay for a trip to Ottawa. If there is not enough room on your farm for us, do not worry. We will find a way to earn our daily bread. Just give us the possibility of immigrating, for the constantly unclear picture of our future is really crushing us down.*

My father surely went to his grave with Martha's words etched on his heart. He knew that others in the small immigrant community had gone to Toronto and Ottawa, or like Mimi, to Montreal, and had failed to gain an entry visa for their loved ones. When he received Martha's letter, my father would have obsessed over what he could do:

> How can I go all the way to Ottawa? Could I hitchhike? Is there a bus? Who would know if there is a bus from Hamilton? Who could go with me to the bus station to ask? How much will it cost? Will it be money well spent or should the money go toward a new plough? Or maybe toward another cow and a few chickens so that there will be food for our first winter in Canada? And will it be time well spent? Would it be better to plant the swampy back field that is just starting to dry out? Even supposing I go to Ottawa, what will I do there? Wander from office to office, being mocked as a greenhorn?

My father never lost the sense of having been a failure. Thanks to the urging of Emil Fränkel, we were safely in Canada, but my father had not managed to return the favour.

> *The days and weeks pass, and dear Emil is mostly very sad and lost in thought. To make matters worse, this week there was a man here from Linz. We probably have to sell our house, although he did promise "perhaps" to help us emigrate.*

I shudder at the bait and switch tactics of this nameless man from Linz, the Austrian city renowned worldwide for its raspberry torte but, in an act of global amnesia, forgotten as Hitler's hometown. Did this unnamed man have connections within the Nazi party? How else would he have been able to extend the ultimate carrot on the stick? Did he really intend to help the Fränkels leave Europe or did he simply want to get his hands on their property?

My dear ones, I'm forcing myself to write these few lines, and I'd
rather be helping you than adding to your sorrows, but I beg you
again from the bottom of my heart, pour us some clear wine and
tell us the truth. Should it be impossible to help us despite your
good intentions, then we will somehow have to find some other
way, because with the children, I cannot go through another win-
ter. We have become quite toughened already, but the autumn is
not supposed to bring anything good.

Did my parents pour that clear wine? Did they tell the Fränkels that the situation in Canada was hopeless? Did they tell them it was the official policy
of the Canadian government to prevent Jews from entering the country?
The autumn that Martha so dreads, the autumn that lurks so ominously, is
the autumn of 1939, the outbreak of World War II.

Now, I want to focus on the sweeter part, and that is our dear
Helly-child. In my imagination, I see her clearly, toddling about
and babbling and throwing herself at Aunt Anny saying, "I'm
hungry." It is really so joyous that the child is thriving there. We all
send her many thousands of kisses.
Dear Anny, you will certainly be very happy to have your little
sister with you and Edi likewise to have found in Ludwig such a
kind partner. When you get everything in order, things will give
you even more pleasure. Our little Dorothy is as brown as a berry
already and has three teeth. Everyone is delighted with her, espe-
cially dear Else. Ilserl now speaks Czech to her friends. Emil visits
your parents daily.

I note with pleasure that Ludwig's kindness was mentioned in the first letter my parents wrote from Canada. I also note that Baby Dorly has three
teeth already, a sharp reminder of the passage of time, as is the fact that
Ilserl has learned to speak Czech. Involuntarily, I wonder if she had already
forgotten me. When this letter was written, I still had no new playmates
and spoke not a word of English.

Now you will soon be in receipt of the lift containing your furniture and possessions, including a good clothes brush and a horsehair broom. These are of the top quality, so take good care of them.

From deep in the recesses of memory springs the smell and the sound of dozens of baby chicks. My parents converted that lift into a chicken coop.

I also remember the special clothes brush my father always used before hanging his good suit in the wardrobe. I wonder what happened to the brush? I still have the wardrobe. It sits, unused, its panels piled in a corner of my garage. Modern closets and low ceilings have rendered it useless, yet I cannot part with this bit of history that came to live in my house along with my aging mother.

Our dear little Mama is supposed to come here soon. We will be very pleased if only our dear parents stay in good health.

For a long time, my thoughts linger on the words "Our dear little Mama." This is the first time Martha has mentioned her mother. Why would Martha have used these words for my grandmother, a strong, capable woman who raised three sons and two daughters?

———

IN HIS PORTION OF THE LETTER, Emil Fränkel makes few concessions to sociability. He congratulates us on the acquisition of the farm but our progress only seems to highlight his own frustration. Dealing with my mother's parents on a daily basis is clearly not easy. My grandmother Resl remains in a state of apathy and deep depression. My grandfather listens to no one and believes that he alone knows best. Everywhere he looks, Emil finds only locked doors and blocked avenues.

Regarding our coming to Canada, I gather from your brief reports that it is hopeless. I have been waiting since March to be called up, but no news to date. People in other categories at least have approval from the local branch of The Canadian and are waiting for the travel permit. If only I were far enough ahead to have something in my hands, I would be less fearful of the future. My dear Edi, words are not enough in such times. Actions alone are what matters.

"*I'm sorry isn't good enough. Apologies don't solve anything. Only your actions matter.*" The very words my father had used to teach me right from wrong. Had Emil's words congealed into a stick with which my father guided me but lashed himself?

From the reports I get from my friends, I gather that eventually everyone over there will find a way to earn his daily bread in peace and freedom. Circumstances are very different here for those who have absolutely no hope of getting out. Here, one day resembles the next and fear about the future keeps growing stronger.

I visit your dear parents every day, but there is little that I can do for them. As soon as they get the exit permit, they will be allowed to leave and I will send their possessions in a lift. Your dear mother's condition has not improved. Two months ago, I told them that they should consult a specialist about the medical treatment that she has received to date, but they refuse to hear of it. There are many days when your dear mother does not want to cook, which sorely vexes your father. Nor do they want to eat in a restaurant. Even if I were to spend the entire day there, I cannot change the situation.

It is not difficult to imagine the effect of this letter on my father. He was not a man given to shrugging things off. He would have consulted all the self-anointed experts among the handful of immigrants that constituted his world, asking everyone he knew whether anything could be done to expedite the Fränkels' immigration to Canada. When everyone replied in the negative, my father would have flogged himself inwardly for all that lay beyond his control. And because my mother clung to the hope that her parents would soon be arriving, my father would not have revealed to her his own despair.

———

AT THE END OF MARTHA's letter, there is a single line in a child's irregular handwriting that triggers my tears.

My dear Hely I think of you often and send you kisses. Ilse.

Searching in Europe
1997–1998

*F*ROM THE DAY THAT I FIRST READ the letters, they have absorbed all of my free time.

I began by making photocopies. A friend with a background in archival preservation techniques showed me how to back the two-sided sheets with plain paper to lessen their transparency. She also insisted that I wear white cotton gloves to handle the fragile originals. Only then did I put the letters away, no longer in their cheerful red box but in acid-free envelopes in the darkness of a safety deposit box.

My next task was to decipher the handwriting. In the case of my grand-parents, I could not even make out the dates or the signatures, for my eyes are not trained in *Kurrentschrift*, the turn of the century writing style that students in German-speaking countries painstakingly practiced. My mother could read entire passages with relative ease, and she did much of this work. By then, she had moved to Vancouver to be with me. Physically frail but mentally alert, she willingly agreed to help me. For months, the clacking of her old Underwood accompanied my household tasks as she transcribed the spindly handwriting into German typescript.

I acquired a scanner to transmit her typed words into my computer, but the scanner balked at the old-fashioned, ink-smudged lettering. Because there was so much that the scanner failed to read, page after page had to be re-entered by hand.

My final challenge was to translate the letters. Because my mother had long ago decided to speak only English, I had not used a word of German since a brief teaching stint in the 1970s. The dictionary became my best friend as I worked from the German column on the left to the English meaning on the right. It was the first stage of a complex process.

The next stage involved moving from literal meaning to colloquial English. Initially, I had planned to publish the letters in their entirety. I had not intended to write a memoir, and saw myself merely as instrumental in bringing to life those who had written the letters. After completing a university course in "creative non-fiction writing," I bowed to the expert advice of seasoned writers and agreed to incorporate my discovery of the letters into the completed work.

As I proceeded, I wrote notes to myself. Every surface in the house soon bore scraps of paper with unanswered questions. My mother filled in some blanks, but countless questions remained. I pored over library books and Internet sites and created lists of people to ask. Still, each answer often led only to more questions.

Not all the letters are dated. Seeking to put events into chronological order, I read and re-read the letters until their contents became stories of individual lives. Thoughts of the family became my daily companions.

The more familiar I became with their letters, the more palpable became my longing for these absent family members. I began to fantasize about family gatherings, with relaxed and happy adults sitting around a table laden with food. Children would be weaving in and out, smaller ones scooped onto laps while older ones boisterously played out of earshot.

I spent time with a friend who does genealogy. Her hallway is a gallery of turn-of-the-century figures whose stiff dignity is captured within simple black frames. I listened with longing as she described her discoveries in a rural Ontario churchyard. I would have to go further afield.

Before long, opportunity literally knocked upon my door. It came on a dreary day in January, 1997, as I sat with magnifying glass in hand, trying to decipher illegible handwriting on a letter that I had already put aside several times. Suddenly a knock on the door accompanied the click of the mail slot.

"Advertising," I thought, as I stooped to pick up the green flyer. I was at that point of non-progress when even a piece of junk mail was a welcome distraction. To my surprise, however, this was no ad for window-washing or gardening help. It was a handwritten note asking if I would be interested in a house exchange. On impulse, I called the number.

The woman who answered the telephone had a strong British accent. *"My mother lives just up the street from you,"* she told me. *"We are here on a visit. My husband and I and our children would like to come for a whole summer, but having all of us for twenty-four hours a day is too much for Mother. We would like to offer our country house in Dorset in exchange for a place in Vancouver. If it would help you to decide, we also have a condo in Switzerland, which you are welcome to use."*

Within twenty-four hours, I had made my decision. I booked a flight and invited family and friends to join me for part of the summer. Because time seemed to stretch ahead, I opted to travel by train for the Swiss leg of the trip. With only a small detour, I discovered that the train would also take me to Austria, specifically to Linz where my friends Martin and Tracey had recently made their home. Linz is the very city where the Fränkels had lived. I longed to see the place that had been home to my Aunt Martha, my Uncle Emil and to my favourite cousin, Ilserl.

I HAD MET MARTIN IN Vancouver many years ago when I was low on cash but rich in empty rooms. I posted a Room-for-Rent notice at the university where it attracted Martin's attention. In addition to being a student, Martin was a handsome outdoorsman with a warm smile and a gentle manner that drew me instantly. We became good friends. Sometimes, I would read his term papers to smooth out awkward phrases and he would reward me with thick slices of the rye loaf he baked each week from his family's bread starter.

Martin brought Tracey into my life. She too was a graduate student, a warm witty redhead with Irish roots and a matching temperament. She was passionate about her studies and fiery in her condemnation of social injustice. Although she is scarcely half my age, Tracey is wise beyond her years. She brought with her a bubbling laughter balanced by deep spiritual insights. I was delighted that she stayed with me long after Martin decided to return to Austria for the completion of his doctoral studies.

It was clear that Tracey missed Martin, and after lengthy deliberation, she agreed to try life in Austria. Because she spoke no German, it meant delaying her own dreams of professional accomplishment. Still, at a deep level, Tracey knew that she must follow her heart. Her intuition was right. Sometime later, they were married. In the photo that they sent me, Martin is proudly attired in lederhosen with embroidered suspenders and a Tyrolean hat, while Tracey wears the traditional Austrian blouse and dirndl. I was eager to witness their happiness first hand.

I was not disappointed. They glowed with joy as we sat in their tiny kitchen, talking with ease as only good friends can. They were supportive of my other mission: to learn about my family. The next morning, Martin accompanied me to city hall where surprises lay in store both for me and for the young archivist in charge of the records.

———

"Ah, if they were born in Linz their names will be here," said the young archivist, proudly pointing to the shelf. *"Volume VI, F for Fränkel."* I shook my head as I glanced at the title: *Baptismal Records for Linz and Surrounding Areas.* I was unable to utter the tangle of thoughts that tied up my tongue. Here, in this silent place filled with long, wooden tables where researchers huddled over their German documents, I felt again the awful shame and weight of my Jewishness. Finally, I managed a semblance of the truth:

"They were not baptized."

Tracey and Martin in traditional Austrian attire for their wedding

The young man stared at me as if I were mad. *"Not baptized? But everyone is baptized! Even the stillborn. Only then can a person be buried in consecrated ground."*

Silence. He was young, and in his lifetime, there had only been Christians in his part of the world. I had to be blunt.

"They were Jews."

Now the light went on, and with mutterings of *"Ein Moment bitte,"* he disappeared into the bowels of the archives. Eventually he emerged, clutching a package of file folders. They were marked with a Star of David and bore the words *"Israelitische Kultusgemeinde."* The Jewish Community.

I found a corner and settled down to work. The papers were all in order and I had no difficulty finding their names. Fränkel, Ilse, born in Linz-on-the-Danube, January 23, 1931, resident of Linz-on-the-Danube. Ditto for her sister Dorothea, born July 10, 1938. Born just a few blocks from this table in the archives.

The records have all been meticulously kept. Even the name of the mid-wife who attended both births is on file. The paper trail confirms that it was not until after Dorly's birth that the Fränkels went to Prague. Where and how did they live during those last months in Austria?

I rechecked the dates. Hitler annexed Austria on March 12, 1938. Because of her pregnancy, Martha must have been unable to travel, for the Fränkels would not otherwise have remained in Austria. They were at an impasse. With Martha in a late stage of pregnancy, travel was risky, but staying was equally risky.

Did they pack a suitcase, ready to flee in the middle of the night? Did they huddle somewhere, Emil, his pregnant wife, and their seven-year-old daughter? From which window did they observe the scene? Was Linz just like Vienna, where Jews were forced to scrub sidewalks with toothbrushes, watched by crowds of jeering spectators?

Where was the Fränkels' home? Had it been looted? Did Emil sell his company? Was it expropriated? In yet another set of archives in yet another government building, I found the address of both the house and of the manufacturing plant owned by Emil Fränkel.

———

NUMBER 28 RUDOLFSTRASSE. The Fränkel house was not far, and I walked there that afternoon. The house was spacious, and seemed to have numerous inhabitants. Although I pressed each doorbell, there was no response. What would I have done if someone had answered?

In my briefcase, I carried the papers from the archives, including the document that had stripped the Fränkels of this house. The document is couched in legalese, but its meaning is clear. It states that one Katharina Bartl gives sworn testimony that she is of pure Aryan stock and that she is therefore entitled to purchase the property of Emil Fränkel for a sum of 60.384 Reich marks, a sum corresponding precisely to an estimate determined by Josef Keplinger, Federal Representative for the Upper Danube. The signature of Emil Fränkel is notably absent. The document is boldly stamped and sealed with the German eagle and the words *Heil Hitler*. Dr.

Fritz Fideo becomes the executor charged with the "de-Jewification" (*entjuden*) of Emil Fränkel's remaining property.

———

I STOOD FOR A LONG TIME IN front of the Fränkel house. Lines from the letters that I had read mingled with my own confused thoughts. This is where my cousin Ilserl had lived before she came to Prague. This is where the cries of Baby Dorly had echoed briefly in the nursery. This is where Martha had opened the door each evening to greet Emil with a kiss. I took a few photos of the building and shifted impatiently. I considered going to a café to sit down, but I had no desire for coffee. Restlessness drove me away.

My footsteps led in the direction of Emil's business address. Because street names had been changed to honour the Nazis and then changed again to cover up that period of history, finding this address proved more challenging. I returned to city hall where willing clerks dug through file after file and sent me from office to office. The paper trail is solid.

The records indicate that Emil had been sole owner of a company engaged in the production of fruit juice and liqueurs. There are documents indicating that Emil was an Austrian citizen to whom many business licenses had been issued over the years. There are also documents dated 1938 that cancel those licenses "in accordance with the ordinances and laws governing Jewish property."

The various clerks, librarians, and archivists that I encountered were all very eager to help. My file folder marked Fränkel soon bulged with business cards, new referrals, and a multitude of photocopies. It was easier to keep collecting papers than to imagine the reality of 1938.

Had the Fränkels been able to stay in their own home while waiting for Dorly to be born? If not, who might have hidden them? Did they dare venture out or had they spent months closeted indoors?

I think involuntarily of Hilderl, a relative on my mother's side. Hilderl was a beautiful child known to me only through my photo album. In the photo, she is perhaps five years old. Her hair is a mass of fluffy curls, her eyes are large and soulfully deep, and her cheeks are rounded. Her name is

"Das arme Hilderl." Poor little Hilda. Neither her name nor the details ever varied as my mother told the story:

"Poor little Hilda was a delightful child, sweet, bright, charming. One day as she was walking home with her mother, a Nazi tank deliberately drove onto the sidewalk and killed Hilderl. I don't know how her mother survived. We all thought she would go crazy."

Here my mother would pause. Her eyes would fill with tears and she would disappear to somewhere deep inside. I tried a few times to push the edges of the envelope, wanting to know more of Hilderl's story. Each time, my mother's voice would change. It became as cold and distant as the voice of a defendant before a hostile inquisitor.

Did the Fränkels know about Hilderl? Did the incident happen in Germany or in Austria? Did it perhaps take place a few years later in Prague when the Fränkels were already there? A life snuffed out, a photo in my album the only evidence that poor little Hilderl existed. There is no one for me to ask.

On the back of one of the documents that I collected in Linz is a handwritten note stating that Emil Fränkel and his family fled to Czechoslovakia in August 1938. I too longed to flee. I longed to flee the archives and to flee Linz with all its reminders of the past.

———

WHEN I RETURNED FROM my impulsive house exchange, my mother relished every detail of my adventures in Europe. I had offered to include her on the trip, but by then, her health had become too fragile. Although she knew that I visited Austria, she asked only about England and Switzerland.

For her, the Swiss mountains were a Sound-of-Music dream, as they had been for me. She loved to hear of my daily alpine walks, each culminating at a different local farm offering coffee and guest services along with unique cheeses made from the milk of their own cows or goats. She loved to hear how I would go out first thing each morning to buy fresh rolls at the local bakery and bring them back, still redolent of yeast and butter. Meanwhile, my friends would brew the coffee and set out the cups and

Das arme Hilderl
(poor little Hilda)

plates on the deck where we would enjoy breakfast with a view of the Eiger and the Jungfrau.

Repeatedly I tried to talk about my time in Linz. My mother was not interested. Invariably, she either left the room or changed the subject.

However, she was happy to talk about growing up in Cham, a small town in Bavaria. After coming to live with me, my mother often regaled my friends with stories that I had heard before. Much to her delight, my friends listened to these stories with fresh ears. They smiled at her tales of getting dressed for Sunday afternoon walks along the river to meet and greet the passing parade of similarly attired townsfolk and their captive children. They showed interest in tales of her long hair and how hard it was to sit still while my grandmother combed it. They laughed at my grandfather's outrage the day my Aunt Anny came home with bobbed hair.

My mother never talked about leaving Europe. Not to others and not to me. The closer the conversation got to 1939, the more visible her upset. I tried to push, but only so far. My questions brought about heart palpitations and a frightening level of agitation.

Whenever I asked her how she was doing with the letters, she would sigh and say, *"It's all so sad."* Several times, I offered to find someone else, perhaps someone at the university to finish the task. Each time, my mother declined. I believe she intended the transcription of the letters to be her last gift to me, as indeed it was.

———

IT WAS WHILE WE WERE working on the letters that my mother first spoke of a phone call from Germany. She had heard from Tini. I remembered the name, if not the person. Tini had been our *Dienstmädel,* a word that it is impossible to translate into the English "maidservant" without its veneer of Victorian class distinction but would be closer to the North American "hired girl," which does not have the same class connotations, as it was often the daughter of a neighbour. Tini was a young girl who helped my mother do things like hand wash the sheets and prepare all meals from scratch in a large household that included my grandparents and me.

"*Tini called last night.*"

From long experience, I had learned to moderate my reaction.

"*Really? She's still alive?*"

"*Hmm. I answered the phone and it was a strange man whose voice I didn't recognize. He said that he was Tini's grandson, and then he said 'Just a minute' and then she came on the line.*"

"*And?*"

"*She said that it was her grandson's idea. He said that there can't be that many people with the name Waldstein in Canada, and that he could find me through the phone company, and he did.*"

My frustration level was climbing sharply and I longed to blurt out some of the questions that would have resulted in clamped lips and the faraway look that I knew all too well.

"*So what did she say?*" I queried, keeping my voice deliberately neutral.

"*She's fine. She's in good health. She lives near her children in Germany.*"

"*In Germany? Where in Germany?*"

Already it was too much. The pursed lips warned me that I had been too eager.

"*I don't know. Some small town in Germany. I forget the name. It doesn't matter.*"

Immediately, my mother changed the subject. I knew the routine. Further questions would get me nowhere. Perhaps in a few weeks I could try again.

Finally, one day my mother said, "*Tini called again. We talked for a long time, until I said 'Tini, this is costing you a fortune.'*"

This time, I asked no questions and simply listened, my thoughts darting about amongst the tangled details that my mother chose to recount. As she wound down, I heard my mother say, "*She gave me her address so I could write to her. And her phone number.*"

At that instant, the idea was born. I would visit Tini. I would ask her all the questions that had welled up inside me for so long. She would know. Perhaps she would tell me.

———

TIME PASSED, BUT IN THE spring of 1998, I was able to plan my visit. I wrote to Tini and gave her the date of my arrival but no specific time. Indeed, I had no sense of distance from the airport or of how long it would take me to get to the little town of Ehningen that I had located in my old school atlas.

Frankfurt airport was large, bustling, and international. Rollaway suitcase in tow, I headed for the information desk where I was directed to the elevator, which emptied directly onto a platform where a train whisked me to the central station to make my next connection. One hour later, I sat back contentedly to watch the countryside fly past. Gardens and neatly cultivated fields alternated with picturesque red-roofed towns. Heavily wooded areas yielded to industrial buildings old and new. Town and country, past and present, all seamlessly interwoven.

Soon it was time to gather my belongings. Across the aisle, I noted a woman also preparing to dismount. I nodded and asked whether she knew Ehningen and could recommend a small hotel. She laughed at my request, and replied that above the butcher shop was the only public accommodation in town. Glancing at my lightweight summer jacket and then at the heavy rain that awaited beyond the open platform, she kindly offered me a ride. Gratefully I followed as she headed for a Mercedes parked in the nearby lot.

"*I work at the Mercedes plant,*" she explained as I hesitated to place my well-travelled bag on the leather seat. "*We get to purchase a car at a reduced price.*"

Moments later, the luxurious sedan pulled up under a sign that read *Fleischer-Metzger-Bierstube-Gäste*. As I struggled to lift out the suitcase, my nameless companion disappeared and returned with a heavy key. Up the stairs and down the hall she marched. Key in hand, she opened the door to a large room dominated by a huge bed buried under a white feather quilt. "*You will be very comfortable here,*" she assured me as she opened a window overlooking the garden.

Though I scarcely knew where to begin, I felt compelled to respond to her kindness. Haltingly I explained how I had come to be so far from the standard tourist haunts.

"I am from Canada and I am looking for a woman whom I do not know but who knows me. Or rather, a woman who knew me. It was a long time ago, when I was small. Sixty years ago. Before the war."

Clearly intrigued, my new acquaintance looked at the address I had pulled out.

"Königsbergerstrasse. Not far at all. Please, let me drive you there. I must be sure that you find this woman."

She remained in the car as I walked up the few steps of the small apartment block. Her name was listed by the intercom. Frau Christine Fuchs. I pushed the buzzer, listened to the electric crackle and then a cautious *"Ja?"*

"Tini, es ist die Helen. Ich bin hier."

"Moment bitte."

Moments later, the door opened and strong arms flung themselves about me. German words burned into my memory.

"Helly! What have I done to deserve this day? Dear God in Heaven! I thank You, dear Father, for allowing me to live so long! I thank You for allowing me to see my Helly-girl again."

Now we wept, both of us, as Tini repeated her words and brought balm to my heart.

"Sixty years ago, they tore you from my arms. Never did I think to see you again. God's Grace has brought you back to me."

My Mercedes woman, whose name I never learned, walked quietly to where we stood. Beaming, she shook hands with Frau Fuchs, but declined the opportunity to linger. She spoke with tact and understanding: *"These moments are for you alone. I leave you to enjoy this special reunion."*

I followed Tini up the stairs to the fourth floor, marvelling at the erect back and powerful legs of this woman in her eighties. Although she barely came up to my shoulder, she gave the impression of strength. She was well built. Not fat, but buxom, her breasts proudly pointing the way. A sheaf of naturally grey hair enveloped a wrinkled face that to me was beautiful.

Words tumbled out of us. She spoke, I spoke, we both spoke, sometimes at once. A thousand questions, each answer leading in turn to fresh

Helen in the arms of Tini, 1937

questions. *"Tell me about… how come… why… when… where… what did you do…?"* My questions continued, not just for hours, but for days. We took time out for other things without interrupting the long conversations about a past that I could not remember, yet that seemed etched into my being.

Tini confided that immediately after our departure, she had approached her boyfriend and announced that she wanted to be married. She had told him that her arms felt unbearably empty. Despite the financial and political uncertainties that swirled about them, he agreed to a hasty wedding. Their son and their daughter Erni were born shortly thereafter.

"It was as if I had to replace the child that had been stolen from my arms," Tini said. *"When they took you away, they tore out a piece of my heart."*

The sound of Tini's voice awoke wordless memories. Her accent itself is a strange clone of my own way of speaking. People used to comment that my accent was different from that of my parents who spoke *Hochdeutsch*, the cultivated German considered to be "classic." It was strange that I spoke more of a dialect than my own family. Now I understood. My first intense exposure to language was through Tini who had spent her days keeping an eye on me as she prepared meals and did all the housework in a pre-electric era.

Tini spoke *"Böhmisch,"* the local dialect of the former kingdom of Bohemia that had become the cornerstone of Czechoslovakia. She was born not far from Strobnitz, the small village near the Austrian border where my father's parents had long owned the town's only store.

Tini told me that she was sure we left Strobnitz in September of 1938 and that we had gone to Prague. I replied that this was impossible because we did not come to Canada until the spring of 1939. Besides, my mother had repeatedly regretted that she had never been to Prague. Tini was unshakable in her version of the story:

> It was right after Hitler made his speech about the Sudeten-land. Usually your parents didn't need me in the evening, but that night they asked me to stay with you because they wanted to hear the speech. The whole family gathered around the radio. There had already been rumours about a place called Dachau and I heard them say that some Jews had just disappeared overnight. You left for Prague the next day, and I helped your grandmother close up the house in Strobnitz. Your grandparents moved to Budweis two or three days after you left, and they gave me a key to the house in Strobnitz. This is not a trust I could forget.

Only when Tini produced a postcard in my mother's handwriting mailed from Prague in November 1938 did I believe her. My mother had sent it to the address of Tini's parents. Tini had kept that postcard through the war and all its attendant dispersals.

My visit was an emotional time for Tini as well as for me. In Germany, the topic of the war had been off-limits both for the millions who had voted for and supported Hitler and for those who were simply victims of the times. Tini described a day when she had been scheduled to take the train on an urgent errand. Some inexplicable premonition had kept her from doing so. At the very moment she would have been there, the railway station had received a direct hit from a bomb and many people had been killed or wounded.

Repeatedly, we returned to the subject of the war, each time from a different angle. There was much that Tini had not told her own children, preferring to put the war years behind her. Tini's daughter Erni had come to meet me the first evening of my arrival. We bonded immediately.

"*I had to come,*" Erni said. "*I have heard about you ever since I was born. My mother has never stopped talking about you, and about the terrible loss that seemed to leave a hole in her heart.*"

Erni and I found that we had much in common, including a reluctance to upset our mothers by asking questions about the past. Erni and her husband Rudi took time off from work to show me Germany. I learned to drink *Hefeweizen* from tall glasses, and to order German dishes that featured more meat than I would normally eat in a month. Arm in arm, Tini and I walked through picturesque towns where geraniums cascaded from every window, where cobbled streets led to historic houses where my favourite poets had once dwelt, where coffee houses and the aroma of freshly baked pastries invited us to linger. To linger and to talk.

It was with real reluctance that I left Tini and her family. She had mothered me in ways that I had missed. For many years, I had experienced myself as parent to my mother, and the recent period of care giving had strengthened that feeling. Tini was able to provide a different kind of love, an unconditional love that I ate up as eagerly as her freshly baked *Vanillakipferln*.

———

My family expands to include Tini, Erni and Rudi
From left to right: Erni, Rudi, Helen, Tini

TINI CONFIRMED WHAT I HAD learned in Linz about the Fränkels.

"*They often visited,*" she told me. "*There would be great excitement as we got the house ready. 'The Linzers are coming,' your grandmother would say. They usually stayed overnight, so I would air all the sheets and bedding and iron the good tablecloths as well as doing some extra cooking and baking. Your grandmother always pitched in, so I never minded the work.*"

She knew no details about the later years, only that she'd heard Frau Martha was expecting a baby. After my family fled, Tini had gone to live nearby with her own parents. She knew nothing further.

Tini did know something about my father's sister Else and her husband. He bore the same name as his brother-in-law Emil, but Else's husband was a doctor. *Herr Doktor Emil Urbach.* He was a renowned specialist and people travelled great distances to consult him. The Urbachs lived in Krumlau, a medieval town popular with visitors from abroad. Tini had been quite in awe of him.

Frau Else had been more approachable, and she often came into the kitchen. Despite being a very elegant lady, always carefully coiffed and attired, she never put on airs. Tini said that on the contrary, Else was very easy to talk to, even if their conversation was rather limited. Still, Tini liked the polite way in which Frau Else always couched her requests: *"Only if you have time, dear Tini. I know how busy you are. Tini, my mother always says that neither she nor my sister-in-law Gretl could manage without you."*

On the last evening of my visit, Tini again fetched the postcard my mother had sent to her from Prague. This time, she pressed it into my hands and told me it was mine.

The card is addressed to Fraulein Christine Trinko, Erdweis bei Gmünd, Sudetenland. The postal stamp is smudged, but the words remain clear.

Prague, November 18, 1938.

Dear Tini

I have written to you several times in Strobnitz, but have received no reply. Now I shall write to your homeland. Perhaps my card will reach you there. If so, please send me a few lines. You know of course that we want to know how you are and what you are doing and whether you are perhaps still in Strobnitz after all and what's new there. We speak a lot about the past. It is all so sad, and yet there is nothing we can do to change it. Helly so often speaks of Tini. The child has not forgotten you nor have we.

We are living here temporarily in very modest circumstances. If you write to me, please address to Ing. Arnold Waldstein, Prague XII, Fochova 20.

What will you do now? Will you accept another position or will you get married right away? You know that I have always been interested in everything that pertains to you and I would like to have some share in your future life, even if at a distance. In any case, I wish you all the best of luck.

You will be interested to know that Aunt Anny and her husband left for Canada/America three weeks ago. We want to go there soon too, but there are still lots of formalities to be completed. My dear parents are in Pilsen and Mother is very sick. Her nerves are very poor as a result of the departure.

I believe that if we could be together, we'd have lots to tell each other. Life in Strobnitz was so pleasant (gemütlich). Please be sure to write to me. Give my regards to your parents. Best regards to you from my husband.

Sincerely,
Gretel Waldstein

———

BEFORE LEAVING GERMANY, there was one more stop I felt compelled to make. Not far from Tini's home in Ehningen lies Cham, my mother's hometown.

"Cham," the conductor announced. *"The next station is Cham. Arrival in three minutes."*

As passengers folded their newspapers and assembled their belongings, I pulled my suitcase from the overhead rack and moved to the aisle. Having had such great luck on the train to Ehningen, I again tried the approach of speaking to a woman waiting to get off the train.

"Excuse me, are you from Cham?"

"Yes, but I haven't lived here long. Do you live here too?"

"No, I'm just visiting. I was hoping you might know of a good Gasthof where I could spend the night."

"Sorry, I can't help you, but there is a small tourist agency just across from the station. The woman who owns it is very helpful. She is an old-time resident who will be able to advise you. You should just be able to catch her before the shops close."

Having expressed my thanks, I hastened across the street to a white frame building with travel posters in the window. A welcoming light still burned in the gathering dusk. A bell tinkled to announce my entry.

"Good evening. How can I help you?"

"I'm sorry; I don't need travel information, just a place to stay here in Cham."

"*Of course. There are many residents who rent out rooms. Cham is gaining popularity as a resort destination because we are so close to lakes and forests. Will you be staying long?*"

"*No, just for one night.*"

"*Oh, so you aren't on holiday. Are you perhaps visiting someone?*"

"*No.*"

An awkward silence ensued. The woman clearly expected further details.

"*My mother is from Cham. My grandparents lived here.*"

"*Oh, but your mother didn't come with you. Where is she now?*"

"*In Canada.*"

"*In Canada! But you speak German. And your mother didn't come with you?*"

"*No.*"

"*You came alone? Didn't she want to come? Surely, she would want to show you where she used to live. Perhaps some of her old friends are still living here.*"

"*No.*"

Another awkward silence. I tried again.

"*My mother will not set foot in Germany. Her memories are bad. She left here in 1939.*"

"*1939? Then she was lucky. That was just before the war. She would have missed all the horror. Cham doesn't have much industry, so we didn't get those terrible bombings, but we had very little food, and many of our soldiers and civilians suffered dreadfully. Your mother escaped all that. How could she have bad memories?*"

I see no way out except the terrible truth.

"*My mother is Jewish. My grandparents were Jewish.*"

I am aware of being looked at with wide-eyed wonder. I suddenly realize that I may be the first Jew that this forty-something woman has ever set eyes upon. Most of the handful of Germany's Jews who survived chose to settle elsewhere after the war.

"*What a shame that my own mother isn't in the shop today. Sometimes she helps me. She may have known your mother. What is her family name?*"

"*Grünhut.*"

"I don't recognize it. There's only one Jew living in Cham now. Everybody knows him. His name is Max Weissglas."

I shifted uncomfortably. A single Jew in a town that once held dozens of Jewish families. Like the last of any species, his name is known to all. My mind flipped back to a short story in our high school English class, "The Last of the passenger pigeons." At one time, there were so many passenger pigeons in America that trains would stop to allow gentleman travellers to stretch their legs and shoot at a sky that was clouded with birds. Then, one day, the last passenger pigeon died and the species was extinct.

A single Jew left in Cham. I could not banish the words from my mind. Soon after arriving at the recommended Gasthaus, I searched through the thin telephone book, and dialled the number for Max Weissglas.

Before I knew what I was going to say, a woman answered. My words simply tumbled out.

"Good evening. I'm a visitor from Canada. My mother was from Cham and my grandparents lived here. They were Jews. When I asked the woman at the travel agency by the railway station for the name of a guesthouse, she gave me the name of Max Weissglas and told me that he is the only Jew in Cham. I would like to meet him, but I'm only here till tomorrow. Is it possible?"

Another long silence. I listened but heard only the thumping of my own heart. At last, the woman sighed deeply, and then asked me to call again in the morning. We agreed to a 9 o'clock call.

Next morning, the same woman answered my call.

"What are your plans for the day?"

"I want to walk around town in the morning, but I don't imagine that will take long. Cham does not appear to be a large town. After that, I'll be free until late afternoon when my train leaves. Could we meet for coffee?"

"Where are you staying?"

"Gasthaus Zum Weissen Schwan. It's near a bridge over the river."

"I know it. I will meet you at noon in the foyer."

I was puzzled by this option and by the fact that she made all the arrangements. Why had she not put Max Weissglas on the phone? Still, I agreed.

My exploration of the town did not take long. Like so many European towns, it is built around a town square with a fountain at its centre. A plaque at its base told me that this fountain is called the *Hexenbrunnen*, the Witches Well. It features a set of bronze witches chasing peasants who are too weak to resist the hex that both draws and pursues them. I found the fountain irritating and irksome. Its modern design dwells uneasily in the ancient square. Besides, blaming evil on witches always triggers my feminist sensibilities. This fountain stirs up an even deeper sensitivity. Is the town attempting to blame its complicity during the war on witchcraft? Has the town revived this ancient denial of responsibility and given it a new twist?

Hexenbrunnen, the Witches Well

The voice of conscience is not far away. Commanding the square is an old stone church that dominates both space and time. Hanging in its tall onion tower is a great bronze bell that is seldom silent. When its deep voice is not reminding townsfolk of the hour and the quarter hour, it is calling them to prayer. I could neither ignore the centrality of the church nor escape its tolling reminder of mortality. For me, each bong carried the name of a Jew for whom Death had come at the hands of the townspeople.

Opposite the church squats a sedate building, prim and orderly as befits the municipal hall. In between, there are small stores, a bank, and several cafés. Their brightly checked tablecloths and umbrellas beckoned, but few clients were sipping coffee in the morning sunshine.

With thoughts of my mother occupying my mind, I wandered disconsolately along the path that follows the curve of the Regen River. My mother had often complained that every Sunday afternoon, she and Anny had been forced to accompany their parents as they strolled sedately along that very path, greeting neighbours and embodying respectability I gazed up at the distinctive twin towers of the medieval Beer-gate and wondered why my mother had never mentioned this unique landmark. I walked past the convent grounds and the adjacent school where Gretl and Anny had sat on a hard wooden bench learning discipline and the ABCs from unsmiling nuns. Just past the convent, I found the small street of shops with the address my mother had given me: *Fuhrmanstrasse, Number 11.*

Number 11 no longer exists. On this short street where every building still stands, on this street that is an exact replica of a photograph in my album, only one building has disappeared from existence. Not modernized, not rebuilt, but simply eliminated. On each side of Number 11, the walls still stand, protecting the small shops within. Number 11 is a paved passageway leading to a small department store on the next street. The store is called *Frey* and pronounced *frei*. The German word *free*. I cannot shake off the multiple meanings of the word or the irony of the large bold sign that beckons people to pass freely through the passageway. I cannot avoid thinking that the passageway is clear and free of obstructions because there is no longer a Jewish-owned building to block the way.

The passageway where Number 11 once stood on Fuhrmanstrasse

I took pictures from every angle and walked up and down the street, scanning my memory for clues to my next step. A butcher shop diagonally across the street triggered memories of my Aunt Anny talking of all the *Wurst* that was forbidden to them because it was not Kosher, and of how good it smelled and how much they longed to taste it. I looked inside, but the store was modern, part of a chain, and its clerks were all young. There was no point in asking.

I walked up the street to a smoke-filled restaurant where a few elderly men were already clustered about tables laden with beer and platters of food. I asked the elderly man behind the bar if he or anyone present might have known my family. Somewhat to my surprise, he was helpful. After animated consultation with his customers, he directed me across the street to the apartment above the bakery where the baker and his wife, residents of Cham since long before the war, would definitely have known my grandparents.

Eagerly, I rang the bell and identified myself through the intercom: the granddaughter of Max Grünhut.

The reluctance I sensed through the intercom became stronger as an elderly woman wearing the expected apron over her housedress opened the door. Without uttering a word, she led me upstairs to the kitchen. An old man sat at the table, coffee mug in one hand, cigarette in the other. He neither stood up nor offered to shake my hand. He did not invite me to sit. His wife did not offer coffee and returned wordlessly to the sink. The message was clear. My presence was unwelcome.

The man said right away that he knew nothing. Yes, there had been a Grünhut who had had a store just down the street, but he never knew him and never knew what happened to him. Although they had lived on the same street, his wife did not know Frau Grünhut nor did their children know my mother or her sister Anny.

How did he know Anny's name? I had not mentioned my aunt.

I backed away from the table, muttering a hasty *"thank-you-goodbye"* and fled.

It was with the foul taste in my mouth of this wilful forgetting of the past that I returned to my room. Quickly, I packed my few belongings, planning only to meet Max Weissglas before washing my hands of Cham. Suitcase in hand, I lumbered down the steps to the small reception area. A well-dressed, middle-aged woman approached, hands extended.

"Frau Wilkes? Melanie Weissglas."

I liked her instantly. Her manner was warm and welcoming, betraying none of the reserve of her telephone voice.

"Would you like to put your suitcase in our car? We thought you might like us to drive you around, and show you as much of Cham as we can. I have made a study of Cham and I have marked on my map all the places where Jews used to live. I have brought along my map, and my husband is in the car."

Somehow, I expected Max to have a physical disability. The ways in which Melanie sheltered him and took the lead in making the arrangements had led me to expect at best a very frail old man. The gentleman who greeted me needed no protection. He stood erect by a dark sedan. His suit was unwrinkled, his tie as straight as the shoulders that sat proudly under their tailored padding. Although he stood stiffly, the smile on his face was sincere as he pumped my hand and welcomed me to *"my ancestral town."*

Questions tumbled from my mouth. Melanie took the wheel, suggesting that we drive and talk lest we never leave the parking lot.

"*Are you from Cham? Did you know my grandparents?*"

"*No, I was born in Poland. I came here after the war. After the concentration camps. I survived several camps. I was just a boy when I was taken away. I lost my whole family. Everyone. I don't know how I survived. Or why.*"

"*I'm so sorry. And Melanie too?*"

"*No. Melanie is not Jewish. Melanie is my saviour. She is my angel. We met after the war, in Belgium. She was a nurse, helping us poor refugees when we emerged from the camps. I was broken. Starved, frightened, as helpless as a baby. Melanie gave me my health and my dignity. Then, she restored my soul. She made me into a human being. A Mensch. Do you speak Yiddish?*"

"*No, my parents only spoke German. But I do understand the word 'Mensch.' It embodies all the good qualities to which most people want to lay claim. To me, a Mensch is more than just a decent person with admirable traits. A Mensch is someone who has integrity and wisdom, but who acts from the heart. A compassionate person. It's a way of being that usually takes a lifetime to learn.*"

Had I earned the right to call myself a Mensch? Melanie had clearly earned that right, and instinct told me that Max had too.

"*But tell me, Max, why did you move to Cham?*"

"*Melanie's family lived nearby. I could not go back to Poland. No one was left. My whole family was wiped out. Everyone was killed. I had no home, so we came here. I opened a little store and slowly, we created a life. We have a daughter who lives in Greece, and now, we even have a grandchild.*"

"*Wonderful. You must be so proud.*"

"*It is Melanie who made me believe in myself. She helped me to believe in life again.*"

Melanie was driving, one eye upon the road, another upon her sheets of paper.

"*Did your mother ever mention the Schwartz family?*" Melanie asked.

"*Of course. She grew up with the Schwartz boys. I think my aunt had a crush on one of them.*"

"*That's their house there, the red brick with the yellow flowers. And what about the Fischers?*"

"*Yes, yes. Martha Fischer was my mother's best friend. She moved to New York and once, they came to visit us on the farm. I remember because Martha was so plump and had dark hair on her upper lip, but her husband was tall and good-looking. My mother said he married her for her money, which I thought was a terrible thing to say about your best friend.*"

Thus, we chatted and reminisced and asked questions and spoke freely as we drove up one street and down another. When we passed through *Judengasse*—*Jew Alley*, I expressed outrage, but Max and Melanie did not seem offended. Perhaps when one has survived so much, a name that may be centuries old loses its power to offend.

When I asked if I might take them out for coffee or lunch, Melanie and Max exchanged glances and asked if I would like to see their home and have a bite to eat there. Indeed, I would.

Their house was high on a hill, quite some distance from the town itself. A modern bungalow with flowers and greenery, not unlike that of my own neighbourhood in Canada. What surprised me upon entering was that the dining room table had already been set for three. Clearly, they had planned to invite me back.

I found myself deeply moved by this incredible hospitality to a stranger. As Melanie opened a bottle of wine, saying this was an occasion to celebrate, I tried to verbalize my feelings. I had been aware only of having intruded, of having brazenly called because of my loneliness in this town once peopled with my mother's family and friends. Instead, Max and Melanie were honoured that I had sought them out. They pointed out that not once in all these years had anyone sought to speak to Max just because he was the only Jew in town. No one had cared to ask about his story. No one in town wanted to know.

While Melanie bustled about the kitchen, Max recounted small bits of his early life, including what he had seen and suffered. Later, Melanie took me aside and thanked me.

"*He never speaks of it,*" she confided. "*I think it is good for him to talk. Not even our children know his story. They know only that he was in the camps. They know none of the details, and even I know very little of what he experienced. The knowledge of what happened will die with him.*"

I tried to tell Max that this would be a loss, terrible in its own way, even if different in quality and degree. To me, the loss of life had been appalling; but to lose even the memory of those lost lives would be to kill them again. That awareness lies at the root of my research, of my translation of the family letters, of my efforts to learn about the past. History erases the individual. Too often, it records only the actions of governments and armies. Ordinary humans are eliminated from consciousness. It is as if they had never been. But they did exist. They lived, they loved, they laughed and cried, and then they were killed. They mattered, these ordinary people.

In times of peace, we go to extraordinary lengths to save a single life. We cheer when the helicopter scoops up the stranded hiker, when doctors save the almost dead patient, when rescuers dig beneath the rubble and find one more living soul. We do not ask if these were special people more worthy of the gift of life than others who were swept away by tragedy. We believe that each life matters. America will never forget the horror of the bombing of the World Trade towers in 2001 where almost three thousand innocent lives were wiped out. How then can we lump together the lives of six million innocents? How can we forget that each one was an individual, and that every individual matters?

Max told me that he no longer believed in God. *"I am a Jew not by belief but by experience. Others have made me into a Jew."*

His history was burned into him as was mine. Although my experience cannot be compared to his suffering, still, a strong bond had grown between us. It was with great sadness that I noted the time had come for my departure.

Max and Melanie insisted on driving me to the station where we embraced like family. A few hours ago, I had not met them and a day ago, I had not even known of their existence. Now I was leaving Cham with a precious gift. Max and Melanie had provided me with a lesson in life and its sometimes miraculous unfolding. Max had also reminded me that the past is always with us, even when we fail to acknowledge its presence. His life provided me with an example of what it is to be human, and how to preserve that humanity in the face of the unthinkable.

My Aunts and Uncles

*I*T WAS ONLY AFTER I RETURNED from my visit to Germany that I realized how deeply I had been affected by the contact with Tini. Strangely, it was a letter dated September 10, 1998, from her daughter Erni that was the trigger to my feelings.

For three weeks, the letter lay on the kitchen counter. Unopened. Sometimes I moved it to the cupboard, into the box of unpaid bills right next to the "to do" list. Then I would bring it back out to where I could see it. Each time the phone rang, each time I plugged in the kettle, each time I passed through the kitchen, the letter reminded me of everything that I did not want to think about. Sometimes I picked the letter up and held it, noting physical details. The way the stamps seemed to be curling away from the blue airmail paper. The faint grease spots that the paper had absorbed as it wandered from place to place. I held it often, thinking about what it might contain. This I could do. What I could not do was open the letter.

Then came the day, no different from the others, a late January day with thick grey clouds when I knew the time had come. Before I could change my mind, I seized the bread knife, inserted the long blade under the flap, and slit open the envelope in one quick motion. With trembling fingers, I removed the contents and began to read.

I read almost to the end before a sob broke the morning stillness. The sob was precursor to the tears that I had held back for so long. When at last they abated, I re-read the words that had opened the floodgate.

> *Perhaps one day we shall walk together in those woods that are our common homeland. I think there is no plural for the word "home-land." Yet for myself, I have decided to have two homelands. I love that sleepy old Bohemia, but these days, I am glad to call Germany my home. For your new homeland, you have chosen what is considered to be the most beautiful metropolis in the world, and Rudi has fetched many illustrated books from the library so that we can have a better sense of Vancouver.*
>
> *Our roots are entwined but our branches stretch out over separate gardens, and if occasionally a little apple in the form of a thought, a greeting, or a visit falls from your branch into my garden, I shall always rejoice. That you exist is beautiful.*

That you exist is beautiful. Words that would bring comfort to any reader. Words that brought particular comfort to me as I sat at my kitchen table, recalling that that I exist only against all the odds.

Why was I wafted across the sea to the safest of all places? What task did the universe lay upon my shoulders like a too short shawl whose design I cannot see? The questions are too big, the mystery too deep. Like a butterfly seeking a floral resting post for its beating wings, so the fluttering heart and darting mind seek momentary repose. There are areas that are safe to think about, others that feel like standing at the edge of a cliff. One misstep and the abyss awaits.

———

SO VIVIDLY HAD THE TRIP to Germany brought members of my family to life that I sometimes found myself withdrawing from my friends. The missing family members totally absorbed me. I threw myself into the task of deciphering and translating their letters with fresh energy.

Because Tini's description of my father's sister Else had awakened my interest, I began this time with the Urbach letters.

It was July 1939, but my aunt Else seemed to be living on another planet where political events did not intrude.

> There are usually visitors here on a Sunday. The children are looking forward to the holidays. Otto wants to go to a student camp for a month and Marianne would like to go away too, because there is nowhere nearby that one can go swimming.

Else's words appeared innocent until I recalled something I had learned long ago: among the first Nazi ordinances had been the banning of Jews from all swimming pools and public bathing areas.

Even as a child, I knew about that ban. From eavesdropping on adult conversations, I also knew that so many Jews had been denied admission to swimming facilities in the Toronto area that some wealthy individual Jews had bought a farm outside the city to establish their own escape from the summer heat. Despite having showered and immersed my feet in the container of disinfectant, I always felt contagious when entering a public swimming pool.

That sense of shame had been reinforced by our first "real Canadian" holiday. I was about 10 years old the summer that my parents loaded up the car, and we drove north to Georgian Bay, Lake Simcoe, and the Muskoka area. It was on that holiday that I saw the posted signs: NO DOGS OR JEWS. Not until 1954, by which time I was in second year university, did Ontario pass fair employment and accomodation legislation that outlawed the advertising of "Gentiles Only" establishments.[4]

It is almost with relief that I turn aside from thoughts of my own past, and bask instead in Else's equanimity. She does not complain. She seems to ask nothing of life beyond what she has been given.

> *There will be no holidays for us this year. We don't need a holiday.*
> *We can sit in the garden if we have time. There is always enough to*
> *do: laundry, cleaning, knitting, etc. A week goes by before you*
> *know it.*

Still, something does not quite ring true. If Else is planning to send both children away for summer holidays, why will she have no time to sit in the garden? Surely not even the most meticulous hausfrau could occupy her entire week with laundry and cleaning! What is it that Else does not say?

I turn to her next letter, written in August 1939, just weeks before the outbreak of war, but this letter is equally placid and bears no trace of anxiety.

> *My Dears,*
> *Your last, thoroughly descriptive reports really brought enormous*
> *pleasure to us all, and we gather that despite all the hard work, you*
> *are well and in good spirits. We sincerely hope that it will continue*
> *thus for you, and that you will be lucky in all that you undertake.*
>
> *We are especially pleased that you are in good health and that*
> *Helly has adapted so well to the new life. I can imagine that she is*
> *everyone's darling, that she will be spoiled and given lots of gifts.*
>
> *How dearly we would like to see your new home in person and*
> *help you just a wee bit with moving in, but unfortunately, we can*
> *only do so in spirit. It must be a nice feeling, to watch everything*
> *grow and thrive on your very doorstep, things that were sown and*
> *planted with your own hands. God grant that your first harvest*
> *will turn out as desired!*
>
> *It really is a stretch of the imagination to picture you, dear Edi,*
> *as country squire. Who would have believed it? Amazing, what*
> *you have become!*
>
> *And you too, dear Gretl. Hats off to you for rapidly developing*
> *into a farmer's wife! It really seems to be true that one's strength*
> *grows along with one's responsibilities.*
>
> *For the last two weeks, we have been "childless." Marianne is*

visiting a friend near Melnik. We visited her there on Sunday. She looks very good, goes dancing twice a week, and has already broken the heart of a butcher and a young apprentice. She is enjoying these few weeks in a village more than summer days in Prague, and everyone is being very nice to her. Otto is in a camp in Vondorf near Budweis. He likes it, and he will visit our dear parents on his way back.

Emil is very pleased that the books arrived, and he will send you something else on raising cattle. I have just finished knitting two little dresses for Dorly, but it is very slow because I have less time than before. Dorly is precious in the truest sense of the word, especially when she isn't wearing panties and is slipping and sliding about in the altogether. Then, we stick her into the washbasin, until everything smells sweet again.

So please continue to be well and be kissed many times by your Else.

Else's urge to make everything smell sweet again touched a chord for me. How often I tell myself to smile though my heart is aching. How often I remind myself that when life has dealt lemons, it is time to make lemonade. Or chicken soup. Knowing the wound is deep, I nonetheless apply band-aids. Sometimes, band-aids are all we have.

Else had a large collection of these. She gave them out freely, to family and friends. She sent them to my parents, in the form of cheerful letters. Her love knew no bounds. Soon, Else sprang to life and became the focus of my thoughts. She became both the person I longed to be and the role model I never had. I envied her warmth, her sensitivity to the needs of others, her ability to make everyone feel welcome and at ease.

———

THE CONTRAST BETWEEN Else's letters and those of Emil and Martha Fränkel in the summer of 1939 could not be more pronounced. Emil Fränkel gets straight to the point. In June he had already reminded my father that in troubled times, it is actions and not words that count. According to Emil, my father has failed to act.

Knowing full well that my parents had barely arrived in Canada, penniless and without a word of English, Emil apologizes for having upset my father, but he does not back away. The situation is critical. On his side of the ocean, Emil is doing everything possible to gain admission to Canada, first for my mother's parents and then, for his own little family. Canadian immigration officials have given full discretionary powers to the CPR whose representatives are playing an unsavoury game: holding out hope as they entangle Emil more tightly in paperwork snares.

July 26, 1939

My dear ones,

It really tore me apart to hear that you could use me there while I cannot hasten my emigration. They are making me wait with enormous patience for a response to all the paperwork I have submitted.

I hope you are not angry with me because of my last letter. My whole thrust in life has been toward the future but with a single blow, that future has been cast into the waters. It will soon be a year that I have been stateless here in Prague. I still do not know whether I will be able to reach my goal in the next while. Thus far, I have received no word from the CANADIAN. *I went to talk to Mr. Steiner a few days ago. He told me that the completion had not yet happened and that I will have to wait a while yet.*

I am already worried about what will happen if I get the okay and I have to come up with the deposit of a thousand dollars that Canada demands. It will be impossible to get dollars here. Dear Edi, it would be a good idea for you to find out whether relatives over there can deposit the money on behalf of the immigrant.

Many friends have permission from the CPR *to immigrate but cannot enter because of the currency issue.*

I am extremely worried about your parents, dear Gretl. They are still waiting for the exit stamp and not surprisingly, they are

both depressed. I am constantly trying to cheer them up. I almost
had all the papers for their lift assembled when I found out yester-
day that all the papers have been cancelled.

Why had Max and Resl's papers all been cancelled? Was this some kind of personal retaliation by a bored bureaucrat? Apparently, it was just part of the bureaucratic insanity that had become the norm for the Jews of Prague. Beyond the mountainous task of getting an entry visa lay packages of up to twenty official forms, all to be completed by typewriter to include half a dozen carbon copies. The would-be immigrant would rush off in search of recent passport photos, birth and marriage certificates, character references no more than six weeks old, proof of both citizenship and residency, tax receipts and official Treasury receipts confirming payment of these taxes. He would also prepare lists of assets, some like real estate and jewellery to be surrendered immediately, others like clothing, furniture, household items and books all to be officially appraised and taxed at up to 100% of their value if taken out of the country. The climate of panic and the need for haste were further intensified by residency visas and other documents that could not be renewed upon expiry.[5]

Like my grandparents, Emil himself was only in Prague on a temporary visa. He must have longed to lunge across the desk where Mr. Steiner sat, complacently counselling patience. Steiner would have known that Canadian officials had not issued Emil an entry visa and that they did not intend ever to do so because Canada's policy was to keep Jewish immigration at a minimum. Prime Minister Mackenzie King was obsessed with the notion that the admission of Jewish refugees might destroy the country.[6]

Somehow, Emil does find the patience that Steiner has urged. He uses that patience to learn a trade: shoemaking. Not only is he taking a course, he is also apprenticing with a nearby cobbler who praises his progress.

I puzzle over the riddle of Emil who felt the first tremors of disaster and took up shoemaking as a response. Was Emil like Hamlet, frozen into inaction by his fear of acting impulsively? Some people did escape by routes as distant as Shanghai and South Africa. Some people did get into Palestine despite the British Mandate against Jewish immigration.

Was it his determination to keep the family together and his desire to join us in Canada that blinded him to other possibilities?

———

MARTHA'S LETTER CAREENS madly between hope and despair. The letter is chaotic, disjointed, and unsettling. One moment Martha is convinced that they will shortly be arriving in Canada, the next, she knows that she is clutching at straws.

> My Dear Ones,
> On Monday evening, Arnold brought us your last letter. What great and powerful joy reigned in the house! Afterwards, I spent a sleepless night imagining each one of you and mulling over every detail of your report. Emil and I got such a hunger to help you that we longed to sprout wings and fly to you.
> What we really regret is that we so depressed you with our last letter. We beg you to excuse us and not to hold it against us. Perhaps you can imagine how desperate we are. There are days when we are totally despondent because there is just no hope at all. So far, we have had no further notification from The Canadian.
> May God grant us only the good fortune of coming to you! Work will never be too much for us.
> As soon as they get the stamps, your parents are supposed to leave immediately. Emil will look after their lift and their belongings. We hope that the expeditor will also succeed in sending off our own two lifts this week.
> Although Ilserl darling is a very quiet little girl, she is so excited now at the prospect of seeing dear Helly again and cannot stop looking at her picture. Write to us soon, dear Helly, if there are nice things that you want us to bring for you.

The fact that Ilserl was so excited at the prospect of seeing me confirms the degree to which Martha and Emil were living in hope. Never would they have encouraged Ilserl unless they really believed that Canada would open its doors to them.

The rest of Martha's letter rambles in a way that we used to think of as "madness." I think involuntarily of Shakespeare's Ophelia as she walks into the river to drown. Martha wanders about, lost in a maze of topics that lead nowhere. Dorly has just eaten tomato juice with sugar. Friends are thinking of trying to immigrate to Australia. Shall we look for a cheese recipe to bring?

———

HOW GREAT WOULD HAVE been the excitement on both sides of the Atlantic! Not only were my mother's parents Max and Resl ready for immediate departure, but the Fränkels too. Their bags were packed and they expected to leave for Canada within days.

Martha seems unwilling and unable to end her letter. Having signed off and sent good wishes to all, she then adds a postscript, as if the letter had become a lifeline that she cannot release.

> Emil will probably still write this week. Is there still no word for us from cousin Hertha in New York? Where is that American affidavit she promised to send?

A flood of long-forgotten memories washes over me with Martha's reference to Cousin Hertha in New York. I am transported back to the farm where from time to time, a parcel would arrive with special items for me. One parcel contained a brown velvet dress that I do not recall ever having had occasion to wear. Another parcel contained a doll with a china face and a floppy body that failed to evoke my maternal instincts. Both parcels came from Cousin Hertha in New York whose daughter Elaine had outgrown their contents.

However, there were other parcels from Cousin Hertha that opened new worlds for me. These contained books. My first books. I read them voraciously, over and over again. *Pollyanna. Nancy Drew. The Bobbsey Twins.* In summer, I retreated with each treasured book to a willow tree down by the brook, a tree whose branches formed a perfect cradle into which I could climb. In winter, I read my books by flashlight under a feather comforter long after my parents had gone to bed.

————

LESS THAN TWO WEEKS LATER, on August 8, 1939, the Fränkels again put pen to paper. Martha claims that she wants to thank us for the photos we sent to my mother's parents, but her letter is a cry of despair.

The delays have become interminable. Although my mother's parents have been told that they will be getting their exit visas within days, the Fränkels still have no documentation in hand. Representatives of the CPR in Prague blame it on Ottawa and Ottawa remains mute. No one is responsible.

> We think of you again and again. How dearly we would like to help you! Instead, we wait from day to day for news from The Canadian, but we wait in vain. Saturday it will be six weeks since Emil talked to Hornath, the CPR representative in Prague, and we have received no notification.
>
> Arnold told us that ships only cross until mid-October, so we do not know what will happen then. Please do not be angry with us if I ask you to intervene again with Mr. Colley and the CPR in Canada to find out what our situation really is. Even if we gather up all our patience, the matter is still taking too long.
>
> As regards your parents, we hope that they will definitely get the exit stamp next week. Emil spent the whole day with them yesterday and has been getting their things ready for the trip. Three days ago, they set up an exit centre where you have to fill out a pile of paperwork in order to leave with a single suitcase.
>
> Your dear parents and Emil are now making every effort toward the emigration and we hope to God that they will soon be safely in your home. Emil is mustering his whole supply of patience, for you

can imagine what a state your parents are in at having to leave. Still, thousands of people today are happy if they can just get out, so one must not complain. Once they are safely with you, then everything will turn out well again.

Emil went to see Mr. Steiner again. He told him that our case should be moving more quickly in Ottawa.

There are days when we are simply broken. The long indefinite waiting grinds us down. We have experienced so much already that we would have to be made of steel to withstand everything. If only there were some way out.

———

IN HIS PART OF THE LETTER, Emil moves quickly to serious matters.

My Dear Ones,
This week I was really busy again with your dear parents. Those are the nicest days for me. We got numerous things ready to take on the trip, prepared an inventory listing the value of each item, and filled out twenty different forms per emigrant. The written tasks took almost three days. Papa has submitted all the completed documents to the central office. They say that it takes a week from the day of submission to get permission to depart.

The lift containing your belongings was a lot of work for me at the time, but there is absolutely no comparison to the present difficulties and paperwork.

I have been very worried about your parents, but if all goes well, they will be able to leave in ten days. They are only taking hand luggage and bare necessities for the trip itself—underwear, clothing, and towels.

Caring for my mother's parents has given shape and purpose to Emil's days. Now that Max and Resl are on the verge of leaving, Emil foresees only the endless wait that lies in store for him.

Regarding my own fate, I still have had no word from The Canadian. Last week I talked to Herr Steiner who told me that my emigration to Canada depends on the government in Ottawa. I beg you, dear Edi, to pursue the matter again and to report to us on the situation.

Other than that, the days are all the same, each day slipping into the next one while we constantly hope for a way out. On many days, I lose the hope that, someday, the happy news will come for us too.

Josef and Fanny Waldstein surrounded by the family
Back row: Edmund Waldstein, Emil Urbach, Emil Fränkel,
unknown, Else Urbach, Arnold Waldstein
Middle row: Martha Fränkel, unknown, Josef Waldstein,
Fanny Waldstein, Vera Waldstein, unknown
Front row: Ilserl Fränkel, Otto Urbach, Marianne Urbach

My Grandparents

As MY MOTHER AND MY AUNT ANNY waited anxiously for the arrival of Max and Resl, the first letter arrived from my father's parents, Josef and Fanny. My own excitement shot up when I found that letter in my father's box.

Although my mother had often spoken of her own parents, whose picture hung in a gold frame over her bed, I knew nothing about my father's parents. My father never spoke of them and my mother rarely did.

My mother recalled Fanny Waldstein primarily as a mother-in-law prone to doling out unwanted advice and Papa Josef as a storekeeper with little to say except to his customers. As grandparents, they had no reality for me, and such was my mother's unacknowledged aversion that she pronounced their handwriting "unreadable." It was only after I called upon the help of a former university colleague with a specialty in German that Fanny and Josef swam into focus.

What emerged were two warm-hearted people with a lively intelligence. Their pet names for me give clear voice to their love. Equally unmistakable is their selfless concern for others. It is from their deep pool of caring that

Ilserl with her grandmother Fanny

my father had drunk deeply. Like him, they saw the goodness in people, and they chose to err on the side of generosity.

Remarkably, they were not only aware, they were quite willing to express their feelings of sorrow and outrage at what was happening. Their world was not just the family circle but also their community of friends and neighbours, people amongst whom they had lived for a lifetime. It is their compassionate observations about a society crumbling before their very eyes that have provided me with the most compelling images.

Among the mysteries of their first letter is the date. The handwriting is perfectly legible: July 27, 1938. However, the fact that the letter is addressed to us in Canada means that the letter can only have been written in 1939. Perhaps my grandfather subconsciously wanted time to stand still.

Another mystery is the fact that Papa Waldstein not only omits their exact address, he omits the city itself. The letter is addressed from "near Budweis." The latter is a name I know well, for Budweis is the city where I was born. I had often heard the story of my mother's refusal to give birth in the family bed attended in the normal way by a local midwife and the old village doctor. After much deliberation, it was decided that my mother would spend the last days of her confinement in Budweis with friends of the family who would take her to hospital at the appropriate time.

I wonder whether it was with these same "friends of the family" that my grandparents stayed after Hitler took over the Sudetenland. My research at the library has produced a map showing the border of the Sudetenland as an extremely jagged line that zigzagged its way around the country. After September 1938, Strobnitz lay in the Nazi-occupied Sudetenland, but only a stone's throw away, Budweis remained in Czechoslovakia, a free and independent country.

My grandfather's letter is direct and to the point.

Nothing new from Strobnitz. The borders are closed now. I have no hopes left of getting anything for the house or the fields.

The letter contains numerous references to people whose names are unknown to me. Nonetheless, the words and actions of these people give shape to my reality. Although none has set sail voluntarily, I see them as bobbing helplessly on a sea of relentless change. A family torn apart when a husband lands a job in Calcutta that enables him to send his wife and children to London. Competent businessmen sent into "retirement" by their Aryan employers. Able young men, including my father's friends, eager to work but forced into idleness. My grandfather names these people who constitute a moving tableau at a time of ever-growing uncertainty.

> We recently received your letter forwarded from Prague, and your lines brought us great pleasure. Mama has probably read it at least ten times to herself and she has read it to Goldschmied and to Katz etc. etc. Everyone is delighted to hear that you are doing well, and everyone wants to go to Canada. Everyone also wants to fall under the umbrella of my protection, thinking that because you succeeded in getting to Canada, I can somehow help them. They don't understand how complicated things are. They don't believe me when I tell them that I cannot even protect my own family.
>
> We are in good health, thank God, and so far, we are doing well. One just has to adjust to the new circumstances. Today it says in the newspapers that people up to age 35 can emigrate to England, but people over 35 have to be professionals, engineers, master builders, etc. They want artisans, not people in business.
>
> We are waiting longingly for better times? Everyone wants to emigrate, but unfortunately, the opportunities are absolutely zero.
>
> Here the harvesting has already begun and the fields are studded with wheat stooks. When does the harvesting start there? There are also many cherries here this year. Do you have some fruit on the farm too? How are you doing, Gretl dear? Do you have calluses on your hands yet, and do they hurt? And what's my Helly-child up to? I'm very lonely for her. Has she stopped speaking of her grandparents, her Opi and Omi? With the passing of time, she will forget us.
>
> You will be sweating a lot now in the great summer heat. Don't worry about it, dear Edi. If you were here, you would also have to

work. It's just that it's easier to work for yourself than for strangers.
Now I don't know anything further to report. For today, I greet
and kiss you all from my heart. Your Papa.

As if reluctant to end his letter, he adds a postscript.

Don't let all the work overwhelm you. In time everything will get
better, and every beginning is hard. Regards to Anny and Ludwig
and especially to my dear Helly.

I find myself dwelling on the smallest details of Papa Josef's letter, including
the fact that he adds a postscript that specifically mentions me. My hunger
for love from a grandparent takes me by surprise. I am also taken aback by
his honesty. In their letters, whether they believe it or not, all other members
of the family maintain the pretense that there is still hope. My grandfather
alone calls it as he sees it: absolutely hopeless. Everyone wants to emigrate,
but the opportunities are absolutely zero. For good measure, he draws a line
through the numeral. He also eliminates both himself and Emil Fränkel
from admission to England by underlining that people over 35 must not be
in business. He cancels out even his one hopeful statement, that *"we are
waiting longingly for better times"* by placing a question mark at its end, as if
to cast doubt upon the likelihood of better times ahead.

Fanny's letter contains no salutation. She plunges directly to the heart of
matters, and her words are like an interrupted conversation, filled with
names that I do not recognize.

I want to add a few lines regarding the letter which Mrs. Gold-
berger sent to Mr. Ornstein. She got the address from Mr. Klein. I
think they might be capable people, but there can be no thought of
moving forward on it.
Engineer Fritz Teller of Krumau is going to Calcutta, India. The
climate there is supposed to be very mild. His wife and child will be
staying in London for the time being. Mr. Rind from Velenic asked
me to send you his regards.

I want to ask you, dear Gretl whether you have to cook the food for the pigs on the kitchen stove. In that case you will need numerous pots every day. I also want to ask how your hands are doing and whether they are still raw and split open. As a precautionary measure, you should rub them every night with something fatty.

I also can't imagine, dear Edmund, how come you are getting wet feet. Aren't you being careful? That would not happen here.

Be well, be kissed by your Mother Fanny

Fanny's words are a harsh reminder of how unprepared my mother was for life on a farm. From my childhood, I remember my mother's hands as chronically red and sore, but in the last year her life, friends often commented on her lovely hands. Her fingers were long and straight, and the rings she loved to wear slipped easily over unswollen knuckles. She filed her own nails and polished them beautifully. Her touch was soft and smooth.

Fanny's words also make me realize what a shock it must have been for my mother who was raised in a kosher home, to find herself now using her pots to prepare slop for the pigs.

Although the other siblings have lauded my mother for adapting so quickly to farm life, Fanny is slow to see her as other than pampered. In a letter to Otto that he must have forwarded to my father, Fanny empathizes only with my father's pain.

The photos of the children arrived today. I cannot get enough of looking at them and I must confess that the first sight of them brought tears to my eyes. Thank God, they are safely provided for, living in their own home and eating their own bread, something that thousands of people today cannot afford.

I feel very sorry for Edmund. How many rays of sun has the poor man endured for his face to have turned so brown? How much sweat has the hard work cost him? Gretl, on the other hand, looks remarkably bright and happy. The hard work has not hurt her a bit.

Although she still has her reservations where my mother is concerned, Fanny expresses compassion for others.

> *Dear Otto, there are many sorrows here. People are running about like chickens with their heads cut off. No one knows what the morrow will bring. Many from our village of Strobnitz had to move out of their homes. It is rumoured that the Jews here will have to move to Prague in stages, but they will first take young people under 35 who plan to emigrate.*
>
> *My sister Jetty also had a summons in Prague, but whether she will emigrate is in doubt. The poor family has suffered so much and they did not plan ahead enough for emigration. The little bit of money that they have is dwindling away, and nothing can be done about it. Like us, everyone is thinking of the future with dread.*
>
> *If God will only grant that Arnold and Vera can stay here! That would be such a comfort for us. My dear Fränkel children must unfortunately leave the country. This is bringing me hours of grief, but I must get used to it.*

I puzzled long and hard about why only the Fränkels had to leave Czechoslovakia. The answer lay in the documents that I had found in the archives in Linz. Emil Fränkel was born in Lemberg, which was then the capital of Galicia and part of the Austro-Hungarian Empire. When new borders were drawn in 1918, Lemberg became part of Poland. Because Emil had settled in Linz, he had to re-apply for the Austrian citizenship that had been his birthright prior to 1918. When the Austrians welcomed Hitler in 1938, they stripped all Jews of their citizenship. The Fränkels had fled to Prague in hopes of finding a safe haven, but when Hitler took Czechoslovakia, Emil became stateless.

There was no country to issue him and his family an exit visa and no border that he and his family could openly cross. At every train station, harbour, or airport, they would be risking seizure and arrest. If Emil could not find a country to accept them immediately (all but impossible), he risked being sent to a concentration camp like Dachau in Germany. In a letter to Otto, my grandfather sums up the situation.

> Our dear ones in Canada are doing well. They still have to work hard, but they are in good health. If only the Fränkels were that far ahead. Arnold and Vera will certainly do their best to make sure that they leave here, and that they get to go somewhere.

Josef grieves for others, but aside from missing his loved ones, he shows not a gram of self-pity for his own lot.

> We are in good health and doing well except for our spirits. To see such misery on a daily basis, to know that there are thousands with no homeland and no means of earning a living is wretched.
>
> Thus, all of you are scattered to the four winds. Who would ever have thought that day would come to pass? Man proposes, God disposes.

———

FANNY AND JOSEF HAD WRITTEN to us in July. In August, Arnold sent several pages of densely written script. His words underline the importance of the letters from my parents and from my father's brother Otto who had also reached safety in Paris.

> Your letter of the May 27th was forwarded to us along with a letter of Otto's. It was a double holiday for us because both of your letters are so comforting, confident, and full of results that one is simply pulled along by this optimism, this trust in God's support, and in a happy, free future.
>
> I need not stress how often and how thoroughly we studied your letter. Even our more distant relatives share our interest in your letters, and feel equal pride and joy in your accomplishments.
>
> Just now, your last letter has returned, having twice been

forwarded to our parents, most recently from Trebitsch by our cousin Martha. She also sent our parents a parcel full of good things and has steadily demonstrated her caring for them, and for you too.

We thank you sincerely for your pictures. They are very good and little Helly is especially cute. We look at the pictures very carefully with a magnifying glass, and our imagination soars and fills in everything that is missing. In this way, we see your whole life before us.

We really are honoured that despite all the work and the intense summer heat, you are taking the time to write in such detail. In this considerable sacrifice, we perceive again and again the proof of your deep attachment, and the deep inner feeling of belonging together that is occasioned by the ties of blood and soul.

Much as I have the urge to do so, there is no way to follow up on all the thoughts that arise when I read your letters, on all the questions that pop into my mind, nor to pick up in writing on all the allusions and interesting things, just as it is impossible for you to portray fully all your impressions, experiences, opinions, and discoveries. But although we can share with each other only the external and the transitory, we still understand each other. Unwritten thoughts enter our consciousness of their own accord.

For this reason, I want to save myself the trouble of entering into each detail of your so very interesting report, but try instead to express my admiration for the way that you are facing up to the powerful demands being made upon you.

Everything in our immediate family circle is all right so far. Everyone is in good health and that is what matters most. Papa wants to come here in the next while to say goodbye to Gretl's parents.

I am surprised that Arnold, a man not given to believing idle rumours, writes definitively that my mother's parents will be coming to Canada. Even more surprising is that Arnold, who thus far has shown not the slightest trace of anxiety over worsening conditions in Europe, has made up his mind to leave.

When he had last written to us on June 25, Arnold had mentioned wanting to spend holidays in Taus. In this letter, Arnold reveals that it was not just a vacation that he sought in Taus, but a series of appointments with his dentist.

> *I did suffer a lot with my teeth. Alfred made me a whole new set of teeth with four bridges, but now my teeth are "fit for overseas" and I hope to have them at least ten years.*

Because of his qualifications as an engineer, Arnold is confident that some country will welcome his skills. One of his friends is urging him to emigrate to Australia and to send all his diplomas and qualifications (translated into English and notarized) within the week. Although Arnold knows people who are doing well there, Australia just doesn't draw him. It is in Canada that he wants to make his home.

> *I would just be terribly sorry if fate were to drive me to another continent. In my fondest dreams, I do see us all together again somewhere, and to this end, you have already made a beginning in Canada. We are counting on it that eventually not only Martha with her family but also our dear parents will be with you.*
>
> *Besides, from an economic and geographic perspective, I can think of no country that seems more propitious than Canada. I consider it a piece of good luck that Canada is precisely where fate has driven you.*

Unlike the Fränkels, Arnold does not press my father. He recognizes the limitations of what my father can do, and has already begun to make his own inquiries.

> *Both Vera and I can see clearly that it is not so easy to get an entry permit, especially as non-farmers, and that it will scarcely be possible for you to have the opportunity, let alone the time to undertake something in this regard. Our request is rather that you make*

inquiries, as time permits, and that you let no opportunity go by to ask whether there exists any interest in our special training and capabilities, and under what conditions an entry visa gets issued.

Since I must give serious thought to getting in somewhere with all my nice little degrees and diplomas, I went to the Canadian Railway yesterday, especially because I heard that with their help, a lumber merchant from Saaz is going to set up a woodchip industry there. Of course, I got nowhere near Herr Hornath, but I did spend quite a while talking to a clerk who gave me all the desired information.

You will be interested in the opinion of the clerk of the Canadian Railway. When I asked him how he could send me as a farmer when he knows I'm an engineer, he replied, "Oh, that doesn't matter. You will learn farming soon enough over there." When I said it would be a shame to waste my expertise, he just shrugged.

There are three possibilities at your end. The first is that you try to arouse the interest of the government in me as an expert (which seems rather problematic to me). The second is that you find a wealthy entrepreneur who would like to set up a manufacturing plant. The third is that you could simply put in a claim for me as your brother to come and farm.

I would not like to say anything about the third possibility until I have heard your considered opinion. Aside from the fact that you cannot bombard Mr. Colley with new requests before Gretl's parents and the Fränkels have even arrived in Canada, I would like to give the advantage to our parents and to the Urbachs (minus the children whom Otto is planning to take). If the Urbachs should have to leave here, they will not have the good prospects that Vera and I have.

You will certainly agree that good advice is priceless, and that under the circumstances here, a decision with lifelong consequences must be taken.

It is only at the end of Arnold's letter that I begin to understand the bigger picture. Although he and Vera are eager to be with us in Canada and are willing to come as farmers, they recognize that my parents must first sponsor my mother's parents, the Fränkels, the Urbachs, and my father's parents. Arnold and Vera will step aside to give immediate priority to the rest of the family who will not have the same good prospects of gaining admission based on their professional qualifications.

Arnold's vision sweeps me along as I imagine my parents' excitement. Soon the entire family will join us in Canada. The plan is that my mother's parents will arrive first. Because their departure is imminent, Arnold's father is coming to Prague specifically to say goodbye to Max and Resl before they leave for Canada. Emil and Martha Fränkel have already packed; they and the children are ready to leave immediately. After that, my father's parents will be coming, as will the Urbachs. Arnold and Vera have decided to join them so that everyone will be together once again.

Buoyed by our letters, Arnold and Vera soak up the pleasures of their last holiday in Europe.

> Now, my dear ones, I want to report a bit about our holiday from which we returned yesterday. It was nice in every way. The weather was good to us, the surrounding countryside was most inviting, and we gave in to our longing for nature and fresh air. We took long hikes from which we returned tired out, we lay in the grass and the hay, we witnessed all phases of the harvest and of country life, we rejoiced in the unspoiled nature and honesty of people who know nothing of discrimination. We had good accommodations and good food and just totally let ourselves enjoy it.

Arnold encloses copies of his professional qualifications to make sure that he gets a suitable job offer. He urges my father to show them to as many people as possible, especially to those who either have influence or could approach those who do.

Vera adds a few lines to express delight in the fact that all remaining obstacles have been removed, and that my mother's parents are finally on their way to Canada.

My maternal grandparents, Resl née Langschur and Max Grünhut

Yesterday there was another family gathering at Elsa's to celebrate our return from holidays. With what great joy we heard that Max and Resl will soon be allowed to leave after all.

Still, there is a hint that Vera has few illusions about what lies ahead.

I can well imagine your impatience to see your parents again, dear Gretl and Anny, but be patient! It will all come to pass if God wills it and nothing interferes. Be patient even if sometimes, it seems to take a long time.

———

LESS THAN A WEEK LATER, whatever hope Arnold and Vera's positive attitude may have inspired is dealt a blow. In a letter ostensibly written for my father's birthday, and belatedly for mine, Martha is strangely distant.

On September 15, your birthday, dear Edi, we will be intensely thinking of you, pleading that the dear Lord keep you in very, very good health. May you be allowed to dwell with your loved ones in peace and freedom!

My dear husband often says that our Dorly reminds him so much of Helly's chatter. She will surely be a charming young girl already. These would be nice playmates now under the supervision of my big daughter.

You are heartily embraced and kissed by your Martha and family.

Else's penmanship follows closely upon Martha's handwritten words. Else's letter is even more remote.

To our dear brother Edi on his birthday we wish every imaginable good thing and love. May he stay in good health and spend the day happily in the circle of his family. His girl must be quite big now and must be bringing lots of life and joy into the house.

At the bottom is a single, rather formal, line in Fanny's handwriting.

I too can send my sincerest regards to congratulate Edi, and Helynka too.

Strangely, it is the only time she signs not as "Fanny," but as "Your Mama." Only the date of the letter provides a clue to its detachment. August 31, 1939. The next day, Germany will invade Poland and trigger the war.

War Breaks Out

$\mathcal{S}$TRANGELY, I HAD NEVER GIVEN thought to the small, inevitable consequences of war. How, for example, did letters continue to arrive from Europe? Now I threw myself into the task of understanding what happened next.

From the notes she scribbled in the margins, I discovered that Cousin Hertha Bloch in New York had agreed to be the go-between for the continuing exchange of family letters. Because the United States did not enter the war until after Pearl Harbour on December 6, 1941, there was a window of time when letters could be forwarded via the U.S. Letters written to my father's brother Otto in Paris were also forwarded by Hertha and made their way into my father's box.

None of the letters directly mentions the war, although Martha does refer to *"this illness that is supposed to last a long time."* Censorship must have begun almost immediately. It lingers like a bad smell in the form of pencil markings and mysterious numbers in strange handwriting superimposed upon the thin sheets of airmail paper. Each letter has two sets of four digit numbers boldly written across the top, reminders that censorship was real, and much more than the stuff of spy novels.

Nevertheless, each family member continued to write. Arnold is the first to send his reassurances that all is well. Despite having written twice in the previous week, on September 3, 1939, two days after Britain and France declare war on Germany, Arnold sends a letter to his brother Otto.

Arnold seems to accept that there is little point in worrying about things one cannot change. With the outbreak of war, his role shifts to reassuring everyone that there is no immediate cause for alarm. On September 3, he writes to Otto saying, *"With us, mercifully, nothing has changed."* Still, there are numerous indicators that change is very much in the air. Arnold reveals that Vera's medical practice has virtually come to a halt, an oblique reference to the Nazi boycott of Jewish professionals. He also admits that my grandmother Fanny has come to Prague specifically to look for accommodations. While Arnold is looking forward to having his parents nearby, he acknowledges that it is not a matter of choice.

> *Dear Otto,*
>
> *Mama surprised us with a visit whose purpose was to look for an apartment, since they have to leave the one in Budweis. Once again our family is almost complete and re-united.*
>
> *I need not stress that we think of you especially often; indeed, you are now my greatest concern. We are already awaiting your next letter with impatience, even though we recently received your letters of August 23 and 26. I wrote to you at the old address on August 23 and 30.*
>
> *With us, mercifully nothing has changed, and we are all in good health. Little Dorly is making special progress. She is already taking a few steps, she can stand up alone by leaning on a heavy object, and she is uncommonly cute.*
>
> *Vera of course has almost nothing to do in her praxis during these times, but I certainly have plenty of work and we are just in the process of enlarging the factory.*
>
> *We are calmly braced for the future, but of course we can have no clear picture of what it may bring. It goes without saying that*

we must be prepared to face all kinds of sacrifices and deprivations, but God will surely continue to help.

Do write diligently, dear Otto, whenever you have a chance, even if it is only a few lines. You will also have to write more often to Edi so that he will not so deeply miss hearing from us. Our good wishes and our prayers accompany you along your paths. Best regards and kisses from your Arnold.

It is a tribute to my grandmother Fanny that in such uncertain times, the few lines that she adds to Arnold's letter indicate that she is more concerned with the welfare of her children than with her own fate.

Your words are like a ray of sunshine in a gloomy hut. With your last letter, you have calmed our heart. May the dear Lord just keep you in good health and may our present anxieties be unfounded. The times give us pause and much food for thought.

I would like to count on another letter soon, but there is some question about how the mail is going to function now. Don't you have some foreign stamps? In the event that it will not be possible for us to write to Edi in Canada, I ask that you do so more often and then report to us.

Puzzled by Fanny's reference to "foreign stamps" and the need to use both Otto and Hertha as direct recipients of mail, I did more research on wartime conditions in Prague. I learned that even writing to the United States was not a simple matter. Eventually, except for two hours in the afternoon at a single location, all post offices in Prague were declared off limits to Jews.

On that same Sunday that he wrote to Otto, Arnold tested the mail and wrote the first wartime letter to my parents. It is largely a repeat of his letter to Otto, but with an even stronger assurance that there is no cause for anxiety.

September 3, 1939

My Dear Ones,
We hope that you have received our last detailed letter of August 24
that included my professional credentials, and the birthday letter
of August 31. We have been without news from you for quite a
while. The last letter was July 27, but we did meanwhile read your
letter to Gretl's parents. We constantly admire how quickly and
how well you have adapted to your new situation and to all the
hard work.

Mama is here in search of an apartment because they have to
leave Budweis. In the meantime, things are going very well for us.
Don't worry, everything will happen the way it will happen. Wor-
rying doesn't help, and one must accept one's fate. All that you can
do is bring us joy through your letters.

Be well and be hugged and kissed by your Arnold.

A month later, Arnold writes another letter that is reassuring in the
extreme. He and Vera hear regularly from Cousin Hertha in New York and
from Hertha's sister Emmy and her mother Jetty (Fanny's sister), both of
whom are still in Prague. Arnold and Vera are now trying to gain entry to
the United States.

I sincerely thank you, dear Hertha for your efforts to persuade
Bella to send us an affidavit. I beg you to continue these efforts
since our hope for the future rests upon getting a visa.

The name "Bella" remains a name totally unknown to me. I checked the
Waldstein family tree but Bella does not appear on it. I acquired a Bloch-
Vogel family tree, thinking she may be related on Fanny's side. No luck. I
remain puzzled about the identity of this woman who promised Arnold
and Vera an affidavit to the United States.

I am puzzled also that Arnold wrote that there were no major changes
and absolutely no food shortages. Other sources indicate that so much was

sucked into the Nazi machine that, almost immediately after the outbreak of war, food was in short supply. In the end, I conclude that not only did Arnold and Vera want to minimize my parents' anxiety, they also wanted to avoid writing anything that the censor might hold against them when the promised affidavit to the U.S. arrived.

> *I can report to you that we are all well, that the whole large family is healthy and that life continues in its old accustomed tracks. The Fränkels and the Urbachs have set up housekeeping together and they live on their savings. Vera and I have our professions. We have enough to eat and there is absolutely no shortage of food here. For now, we even have our croissants for breakfast.*

———

ATTACHED TO ARNOLD'S September missive is a lengthy letter from my grandmother Fanny. Like Arnold, she is reassuring, and her words must have greatly comforted my parents.

I am also astounded by her informed comments on farming life. She seems to know so much that my parents were only gradually learning. That cream must be just at the right temperature to be successfully churned into butter. That hay is grown and mown for feed, but that straw (to provide clean bedding for animals) is part of a longer, two-step process and is actually a by-product of the harvesting of wheat.

> *My Dear Children,*
> *I happen to be in Prague for a few days and yesterday, I went to visit your dear parents Max and Resl. I found them both well, thank goodness. I must say that Papa has made a great recovery, and he seems well rested. Dear Mama is also doing quite well. Uncle Ignatz Grünhut was just there too.*
> *Don't worry, children, Max and Resl are not lacking anything. They have some store of food supplies and they have taken my advice and bought extra in case there should come a time of*

shortage. I also offered them anything of ours that they might need, but thank goodness, they still have all they need or have requested. We won't let them do without, you can be quite sure of that. Besides, dear Emil visits them daily. He tries so hard and I really admire him. All else we must leave to God. Who knows what still lies ahead? May we all stay in good health!

And now, to the point. I read your last letter, dear Gretl and Anny, and I am reassured to learn that you have completed the biggest task of all—the harvest. That is the real proof of a capable farmer, to even guess the weather, so that everything reaches the barn in a dry state. How much oats did you plant? Do both of the men now have to repay the neighbours in kind for their help?

I'm not very pleased with you for acquiring a bull. Why on earth are you doing that? It's a very dangerous experiment, and you could have acquired two cows for the price. I'd be very happy if the wild animal were off the premises again. You'd better look after your precious health! I beg you! Listen to me!

I hope that the work ahead won't cost you so much sweat, especially now that the summer heat is over. Are you already planting fall wheat? And how are the vegetables doing? Did you plant turnips? They are nourishing both for cattle and pigs. How is the milk separator working out? I suppose one of the men will have to churn the cream. It's very hard work and has to be done just so, as is the case with the temperature of the milk.

Splurge on a bit of cream for your elevenses, dear Anny and Gretl. I am sorry to read that you haven't gained any weight. You must do so by consuming good cream and butter. Helenchen will probably also enjoy some bread and butter. Gretl, try to put up some cottage cheese. It makes a nice change.

I forgot to send you congratulations on Helynka's birthday. May you all experience great joy from her. Now I close with the sincerest of greetings to you all. Stay well and be heartily hugged and kissed by your faithful Mother Fanny

Give lots of good kisses to Helynka from me.

No one has ever called me Helynka, and I seize the Czech diminutive as symbolic of my grandmother's love. In an orgy of self-centredness, my eyes scan the remaining letters from my grandmother in the fall of 1939, searching for my name.

> My dear children,
> How overjoyed we were to receive your photos! Please accept my sincerest thanks. I take them out several times a day to look at them. Really, I just can't get enough of looking at them. The pictures of each one of you are good, but I must confess that when I first saw you, I cried a lot. I thank the dear Lord to see you standing in front of your own home with a roof over your head, even if there is a long hard road ahead of you. And dear sweet Helynka, I like her in every way. I always give her photo lots of kisses.

In another letter, she calls me *Helimäderl* and says that I am cute enough to kiss. However, neither references to my cuteness nor distracting comments on farm life can hide the fact that things are no longer the same. My grandmother's birthday wishes for my father are a tacit acknowledgement of the momentous changes that have taken place.

> Now I come to you, dear Edmund, in order to offer you my most heartfelt good wishes on the occasion of your birthday on September 15. May you always be healthy and strong.
> May you meet your own expectations as a farmer and in an honest fashion so that we parents can take pride in you.

On September 15, 1938, my father would have celebrated his birthday in the family home surrounded by his parents, his siblings and in-laws, his nieces and nephews, and many friends with whom he had grown up in Strobnitz. Less than two weeks later, the British Prime Minister, Neville Chamberlain would fly to Munich and give Hitler the Sudetenland in return for "peace in our time." Leaving everything behind, my parents would flee to Prague, and less than six months later, when all of Czechoslovakia had become Nazi

territory, my parents and I would flee again, this time across the sea to
Canada.

Fanny's words underscore the magnitude of all that has happened.

> *How much has changed in the course of a year! But you, dear chil-*
> *dren, all of you there, be of good cheer! You are the lucky ones.*
> *What sorrows there are here! I cannot begin to describe the suffer-*
> *ing that people are experiencing.*
>
> *Our own dear Martha is so worn down by the constant worries*
> *and upsets that she has positively turned gray. She is beside herself*
> *with anxiety. If only the Fränkels could come to you! That is our*
> *greatest worry. Now they are being asked for proof of origin of the*
> *parents on both sides of the family. The paperwork is taking for-*
> *ever.*
>
> *Thankfully, your dear mother Resl is supposed to be doing very*
> *well, or so Emil informed us. He was here this week to meet Rudolf*
> *Ziegler. He has become quite slim as have we all, and he has asked*
> *me to send you his very best wishes. How gladly he'd help you with*
> *your work on the farm, if only it were possible! They want to send*
> *Erica to London.*
>
> *My heart aches for these good people. Where are they all sup-*
> *posed to go? Leaving such a good way of life is painful.*

In an undated letter also written in the fall of 1939, Fanny reports that
among Else's many visitors, there are some who are trying to send their
children to England. *"How does one part with a child?"* I ask myself again.
"How does one know if the worst is yet to come?"

Today, as I watch my own toddler grandchildren seek shelter in their
mother's arms, I cannot imagine the courageous parents who prematurely
parted with their children.

Fanny's heart breaks for her daughter and for *"all these good people"* who
are leaving. As she points out, they are not leaving in search of a better life
but because their own peaceful existence has been shattered, much like the
ultra-modern Bata shoe factory whose demise she describes.

My dear children,
I thank you very much for your kind and detailed letter and I am answering it right away so that we will soon be lucky enough to hear more news from you. How nice it is to read your letters, my dear children. I follow your lines while imagining everything in my mind.

Now the hay has been brought in. It was surely a more difficult undertaking than in than our little fields in Strobnitz, especially since you have so few wagons.

Here, the weather has been mostly bad. Sunday night we had such bad thunderstorms in the area between Iglau and Zlin (hailstones weighing ¼ kg.) that all crops were destroyed and the roofs of most houses were blown away or smashed. The Bata factory in Zlin was totally demolished. Its vaulted glass roof caved in and all the machines are unusable. Thousands of windowpanes have been reduced to a heap of shattered glass.

Now you will have finished unpacking the lift. Did everything arrive unbroken? Do you, dear Gretl, feel more comfortable in your new home? Is Helenka happy too to have her own things again? How many rooms are there in your house? And that reminds me, where do you get the wood for the stove? Do your woods produce some fuel? I have another idea. Could you create some kind of bathing facility in your little creek, even if it were only a Sitzbad? Could the water be dammed up?

Now I close with the sincerest of greetings and kisses to you, my dear Hellygirl and a request that you bring us pleasure soon again with your news. Your faithful mother Fanny.

I smile to be called *Helenchen* and at the idea of a Sitzbad in our mud-bottomed creek. From the house to the creek involved a good twenty-minute walk through the fields. Still, my grandmother's questions speak to me of a vibrant curiosity that reflects the depth of her caring.

To her son Otto in Paris, Fanny writes a similar letter, but with a paragraph underscoring the difficulties that others are experiencing.

Sorrows are rampant here. Like headless chickens, people are scattering in all directions, not knowing what tomorrow will bring. People from Strobnitz have had to leave their homes, and all Jews are supposed to move to Prague in stages. Young people under 35 will be first on the list, and many will try to leave the country. My sister Jetty has been interrogated, but there is some doubt about whether she will be allowed to emigrate. They are claiming that her taxes have not been paid. She and her family have suffered so much, and they did not put enough money aside. The little cash that they have is being eaten up. Like others, they dread the future, imagining themselves penniless in a foreign land. And now, we have this latest decree—moving to Prague where life will be much more expensive than here in Budweis.

————

DESPITE ALL THAT HAS happened, my grandfather Josef views himself as a lucky man. *"One of God's favourites,"* he calls himself in his first post-war letter. He now accepts the fact that his entire family is planning to regroup in Canada. His joy is tempered only by his awareness of what is happening to the Jews in Europe.

Budweis, Sept. 26, 1939

With today's letter we come to inquire about your well-being. We are in good health and hope the same is true of you all. Your last letter gave us great pleasure, as did the photos that we received this week. We are really impressed and everyone looks great, especially dear little Helly.

Still, when I look at you, dear Edi, my heart aches. How many rays of sun must burn down before a face becomes so blackened? But still, take a look at your magnificent achievements of the last few months. We are proud of what you own and of what you have accomplished.

I showed the pictures at F. P. today and everyone was full of enthusiasm. Mrs P. would gladly trade her whole house for what you have. Despite all your hard work, people here envy you. Here, there are young, strong Jews wandering about, unemployed. They would gladly work in return for a meal. Young Rosenberg goes to the brickyard every day to earn a handful of change for a whole week's work.

And now, dear Edi, for your birthday I wish you all the best, especially an iron constitution, and may all your wishes come true. I hope that with the hard work and the energy that you are expending, you will advance further than here in Strobnitz.

I like to imagine that I am one of God's favourites, and I pray that you will soon be well established. As soon as the Fränkels leave for Canada, half of us will be across the ocean.

It will be easier for Arnold and Vera. Be glad, dear Edi, that you have gotten so far ahead. When I look at your friends here, my heart aches. Everybody wants to emigrate, but nobody can. Nothing but problems.

I close for today, wishing you all the best again, my dear Edi. Regards to Gretl, Anny, Ludwig, and to my dear Helly-child. In my imagination, I still see her playing about in the garden in Strobnitz.

Your faithful Papa.

———

AS FALL TURNS TO WINTER, Fanny worries about her adult children. Has Otto thought to pack warm underwear? She assures her son that she and his father will survive the winter by keeping their heads down and not drawing attention to themselves.

I am able to decline with thanks your question about whether we need anything for the household. We get everything that we need

*here using ration cards, and you can otherwise be assured that we
don't lack anything. If we can receive good news from you children
abroad, that is our joy.*

My grandfather Josef's letter to Otto is brief but melancholy. His loved ones
are scattered in all directions and there is little to break the monotony of
his days.

*We were very pleased when we got your last letter. You are always
the old Otto, always in a good mood, even in these hard times.*

*Thank God, we are all in good health, we have enough to eat
and we are satisfied. If only God would grant us the good fortune
to all be together again as a family. Sadly, you are now scattered
about in all directions. This is not something we ever thought
would happen.*

*I don't know anything special for today. We had two letters from
Edi via Prague. It is a delight to read these. He really hit the jackpot.*

———

IN NOVEMBER, BOTH Fanny and Josef write again. Visitors from Strobnitz
have brought the village news, mostly about young people who have left or
married or joined the army. These visitors have also brought the name of
the villager who "took" the store. Like any legitimate owner, he is now
pocketing the profits.

Fanny's letter is her trademark blend of pertinent questions and worried
motherly advice. Because our sows have failed to produce enough piglets,
Fanny suggests that we not feed the brood sow so well, and that we give her
"more slimey food, not too rich" so that she will produce more piglets. She
advises us to plant "noble" trees in the orchard, like those bearing the winter apples that are shipped to Europe. Although she admits that plucking
and gutting chickens is not a pleasant task, she suggests that it is easier in
the long run and more profitable than transporting live chickens to market.
In large measure, our life has become her life.

Believe me, dear children, I am running a farm in my thoughts and would dearly like to help you with yours.

Fanny seems obsessed by the issue of gathering fuel from the woods, and a variation of the same paragraph appears twice in her letter.

How are things with the fuel? Do your woods produce wood for burning? I beg you to be very careful, especially in chopping. You will remember well, dear Edi, the scare we had earlier.

My grandfather is less garrulous but clearly lonely for his family. He rues a way of life that now seems like a fairy tale. "*Someday, we will tell you every-thing,*" he promises my parents:

If at all possible, write us a letter again. A letter from you is a day of celebration for us. We do not hear much from Strobnitz. That was once upon a time.
> *A thousand kisses to my dear Helly-child.*
> *Your faithful Papa.*

Before forwarding the letter, Arnold and Vera add a few lines in the margins to reassure my parents that all is well.

We received your letter of October 9 addressed to Gretl's parents. We ourselves have been without direct news from you for months. We are all doing well, and so far, everything is as it was. Do not worry. We are working and we have enough to eat.

————

MARTHA FRÄNKEL'S FIRST letter after the outbreak of war contrasts sharply with the comforting words penned by Arnold and by my grandparents. My father's sister indicates that the Fränkels are coping but, as predicted, the fall has not been pretty. Clearly, she is speaking of more than the colour of the autumn leaves.

Prague, Oct. 17, 1939

My dear ones,

How precious your recent lines addressed to Gretl's parents were for us! You can well imagine how happy we were to know that, thank God, you are all well. To be without news from you casts a shadow over our mood, especially since our thoughts always dwell with you.

In one of my last letters I wrote to you that the fall here was not going to be pretty, and it has not been. How nice it would have been if we had been with you in time for your harvest! But just as with Gretl's parents Max and Resl, everything is a matter of fate, and we are all in God's hands.

Your progress in the running of the farm brings us great pleasure, and in our mind, we form nice pictures of everything. Dear Anny, I admire your business acumen. You are a woman of the times, and may Ludwig and everyone be happy with your ideas.

You, dear Gretelein, are probably already mistress within your sphere of expertise. With united strengths, you will soon create a nice agricultural enterprise. I keep seeing all of you in my mind. My dear little brother, how I'd love to give a few good kisses to you and to sweet Helly-child who is probably a very good little girl.

Sunday Max and Resl were here. I like them. They look well, thank God, but of course they would like most of all to be with you.

As Elsa has written, our little Dorly is walking already. She still wobbles a bit, but she is really cute in her ways. Ilserl can already speak Czech with her friends and Trude's cousin is giving her English lessons free of charge. Unfortunately, the school here in the district of Straschnitz where we are staying is unhealthy and primitive.

Emil has been working hard as an apprentice shoemaker and he's up to nine soles redone in a day. As of today he got a small job as cashier at the emigration office of the NZO, the National Zionist Organization. Emil is delighted to have something to do. Besides, if there is no other way, then we will have to go to Palestine illegally if that becomes a possibility. When all is said and done, one is only human, and this illness is supposed to last a long time.

Trude wrote us a moving letter of farewell. She is on her way to N.Y. where her sister-in-law has opened a hat salon. They want to help us, but I can't imagine how. We were very happy to have news from our brother Otto. I had been thinking of him all the time. Alone in a foreign country, he must experience events even more sharply. Yesterday we received a little 5 gr. package that he sent. It was touching. For the moment, we have enough to eat. Arnold has also just received a package from Otto. Our own dear parents in Budweis are doing quite well, thank God. Unfortunately they have to cope with all the new conditions, as do we all.

Now I want to close with the best of wishes. Stay very, very well, all of you!! You are heartily hugged and kissed by your Martha.

The letter ends with greetings from my cousin Ilserl whose handwriting has improved greatly despite the lack of formal schooling. I linger longest over her simple words.

Best regards and kisses from your Ilse

Over each detail of Martha's letter, I reflect at length. With his usual foresight, Emil has taken on two jobs. Shoemaking, always a practical skill, was doubly so in 1939, given the reality that "every army marches on its feet." Emil's second job, his work at the office of the National Zionist Organization would provide a different advantage. It meant that Emil would be among the first to hear news of any opportunity for reaching Palestine safely.

Although it is too late for the Fränkels to come to Canada, Ilserl is being tutored in English. To me, it is an indicator that the Fränkels have not completely relinquished their dream of crossing the Atlantic.

Because Martha's letter is so filled with news and because Emil seems so enterprising, I am reassured. It is my research into historical events of 1939 that uncovers two deeply disturbing facts. On the Internet, I find the following:

Middle of September 1939: ESTABLISHMENT OF JEWS WITH POLISH NATIONALITY. By searching houses and flats in Prague, those Jews who formerly had held Polish nationality were found.

27 September 1939: REMOVAL OF POLISH NATIONALS. By Transportation.[7]

The words jump from my computer screen. Removal. Transportation. Former Polish Nationals. Emil was a former Polish National.

Anxiously, I scan the remaining 1939 letters for further news. How did the Fränkels manage, when other Jews with Polish nationality were being "removed by transportation"? These words were the standard euphemism for "shipped to a concentration camp."

Two letters from Else and Emil Urbach provide clues, but no clear answers. In a letter dated October 13, 1939, Else directs the focus to family news. She refers to changing conditions almost in passing, as if they do not really apply to the Urbachs. Others may be rushing to emigrate, but she is waiting for the storm to pass, painting a rather tranquil picture of daily life.

My Dear Ones,

It was a nice surprise for us all when, after a long pause, we again received a letter from you. We are very glad that you are in good health, and thank God I can report the same of our parents and of everyone here.

Our Marianne is in a French school now. She is also taking a sewing course so that she will be well prepared to help our brother Otto produce women's knitwear fashions in Paris. To our delight, we had pleasant news from him several times lately. He has probably also written to you several times.

Last week we visited Gretl's parents. They went to the syna-
gogue during all the High Holidays and have adapted well to the
circumstances. I can imagine how much you wish you already had
them with you. You must not lose courage that it will come to pass,
and when it does, your delight will be doubly great.

Helly will surely already be a big girl and bring lots of life to the
house. She could play nicely now with Dorly, who is very cute and
is toddling about, babbling continuously in her own language.

It is only Else's reference to problems experienced by *"our people"* in finding accommodation that strikes a jarring note:

Despite all the sorrows, time flies and before we noticed, the sum-
mer had passed. We are now in search of a suitable place to live
since we must move within the next three months. Today we found
out that there is an apartment in a large house across the street. We
looked at it right away. It is quite modern, with central heating
and balconies, but it is very expensive. We are to hear in three days
whether they will rent it to us. These days, they do not like to rent
to so many people and not everywhere to our people, so there is not
much choice.

Strangely, toward the end of the letter, Else's handwritten words transition
in mid-sentence to typed lines offering concrete suggestions that can only
be from Emil Urbach.

I hope that the winter will pass well. It will certainly be quite
severe where you are, and I hope that you have enough fuel from
your woods and dry plants. Did you ever get the book on raising
pigs and cattle? I also wanted to send you a book on gardening, but
I was waiting to hear whether you received the other books. Dogs
have risen very much in price recently and are used for a variety of
purposes: fat, hides, hunting and tracking, guarding property, etc. I
suppose you wouldn't have time to raise bees? Honey would be a

good item to sell, especially if you had honey-bearing plants in the fields.

Emil's final paragraph strikes a chilling note. Unlike my parents and the rest of the family, he harbours no dreams that "someday" we will all meet again.

> *We did not know what to do with your reference to "holding on to the thought of seeing one another again here at home." We still do not know how to take this comment. It is our opinion that every single person who is outside of Europe is to be considered fortunate. You are heartily greeted by the whole Urbach family.*

What prompted Emil's words remains a mystery. The only logical possibility is that my parents had written a letter expressing their own loneliness, and wondering if someday, they would all be re-united back in Strobnitz, the place where they had experienced the simple joys of family and had known happiness.

Emil pours cold water upon that dream with his blunt reminder that anyone who has managed to leave Europe is indeed fortunate. Remarkably, in his last unsigned letter of 1939, Emil does not mention the Fränkels in the catalogue of family news.

Dec. 6, 1939

My dear ones,
We were very pleased the other day to have seen your lines to our dear parents in Budweis and to the other relatives. From them, we gather that you are doing well and that the state of your cattle and the marketing possibilities for butter have improved.

At the usual Sunday gatherings, you always occupy an important place on the program. We wrote to you a while ago, but the letter seems to have gotten lost. That is why your remark that you had not heard from us in two months rather surprised us.

One of us regularly visits your dear parents, Max and Resl Grünhut. They live quietly and modestly, lacking for nothing aside from their wish to leave, which unfortunately is still rather difficult. Your dear mother is in good health, gets distracted by your dear father from the everyday routine through visits, board games, etc. They often go for walks or visit relatives and acquaintances. They also go to the synagogue assiduously. Thus, they pass the time that they would like so much to be spending with you. Our dear parents in Budweis are living in a similar way

As of January, we will be living near Arnold. Else will be able to enjoy the city more, since she has been spending lots of time now on the acquisition of food because of the considerable distance from the stores. The children are still attending school. Marianne is learning French, and our Otto is completing the last year of Gymnasium. Time will teach us what they should do a year from now.

We get comforting reports from your brother Otto from time to time. Let us hope that they correspond to reality and that it will remain thus.

Many people from here are immigrating to Palestine now. Manni and his wife have already landed there. We do not lack food. Everything is very purposefully regulated, well organized.

Edi, did you ever receive the books? The one on raising cattle too? I still have a book on horticulture and a flyer and a chart on combating the Colorado beetle, but do not know if these would reach you. I will leave it for later times.

With best regards

The Family Copes

*T*HE YEAR 1940 BEGINS WITH A LETTER from my Grandmother Fanny, who hungers for news about us and the farm.

> *I want to end the old year and start the new by writing to you, my dear children. My thoughts dwell constantly upon you and I cannot hide from you how lonely we are for you. We received a copy of the letter that you, dear Anny and Gretl, wrote to your parents, but we were doubly pleased with the letter you addressed directly to us, especially since it was quite detailed. We long to know everything about your new life.*
>
> *Still, one cannot change things. You are fortunate that work is all you have to worry about and that you are adapting so well. Especially you, dear Gretl and Anny. Who would have believed you'd have the strength for hard labour? I beg you to eat heartily, for that makes quite a difference.*
>
> *We've had severe frost for several days now, which again makes me think of you often in regards to having to get up early. But it*

has to be done, doesn't it, my dear Edmund. You've no other choice. If you don't do it, the animals will do you in.

Fanny shows our photos at every opportunity, including to the visitors from back home in Strobnitz.

I've been asked to send best regards from Mr. and Mrs. Chief Postmaster and from Mrs. Head Watchman who visited us from Strobnitz. They were delighted with your pictures. "O Boze! Helenka!" they exclaimed.

The Czech words bring me a smile. Although Ludwig and his cousins were fluent speakers of Czech, the language was spoken only occasionally by visitors to our house. My mother revered Goethe and Schiller and the greats of German culture. For her, Czech was a lesser tongue. During the first year of her marriage, my mother had been the belle of the annual Fireman's Ball in Strobnitz. Fanny warned her to learn Czech if she wanted to retain that position. With faith that her beauty would carry the day, my mother had refused to stoop so low. Sadly, the issue was never put to the test. The next year, my mother was pregnant. The following year, as Jews, my parents were no longer welcome at the village ball.

I smile also to see that my grandmother carries no grudges. She welcomes everyone from Strobnitz who comes to visit her. Clearly, Aryans could easily cross the border to Budweis, but for Jews, this was impossible. Fanny's letter with its professional appellatives in the place of family names reminds me of the German cemetery that I visited in 1998 on my trip to meet Tini, our former family nanny. Tini took me to the cemetery to "introduce me" to her late husband. As her spoken words morphed into silent communing with the deceased, I wandered off. I was surprised to see that many of the tombstones were engraved with reminders of the professional status of the dead, and that many of these titles seemed less than noble callings. Chief Accountant. Director of Sanitation. Municipal Maintenance Controller.

Later, I asked Tini about immortalizing such titles in stone. Did she not view death as the great equalizer who makes all earthly titles null and void? Tini's response was simple: a man is forever defined by what he makes of himself.

———

FOR MY GRANDFATHER JOSEF, the inability to work threads its way through all of his letters. Despite the clear mark of the censor across the page, he slips in the comment that "*much has changed in the business world.*" It has been more than a year since he and my father had been forced to leave Strobnitz and the store that had been their livelihood, yet my grandfather is still smarting from the wound.

Aside from that single comment, my grandfather's letter is uncharacteristically flat and somewhat disjointed.

> *My dear Children*
> *After a lengthy silence we are coming again to send you a sign of life. Thank God we are all in good health and doing relatively well. Gretl's parents wrote to us last week that everything is okay with you. We are happy to know that you are safe.*
> *How is my little Helly-child, I long so much for you. If only I could see you, even for five minutes!*
> *As far as business goes, much has changed here. Now in the winter you will also have a chance to recover a little, although there is lots to do even in the winter on a farm. I also have the happy hope that within a few years, you will get ahead through your hard work.*
> *Otherwise, we don't hear anything; everything is as it was. Write us another detailed letter, for it is always a joyful day when we hear from you. Best regards to you all.*
> *Your faithful Papa*

———

IN THE MARGIN ARE A few lines from Arnold and Vera. The date indicates that Fanny and Josef had forwarded their letter of January 2 to Arnold and Vera in Prague. Perhaps this was because they were unable to purchase foreign stamps in Budweis. More likely, Arnold had advised against sending mail to countries hostile to Nazi interests. For a Jew to write frequently to France and the United States may well have been a risk that he chose to reserve only for himself.

January 8, 1940

My dear ones, reporting to you that everything is as it was. Without exception, we are all doing well, thank God, so that you need in no way be concerned for us. Unfortunately, we don't get mail from you often enough, and I especially haven't seen so much as a line from you for months, dear Edi. Best regards and kisses to you all from Vera and Arnold.

———

IN A LETTER TO THEIR SON Otto who forwarded it to my father, Fanny and Josef openly confess their loneliness. In addition to being deprived of their children, they are in the grip of a severe winter that is chaining them indoors.

Dear child, are you often homesick for us? I think of you so much, and many nights I even dream of you. Still, everything must be borne calmly and patiently.

After a very long interval, we received your card. Was this the mail's fault or yours? Well, we thank God that you are okay, which is all that matters. We too are well, but having a very severe winter that is keeping us shackled up in our room.

Is Fanny's unnecessarily strong terminology of imprisonment another example of communication in a time of censorship? With increasingly restrictive curfews for Jews, it is more than the cold, in all likelihood, that confines them to their quarters.

Fanny asks questions about Otto's life in Paris and also makes observations about *"the Canadian contingent"*:

> *I remain amazed by the hard work of the dear children. Who would have sought such strengths in Gretl? The zeal with which she tackles her work is unbelievable. Indeed, she wrote that they would like to expand if only they had the money.*
>
> *Apparently little Helen is growing into a sturdy little girl. She consumes her meals with a great appetite. Back home in Strobnitz we would have said she is laying the groundwork for becoming a farm wife.*

Josef expresses regret that his family is no longer together, but he reveals no personal fear of what the future will bring.

> *So pleased that you are okay. That's all we need to know. We are in good health, thank God, and hoping for sunshine. But there you are, all of you scattered about again. At least you are in a nice place. I have so much to ask you, but I must tame my curiosity for now and wait for better times. Please write to us soon again. Your faithful Papa.*

———

ON JANUARY 29, 1940, Martha Fränkel also writes to her brother Otto. The Fränkel's situation is grim. Emigrating to Canada is no longer a possibility. She and Emil have decided that their only option is emigration to Palestine, an illegal and uncertain venture.

> *My dear husband is at the office daily until ten o'clock. Our goal is to go to Israel illegally as soon as possible, even though it will take two or three months and will be very hard on the children.*

Unfortunately, it looks like there is no other way.

Ilserl was nine years old yesterday. She is a quiet, dear little girl, and she studies hard. Dorothy is a dear. She runs and shouts and cries aloud, and she totally brightens our existence.

I picture my little cousins, Dorly the toddler and Ilserl, the *"quiet, dear little girl"* whose birthday Martha and Emil have managed to celebrate. My mind flits back to reports I've read about ships that arrived in Palestine with no landing permit. Their passengers were simply told to swim ashore.

All of Martha's letters have been emotionally intense, but the final paragraph of this one is uncharacteristically effusive. Her words border on the mawkish as she pleads with Otto to write to cousin Hertha in pursuit of an affidavit, a letter from an American citizen indicating that the Fränkels will request no government handouts if the United States will allow them to emigrate.

I still want to try one more thing. When you were still resident in Vienna, you had us registered as of June 1938. Since other Austrians who were registered in May 1938 are now getting visas, my husband made some inquiries. A reliable source told him that if we were in possession of an affidavit, there would be a possibility of getting a visa in two or three months.

The affidavit originally intended for Edi has been signed over to Arnold, and it's good for him to have something in hand too. I'm writing to Hertha again today. Perhaps helping us will be in her power after all, and perhaps some noble soul will be found to issue us an affidavit. So I wanted to ask you, Otto-kins, whether it is in the scope of your possibilities to write to Hertha in this regard. You know our dates.

Not a single day goes by without my heart being with you. How I beg God each day for your health, Otto-kins, my dear, good, sweet honey. How long it's been since we saw each other, and even worse, it's your dear birthday, I think so-o-o-o often of you. The older you get, the more ardent my wishes for you become. I feel

such a deep, devoted love for you that truly, words fail me in order
to convey my wishes to you. May it be, beloved little Otto, that you
stay in good health (our souls cry out for it), and may God grant
you the strength to bear all that lies ahead. A friend told us that
you got a new suit for your birthday, and so I say to you, beloved
Otto-kins, God grant that you wear it in good health. Whenever
you send us a few lines, we are happy, and we always thank you
very much.

Emil Fränkel sends only a few lines, but his condensed words are all the
more powerful.

Dearest Brother-in-law
Above all, the best of everything for your birthday. May God keep
you in good health to bear the difficult times ahead. Do us the
favour and write to Hertha. I'd be very happy if there were any
hope for us. Things are going well for me in the office, but being
occupied only helps distract me for ten minutes. Many kisses Emil

———

IN HER NEXT LETTER DATED March 3, my grandmother Fanny indicates that
sending and receiving mail has become problematic. She writes that letters
now take at least three months, and that the last letter they received from us
is dated December 1939. Because no one wants to part with original letters,
Emil Fränkel has assumed the role of scribe. He copies by hand our letters
to the family in Prague and forwards them to Fanny and Josef who are still
in Budweis. Fanny's letter suggests that conditions in Europe are deterio-
rating, and that it has been a harsh winter.

I have been waiting from week to week for news. It probably seems
exactly the same to you. My dear children, I would very much like
to ask you to try to write to us again, but I don't know to which
address. I must leave that to Arnold.

I thought of you every morning during the winter. We stayed under the covers until 9 o'clock because there was a dreadful cold spell and we had to be frugal with our fuel.

My grandfather Josef fills his part of the letter with pertinent questions about the farm.

What is the state of your cattle population? Has it expanded? Write everything, even how many cows, horses, pigs, and chickens you have. How I'd love to see them and feed them! I have always hankered for life on a country estate. The exercise and being in nature all day long is very good for you. Besides, it helps you forget your troubles.

Now it will soon be your busy season again. We are all overjoyed that you are there and that you can go to bed in peace and get up in peace. Let us pray to God that there will be sunshine for all of us again someday.

New handwriting in that same letter plus the date of March 10, 1940 indicate that Arnold has once again taken responsibility for mailing his parents' letter. His brief words must have brought comfort to my parents.

Although I just wrote to you a week ago c/o Hertha in N.Y., I am sending you this letter so that you can see that your dear parents in Budweis are also are doing well.

Nothing has changed for us, thank God, and work is our greatest joy. We think of you often and we are happy to know that you are safe. You need not worry about us. We are not in need and we are satisfied.

———

INITIALLY, I TOO WAS reassured by Arnold's words. However, the constant presence of the censor gives me pause. Arnold's *"work is our greatest joy"* now rings false, like an echo of the Nazi dictum "*Arbeit Macht Frei—work is liberation.*" As an engineer, Arnold's expertise would have been in demand as the Nazi war machine moved into high gear, but Vera? How can work have been her greatest source of joy if she had been forbidden to practice medicine since 1939 when the offices of Jewish doctors in Prague had been shut down?

For my grandfather Josef, the enforced idleness has become intolerable. The contrast between Arnold's note of March 10 and Josef's next letter dated April 29, 1940 is remarkable. Josef yearns to be useful, and his letter is laden with irony. For him, useful work is the mark of a human being. The days drag by as he contemplates the waste unfolding before his eyes. He watches as younger Jews shift piles of sand from one place to another, and then shift them back again. Education and talent wasted.

> *If only I had something to do! Idling away my time is too boring. Send me your piglets and your chickens so that I can feed them! Dear Edi, your colleagues go to work daily. Flood control, they call it. I would like to write you many interesting things, but another time. Meier is working too. His task is a healthy one, with pickaxe and shovel, one that makes your back strong.*
>
> *So many people wish they could trade with you now. I have just spent a week in Prague where I attended services with Gretl's father, Papa Grünhut. At the Urbach's, Else organized a big afternoon gathering to welcome me. She invited at least thirty people, the whole assembly of relatives. Everyone is in good health and trusts God concerning the future.*

In this letter, Fanny does not reveal her own feelings about the changes that have stripped her husband of purpose. Instead, she diverts attention to us, asking whether my mother has managed to gain a few kilos (she had not, and despite a penchant for sweets, remained fashionably thin to the end of her days), and whether my father has help with the milking (he did, for as our livestock increased, my mother hand-milked all forty cows).

What is striking, however, is the frequency with which Fanny and all my non-religious relatives have begun to insert the word "God" into their letters.

> There can be no greater joy than to read your reports. We are amazed at the zeal with which you tackle this huge job, but then you have no choice. We pray to God that the rewards for all your diligence will continue to flow.

———

FANNY ALSO MENTIONS WRITING numerous letters that apparently did not arrive in Canada. This led me to assume that letters had been lost en route, including perhaps one from Else and Emil Urbach. However, Emil's next letter suggests that he had held back from communicating since December 6, 1939, because of my father's unexplained (and to me, inexplicable) failure to express his thanks for a book Emil had sent.

> April 21, 1940
>
> My dear ones
> In his last letter, dear Edi is justified in complaining that it has been a long while since he heard from us.
> Last time we sent a book on raising cattle or pigs. Because the shipment has not been acknowledged, a further book on horticulture has not been mailed. Perhaps I can send it along at some time or other.
> Your interesting letters to Gretl's parents are being sent to all the brothers and sisters and to Josef and Fanny. Everyone feeds on their content and is delighted with the success you've had. Judging by the letter numbers, there are still several en route. We all longingly await news from you.
> It brings us pleasure to note that, although your work has been undertaken with a huge expenditure of energy, it is connected to a

gradual but measurable degree of progress. We wish you the best of continuing good luck.

For Gretl's parents Max and Resl, it would be the greatest stroke of good fortune if they could already be with you. They have a nice apartment in the neighbourhood now, and we will be able to visit back and forth more often. They live simply, they are not suffering from any lack, and they go for walks, visit relatives, or go to church (sic). You must not worry on their account. If only you could be successful in prevailing on the authorities to finally ensure their departure!

Martha and Emil are waiting impatiently for the chance to leave. They are wavering between Palestine and the USA. They've been registered to leave since 1938. If their affidavit were to arrive in time, then they might soon get their visa. Maybe Hertha or Trude in N.Y. could do something for them. Ilse is learning English. Dorly is a bright and a good child, and she is growing rapidly.

Josef Waldstein is living in Budweis with his dear wife Fanny. They are happy to have news periodically from their dear ones. You need not have the least bit of anxiety on their account either, even if they don't write. They think of their children regularly, and wish each of them every success.

Arnold along with his wife are busy with their professions and report everything to you from time to time. Our son Otto is matriculating this year. We are not racking our brains about his future nor about that of our daughter Manci who is sewing dresses and mastering languages.

We are happy about the reports concerning your child; is she Americanized now? You are wished lots of continuing sucesses and greeted by

Your

Emil's typed and unsigned letters are so formal in tone that somehow, they seem more factual to me than some of the other letters.

I am especially interested in Emil's comments about Martha and Emil Fränkel for whom the sands of time are running out. Emil and Martha must leave Prague, yet there is not a single country prepared to admit them. They cannot stay, but there is nowhere to go.

Was there not one person in the entire United States of America willing to sponsor this capable, hard-working man and his little family? Aside from the mysterious "Bella," did neither my father nor Hertha have any contacts? Even if Hertha's first line of responsibility was her own mother and sister, did no one have "a friend of a friend" who might have helped?

———

ONLY A FEW DAYS LATER, a letter written by Arnold reveals that Vera's work is indeed ending. Strangely, Arnold does not even mention the urgency of the Fränkels' situation.

> *May 1, 1940*
>
> *My Dear Ones,*
>
> *After an unusually long time, a letter of yours has arrived again. You can imagine the joy released by your words of February 8 that arrived here last week. We are often with you in our thoughts, picturing your life and your doings. We are absolutely delighted at the progress you are making, and are happy knowing that you can peacefully pursue your work. I am convinced that, slowly but surely, you will reach a reasonable level of prosperity.*
>
> *About our fate, please continue not to worry. Like every human fate, it rests in God's hands. So far, we have done well in every respect, and we hope that this will be equally true in the future. We are not suffering from any particular need. We earn a reasonable amount, and so far, there has been no problem getting food. One change that does await us is that in the summer, Vera will resume private life. To compensate for the resulting drop in income, we plan to rent out the second room, let the maid go, and dissolve the household. Every morning, Vera will go to her mother's to help*

with the cooking, and we will eat lunch there. Besides, my salary
has risen so dramatically lately (almost 3000 Kronen) that we will
manage, barring the unforeseen. Generally, we are hopeful, so
please don't worry about us.
  I greet and kiss each one of you from my heart. Your Arnold

Days later, Emil Fränkel sends a typed letter addressed primarily to Hertha.
He is losing hope. They must leave Prague, but they have nowhere to go.

Arnold and Vera have stepped forward. They will relinquish my father's
affidavit in order to save the Fränkels. How or why this affidavit was originally issued to my father is a puzzle. To my knowledge, he had no friends
or relatives in the U.S. except Hertha. Given that we were already in
Canada, given that Emil Fränkel was my father's closest friend, and given
that initially, Arnold showed little interest in emigrating, I have no idea
why the "Bella affidavit" was not immediately transferred to the Fränkels.
Instead, the affidavit expired, and Emil must beg Hertha to ask Bella to
issue a new one.

May 7, 1940
Regarding your inquiries about us, dear Hertha, we were very sad.
Since we were registered on April 6, 1938, and the local weekly
paper stated that those who had been registered by the above date
are now being summoned for the purpose of emigrating, we are
prompted to ask you again for the affidavit.
  Because of your last communication, dear Hertha, I went to the
American Consulate to get information. To our utter amazement,
they told us that our waiting time on the Polish quota has been
exceeded and that we can be allowed to leave immediately if we
are in possession of an affidavit. Now, dear Hertha, you can well
imagine my situation, to see the goal so near and not to possess the
fervently longed for affidavit.
  On the very same evening, I spoke to Arnold who immediately
pronounced himself ready to give us his affidavit. Now it's in your
hands to help us, and we beg you, from the bottom of our hearts, to

come immediately to an understanding with Bella. The affidavit that was issued to Edi in 1938 has now expired. Bella would have to issue a whole new affidavit for us and we give you our dates as follows:

Emil, born February 6, 1894 in Lemberg, resident of Linz on the Danube.

Martha /Waldstein/, born September 26, 1908 in Strobnitz, resident of Linz on the Danube.

Ilse, born January 23, 1931 in Linz on the Danube, resident of Linz on the Danube.

Dorothea, born July 10, 1938 in Linz on the Danube, resident of Linz on the Danube.

Dear Hertha, since you have had the experience of filling out affidavits for your mother and your sister, please help Bella so that no unnecessary delays will occur. Especially these days, the slightest obstacle could cause months of delay.

Please reassure Bella that, as much as it is in our power, we will not become a burden on her, and we will always be grateful to her for her kindness.

Since we know from what you wrote that Bella always goes on her summer holidays very early, please don't be angry with us, dear Hertha, if we remind you once again of the urgency of this situation. Besides, no matter how fast we do the documentation, things still take a long time.

Should you be successful in this good and noble deed, be assured that you will have our undying gratitude. May God reward you upon the head of your dear child!

Perhaps it would be possible for you to convey the contents of this letter to Edi. This time, we finally hope for the best. Many sincere thanks in advance.

Yours
Emil

Re-reading this letter, I was enraged by the unknown Bella who contemplated the luxury of an extended summer vacation. How could she have ignored the desperation of Emil's words? Until the fall of 1941, Germany's policy was one of extrusion, and any Jew could leave if he had a place to go. It was mainly because the rest of the world would not take them in that relatively few Jews got out.[8]

Even though he had no answers and no power to change Canadian policy, I wonder if Emil's words left my father feeling that he had not done enough? Given the reality of a Canadian Immigration Act that "ranked would-be settlers by their racial characteristics, that distinguished Jews from non-Jews of the same citizenship, and that pre-dated Hitler's Nuremberg laws by more than ten years,"[9] is there anything my father could have done?

At the end of Emil's impassioned letter to Hertha, Martha adds only a few lines. She makes no pretence at lighthearted news.

> Well dear Hertha, the great undertaking will have to be accomplished after all. Although we would like to have sheltered you from it, the hard "we must" and the saying "only to the valiant belongs the world" is now our password.

The Letters Stop

ARNOLD DOES NOT WRITE AGAIN until July 21, 1940. Surprisingly, he mentions neither the Fränkels' situation nor the affidavit. Instead, he maintains a studied calm that masks the upheavals that are transforming life in Prague. Street names are being changed to honour German heroes. Vera's medical practice has come to an enforced end. They will soon be moving out of their apartment. Arnold does not dwell upon these changes. Instead, he draws attention to the progress that we have made, and to the stability of the family. His letter reminds me again that the letters travelled from person to person on both sides of the Atlantic.

> *My dear ones,*
> *Great joy reigns in the family whenever your written lines reach us, and every letter wanders from hand to hand. Then we all give thanks to God who has guided your fate along such peaceful paths. We rejoice at every little step forward that you are able to record.*
> *Our joy was especially great when we gathered from your letter of June 28, dear Hertha, that our brother Otto is also in good*

health and doing well. If we aren't as diligent about writing as you might perhaps wish, please don't take it amiss. Circumstances do not always make it possible to write. Nonetheless, our thoughts are constantly with you, and we follow every phase of your existence, from your work to your home life, which we can easily picture thanks to your descriptions.

In contrast to all the progress that you have to report, I can say only that as far as we are concerned, things are unchanged or almost unchanged. The old circle of family and relatives is still the same. At Else's, who somehow has a special knack for making guests feel welcome and where the uncommonly sweet little Dorly becomes the centre of attraction, we all get together, often by chance.

Mama is also there. She is living with Else and will stay for quite a while. She has a mild weakness of the heart, so we would rather have her in the care and control of family. Dear Vera will be closing her practice in a few days. We will keep our apartment for another three months and then we will probably move to a smaller one in the same house. Our street, by the way, is now called Schwerinova (Schwerinstrasse).

And now, one little favour that I ask of you, dear Edi. Please add a few lines in your own hand to Gretl's letters, and address these specifically to our parents who derive pleasure from every word. Now, be well, my dear ones, and may God be with you!

Your Arnold.

I marvel at how smoothly Arnold has slipped in the new development that would give my father cause for concern: his mother's health. Clearly, Arnold is trying to be truthful while avoiding unnecessary upset. Still, the suggestion that my father not leave letter writing in the hands of my mother is a sharp reminder of how carefully the family reads each letter, searching, as do I, for those small but revealing differences that characterize each individual.

―――――

ON AUGUST 25, WHEN HE writes again, Arnold no longer minimizes the seriousness of Fanny's condition. While he tries to put a positive spin on events, even going so far as to pretend that Vera has stopped practicing medicine in order to learn to cook and clean the house, his humour is transparent.

> *My dear ones,*
> *Our thoughts are often with you, much more often than it is possible for us to write. This time, dear Edi, it is the occasion of your birthday that gives rise in even stronger measure to our best wishes for your well-being.*
>
> *Everything here is more or less okay. It is only the health of dear Mama that unfortunately leaves a bit to be desired. She has a weakness of the heart and has lost a lot of weight. Else and Martha and Vera are caring for her as best they can, and a competent heart specialist is treating her, so that we hope, now that she is feeling better, she will soon recover.*
>
> *Vera is now running the household alone, which is greatly to her credit under the existing circumstances. Above all, she wants to get some practice in the domestic arts. So far, my stomach pronounces it good.*
>
> *I have lots of work in the factory, especially since the old boss died and his son took over the firm. The number of orders has doubled. I have not yet taken my holidays this year because of the continuing bad weather. However, we usually go for nice bike rides on Sunday, often 70-80 km.*
>
> *Now my dear ones, be well, write soon and more often than we do. Hugs and kisses to every one of you from your Arnold.*

On September 26, Arnold and Vera write again. Their letter provides me with a date that I quickly entered into my book of birthdays. Martha, the youngest of my father's siblings was born on September 26, the same day as her mother Fanny's birthday.

For 34 years, there would have been great rejoicing as the family celebrated the joint event. This year, Arnold makes no mention of even a simple family dinner. The omission startles me.

My dear ones,

Today, on Mama and Martha's birthday, our thoughts are especially intensively with you in the distance. We received your last letter and read it with pleasure. God grant that you continue to prosper, that your labour bear fruit, and that contentment be granted to you.

About the state of Mama's health, I can report joyful progress. A great improvement has taken place. She is already spending several hours a day out of bed, although she is, of course, still very weak and thin. She has gained some weight, and she is able to walk about in the room. Naturally, she is still under doctor's care and gets injections and medication, though not as frequently. The symptoms of heart trouble only occur now and then. Dear Vera takes care of her as much as ever and Else does her best to brighten her spirits. So we hope that dear Mama will soon be in full possession of her strength, and I think we need no longer be so concerned.

About us, I can report that, considering the circumstances, we are doing well, especially given that we are fairly modest people. You need not worry about us in this regard.

Dear Vera is bravely running the household, even though it is often beyond her capacity. She is often held up elsewhere. In a few weeks, the Fränkels will move in with us. We have reserved the two rooms upstairs that are not being used at the moment. Papa will move in with Else and the Fränkels will then use his furniture.

I continue to work hard in the factory, and although we have orders and enough raw materials, there have been some administrative changes. As a result, we must count on my leaving the firm in the next few weeks. Well, no panic, somehow we'll manage.

As I kiss you and embrace you from the heart, I remain your old Arnold

As I analyse Arnold's letter, I note that although Fanny may be on the mend, all else in Arnold's world is crumbling. Despite the fact that his skills as an engineer are in demand, his work life is ending. Ever conscious of the all-seeing censors, Arnold attempts to make his dismissal seem plausible. However, the "administrative changes" at the factory that will terminate Arnold's employment can only be a metaphor for the Nazi takeover and for the new laws that exclude Jews from the world of gainful employment.

The fact that Vera is "bravely" running the household appears to be a veiled reference to the long line-ups for Jews in Prague who were allowed to shop only between 11 a.m. and 3 p.m. They were also denied ration cards for a range of goods, including vegetables, fruits (fresh, dried, or canned), sugar, nuts, cheese, fish, poultry, and more.[10] Plans for the Fränkels to move in with Arnold and Vera, and for my grandfather to move in with Elsa are evidence that Jews are being compelled to live in ever more cramped quarters.

———

ARNOLD'S NEXT LETTER dated October 26, 1940, mentions the word "war" for the first and only time. It is a very strange letter in which the truth is veiled. Arnold chooses his words so carefully that he does not even use his brother Otto's name. Instead, Arnold refers to "Ingwa," as if this were a woman's name. I know that Ingwa is an abbreviation of Ingenieur Waldstein, and that Ingwa is the name Otto used as his knitwear label. Arnold uses a similar code for others. He refers to an uncle whose improbable Hungarian name "Fekete" I have never heard. This "uncle" has received news that two women for whom Arnold uses only first names are with Otto in an unspecified safe place.

Arnold reports, *"Mama can almost be called well again."* Sobering news, however, is the fact that the Fränkels will be moving out of the home they have been sharing with the Urbachs, yet they will not be allowed to move in with Arnold and Vera. Clearly, as the Nazis tightened every loophole, the decision of where to live is no longer a matter of personal choice.

My dear ones,

As always, we were delighted with your lines, and these are now making the rounds of the whole family both in the original and in a copy.

From Ingwa too we had the first news in a long time. Together with Dita and Liselotte, she (sic) telegraphed Uncle Fekete that they are all doing well. From us too, I can report that we are all doing relatively well. Above all, we are pleased to be in good health, and of course, that is what matters most. Dear Mama is now also sufficiently restored that one could almost call her well. She now spends most of her time out of bed, has a good appetite and is gaining a bit in weight and strength.

Meanwhile Papa is living alone in Budweis, though he will probably move to the Urbachs' in the new year when the Fränkels will move away from there. Because they are not allowed to move in with us, they will have to try to find a furnished place somewhere. Dorly is very cute now. She is starting to talk, chattering equally well in German and Czech.

In the factory, circumstances have improved to the extent that I'm staying for now, presumably to the end of the year. Vera bravely runs the household but at noon, we go to a lunch table because she is short of time. We eat very well there, and for a while, one forgets that there is war.

Now, my dear ones, accept all my best wishes for your further well-being and the assurance that our thoughts abide steadfastly with you.

I kiss and embrace you from the heart. Your Arnold.

My dear ones,

If I have been somewhat monosyllabic in my latest letters, my thoughts are nonetheless with you in all the old love and fondness. I am always so happy at the reports of your well-being and the successful progress of your work. I have moved into my new duty circle in quite good spirits, all the more so because my

old duty circle still continues in part. Best regards and kisses.
Your Vera.

LINE BY LINE, I HAVE PORED over this letter from Arnold and Vera, seeking to move beyond the words and to grasp all that they were trying to convey. I still have more questions than answers.

Only a month ago, the Fränkels had been planning to move in with Arnold and Vera. Why did they now have to look for a furnished place instead of using Papa's furniture? Why would they have been moving in the first place? Had the Nazis first turned the spotlight on the "less desirable" Eastern Jews, those from Poland, Russia, and Romania, and only later focussed attention on the more integrated Czech, German, and Austrian Jews?

Since first encountering Emil Fränkel's letters, I have done considerable research to learn more about this uncle by marriage. On impulse, I Googled his birthplace of Lemberg in Galicia, and found that Wikipedia lists Galicia as the largest province of Austria until 1918 and that its full official title was "Kingdom of Galicia and Lodomeria with the Duchies of Zator and Auschwitz." My body shuddered involuntarily as I saw the dreaded word *Auschwitz* that I only knew in its more sinister context.

Vera is still "bravely" running the house, but because she is short of time, they eat their noon meal at a *Mittagstisch—lunch table.*

I pictured the "lunch table" as a soup kitchen, the next step down for Jews who have been denied access to shops and food supplies. My research confirms that these soup kitchens set up by Jewish welfare agencies distributed not only meals but also clothing, coal, potatoes, medicine, and whatever they could to the growing number of destitute Jews.

I forced my thoughts back to Arnold's letter. *"We eat very well there,"* he says, *"and for a while, one forgets that there is war."* It is the first and only direct mention of the war in any of the letters.

For me, whenever I immerse myself in books or distractions to hide from the daily headlines, I think of the Jews of Europe who had nowhere to hide. How was it possible, even momentarily, to forget the war? For Arnold, the fact that he was still working must have provided consolation and hope.

It also leads me to believe that his factory produced goods essential to the German war effort.

Arnold's closing words draw my attention: *"Now, my dear ones, accept the assurance… that our thoughts abide steadfastly with you."* Increasingly, his language has a biblical ring, as if each letter to us might be his last.

Vera's greetings tell me that she too feared that the exchange of letters might end. She hints that she is still seeing some of her old circle of patients. I assume that these would all have been Jews. Aryans would not have dared to continue to visit a Jewish doctor, no matter how attached they had become to her in earlier years. Examples abound in the literature of Aryans dragged though the streets in disgrace for having patronized a Jewish place of business.

Still, I had trouble picturing the scenario. Too much coming and going in a private residence would have alerted the neighbours. Did Vera only do house calls at this time? Sometimes, this must have been in violation of the strict curfews. Did she dare to carry a bag containing supplies? How would she have obtained even the most basic of medications after they closed down her practice? Did people only call if they thought the illness was life threatening?

———

THE NEXT LETTER IS AN undated one from my Grandfather Josef. He says very little beyond expressing his love and his nostalgia for carefree days when he played with me.

> *My dear Edi, dear Gretl, and my dearest Helly-child,*
> *After a long silence, I want to send you a few lines again. I am in good health and doing well and your letters are always a joyful day for me. Dear Edi, we thank the dear Lord that you are doing so well. I think of you every day. Everyone asks about you and sends regards.*
> *How are you, dear Gretl, and our cute Helly? Where are the days when we played together in the park? Remember, Helly, you*

and Opi? I have a single wish left, to play one more time with
Helly. May the dear Lord grant our wishes.

Dear Mama and the sisters probably are writing everything to
you and keeping you up to date, so I close my letter today and hug
and kiss you all in spirit. Stay well and write soon again.

Your faithful Papa

Attached to my grandfather's handwritten words is a typed and factual
letter that is unmistakably from Emil Urbach. What puzzles me is that
Emil, who has never signed his letters and whose typing has always been
accurate, appears to be giving a false name.

We really liked the little picture of you and we look forward to the
next ones. We read your reports with great pleasure. All our friends
and relatives are doing well, thank God, and send you best regards.
We hope that in the coming year that you will have a really good
harvest as the crowning point of all your hard work.

To you, dear Gretl, we wish all the best for your coming birth-
day in January. May you remain in good health, and above all,
may you experience great joy from Helly.

Dear Mama is feeling better, thank God. She is darning socks
these days, and thinking of you a lot. She always wishes that she
could help you in your work. Our Otto is tutoring children in a
large town nearby. He is doing well and likes it there. Our Manci is
learning to become a seamstress. She leaves the house very early
and returns very late. Nevertheless, she feels lucky.

Anny's humorous way of writing always makes us smile. With
best regards to every one of you, we remain the family who loves
you

Auerbach

Following closely upon the typed words are a few lines in Martha's handwriting.

Perhaps you will still get some results. What a joy that would be for us all! Again, dear sister-in-law, all the best. We greet and kiss you all. Your Martha and Emil.

———

THE NEXT LETTER IS FROM my grandparents Fanny and Josef. Several things in the letter puzzle me. Why has my grandfather signed it as "Josef" rather than his usual "Papa"? Why didn't he move in with the Urbachs as projected in Arnold's letter of September 26? Most of all, if my grandparents are now living with Arnold and Vera, then what has happened to the Fränkels? Where and how are they living?

I was very pleased to receive your letter and the little photo. You all look great. As to my health, I feel stronger already. My heart suffered from weakness. We live at Arnold's where we use Vera's old waiting room. Because I cook separately for us, I am busy every morning. I spend the afternoons darning stockings for the Urbachs because dear Elsa is busy enough as it is. Thank goodness we are all well and busy. Dorly is a delightful child and Ilserl is a good student. Emil works at the office.

My thoughts have been with you constantly, and all the cousins send their regards. I often spend time with the in-laws and we go for walks together. Resl is much recovered.

Now, my dear ones, accept from all of us our best regards and kisses. Please write again soon. We very much look forward to your letters.

Your faithful mother Fanny.

P.S. I beg you to pardon my bad handwriting. That's what remains from the weakness.

And from me too, sincerest regards and kisses. Write to us again soon. Your Josef

———

ONCE A MONTH, DEPENDABLY, Arnold sends a letter. On November 28, 1940, he writes that despite Germany's need for technicians and engineers, his work at the factory has been terminated. He refers to his "old evil" and to his "defect," words that are clearly euphemisms for being a Jew.

> *My dear ones,*
>
> *Today your September letter arrived, so of course, there was great joy here. I'm sure you have some idea of what your letters mean for us at this time, especially when they bring us good news of your well-being and also calm us about Otto's welfare. I thank every one of you for your best regards and at the same time, I beg you to continue to write to us at least once a month.*
>
> *Here, everyone is in good health, and except for professional changes, everything is as it was. Dear Mama has now almost totally recovered. She is out of bed all day, is gaining weight, and is feeling generally stronger, so that one can virtually consider her healthy. The doctor, who really performed a miracle on her—he himself never doubted her recovery, but we all did and she herself had deep-seated fears—just comes once in a while now, leaving routine caretaking to Vera.*
>
> *As indicated earlier, for me there has been a major professional change. Recently, because of my old evil, I couldn't manage the difficult demands of my job and had to leave the company.*
>
> *Fortunately, I immediately found work again. I'm not working in my old capacity but rather as controller in a small metal manufacturing company in Smichov. The pay is modest but otherwise it's quite nice and I am totally satisfied. I do have to get up at 5:30 because it's the early shift. For lunch, there is just a cold snack, but it means that I'm home after 3 o'clock, in time for afternoon tea, which has not been the case for me in years.*
>
> *Vera goes to a lunch table and brings my lunch home, which we then share for supper.*
>
> *You see how well I hit it by choosing a technical profession— technicians are in great demand these days and are also well paid.*

If I didn't have this defect, I could easily earn 5-6000 Kronen and even more in Germany.

Now I want to close for today and I send to each of you my sincerest regards and kisses. I am always with you in my thoughts, and I remain

Your Old Arnold

Again and again, I pore over Arnold's words. His Jewish birth means that the job he had hoped to keep till the end of the year has been terminated. Still, his expertise as a metals engineer in wartime means that he is snapped up by another firm that is clearly working around the clock. Although it is painfully evident that he had no choice, Arnold minimizes the deprivations involved in his new position.

Meanwhile, Vera has given up all pretense of wanting to be a homemaker. She no longer hides behind a curtain of sociability as the draw to the lunch table. She brings home Arnold's lunch and they share it for their evening meal.

———

IN DECEMBER 1940, Fanny has recovered sufficiently to write a few lines to wish my mother well on her birthday, January 5. Fanny's few words are but the prelude to another desperate plea from my father's sister Martha. In her dreams Martha is talking to my father, longing for the day when fate will bring them together again:

My dear ones,
We were very pleased with your little picture. Dear sister-in-law, you look fabulous and your sweet little child is precious. Today I dreamt of you, my darling little brother, and in my dream, I told you all kinds of things. We'd have so many true tales to tell one another... if only we could!

Little Helly-child is probably your best source of distraction with all the work you have. Dear sister-in-law, your sister Anny is really a brilliant businesswoman; we admire her cleverness. Best and sincerest regards to her and to her husband from us all.

Ilserl is a big girl now. She has to study privately because there are no schools for our kind of people. She is being very reasonable about it.

Maybe fate will want us to see one another again after all. Please, dear little brother, contact Bella directly. If she has already filled out the form, then she could really do the good deed.

––––––––

THERE ARE NO MORE LETTERS until March 10, 1941. Like the other wartime letters, this one has handwritten numbers at the top. The mark of the censor. The letter is from Arnold who says very little this time. Still, I sense his loneliness for family.

My dear ones,
Lately there was an occasion for great joy as your letter of January 10 arrived. In the meantime, a letter from Otto has also arrived, so that we again feel reassured for a while. We live through your reports and in our imagination, we see every single one of you at work, including sweet little Helly who is watching whatever is happening.

In the meantime, little Dorly has gotten as big as Helly was when you left us. She is exceptionally dear and bright and babbles in both languages. Thank God, I can report that we are well, and that we have survived this whole time better than you probably imagine. I perform my work diligently and Vera is working hard too.

I send you our best wishes for your well-being, and remain with the sincerest of hugs and kisses, Your Arnold

Abruptly, the wartime letters end. *"Wait!"* I call out. *"Do not disappear! It is only March. Pearl Harbour will not happen until December 1941. Why have you stopped writing? Where are you? What is happening?"*

Imagining

*I*CANNOT YET REACH FOR THE HANDFUL of post-war letters. I procrastinate instead, allowing my imagination to float to an earlier time. In my
head, I create vivid scenes of the family. Mostly, I imagine them at the train
station, everyone waving goodbye to us.

"*Write often!*"

"*Don't forget to take photos!*"

"*Watch out for snakes and wild animals!*"

"*Eat as much as you can on the ship! You'll need strength.*"

*The sharp whistle of the train cut through the babble of last minute sugges-
tions. A sudden silence fell over the little group huddled on the platform. Tears
streaming down her cheeks, Gretl leaned once more out the window, waving
wordlessly. At her side, Edi stood woodenly, his arms wrapped tightly around
little Helly. Squirming with excitement, she alone seemed happy as the train
lurched, then slowly inched forward.*

*A final chorus of shouts and a single deep-voiced "farewell" floated forward
from the platform as the train gathered momentum. Not "goodbye" with its*

cheerful hope of early reunion, but "farewell" with the full weight of resignation to a final parting.

"Whose voice had it been?" Edi wondered as he set down the child and took her hand. Had it been his father, the family patriarch whom everyone called Papa Waldstein? Or had it been Gretl's father, Max Grünhut? Perhaps it was his brother Arnold, the eternal optimist experiencing a rare moment of doubt. More likely, the voice had belonged to one of the two Emils, the brothers-in-law who shared more than the coincidence of their first names.

Emil Urbach was the older man, and the vest of his dark three-piece suit seemed a trifle snug, as befitted the prosperous father of two teenagers. Edi imagined the four Urbachs walking arm in arm along the platform, then stopping by the exit to wait for "the old folks." The four grandparents would walk more slowly as would Emil and Martha Fränkel with their young family. Martha would be carrying the baby while Emil strolled hand in hand with Ilserl. She would be bombarding him with questions.

"Papa, will it be a very big ship? Bigger than the castle on the hill? Papa, is it true that Canada is full of bears? Won't Helly be scared?"

And finally, the most important question of all, the one he so desperately wished he could answer. "Papa, when will we see them again?"

As Emil lifted his eyes, he saw that the Urbachs had indeed stopped to wait at the exit.

"There's Uncle Emil and Tante Elsa. Wait with them while I help Mama. Her arms must be getting tired."

Iserl skipped ahead, and seconds later, she had been scooped up by her cousin Otto Urbach and placed on his shoulders. From her perch, she surveyed the train station. What a giant place it was! Higher than her head, a few pigeons roosted on metal girders, and higher still, beyond the sooty glass roof, grey clouds hovered. Her ears rang with the buzz of voices and the creaking of luggage carts and the hissing of trains waiting impatiently on their tracks.

Just then, she caught sight of her Omi and Opi. They were walking slowly. Opi had given his arm to Helly's grandmother, Oma Grünhut. Opa Grünhut seemed to be making a speech. His moustache twitched and his arms flayed the air as he spoke. How strange it was to see her grandparents dressed for travel. They were probably taking the late train to Budweis. Ilserl wanted to go with them, but her parents had already said "no" in that strange, tight voice that warned her not to ask again.

Not that it would be the same without Helly there. The grown-ups never seemed to have time for anything these days. Whenever the family got together, all they did was sit around talking politics. Often the talk sounded like an argument, and nobody seemed to be happy anymore.

Maybe this afternoon they could at least go to a park, and if Otto and Marianne came along, they might play hide and seek in the bushes. But lately, even Otto and Marianne seemed different. Just now, Otto had scooped her up onto his shoulders, but he hadn't even teased her about her curly braids looking like pigs' tails. Something was very wrong.

Of course, they were all sad that Helly and Uncle Edi and Tante Gretl were leaving, but surely, they would be back, even if it took a long time. Meanwhile, there would be letters from Canada. Ilserl could read quite well, and Mama had promised to look for a new school where Ilserl could also learn to write. Then she could send letters to Helly, and they would not forget each other, not ever, no matter how long it took until they could see each other again.

Otto reached up and set her down carefully. Ilserl pushed back her right braid just as Tante Elsa issued the expected invitation: "Let's all go back to our house. We can have coffee and Kuchen. The children can play in the garden while we talk. It will make us all feel less lonely if we are together."

"Great idea" echoed her Emil, smiling as he thought of the ramshackle villa at the edge of town that seemed always to be full of friends and family. How lucky they had been to live there since the hasty sale of their house in the Sudetenland. Remembering those tense days, Emil's smile faded. Despite the rumours, surely that was all behind them now!

Emil pictured the villa as they had first seen it. The windows had been grey with soot from a nearby factory, and the whole building had smelled dank. The kitchen speckled with mouse droppings had been particularly foul. A decaying broom propped open the pantry door, but the pile of debris had been left to rot in a corner.

Afraid to see disappointment written across Elsa's dear face, he had uttered the thought that was uppermost in his mind.

"Small wonder they were willing to let Jews live here. No one else would want it."

To his surprise, Else had reached out a gloved hand and smiled.

"Let's take it. It has many rooms, and we'll need the space if we are going to share with the Fränkels. Marianne and Otto could each have their own bedroom, and if we're lucky enough to find a maid willing to work for Jews, there will be room for her too."

"But it's so dirty, so unlike our beautiful house in…"

"Never mind," she interrupted. "I know how to work. My mother taught us well. Besides, I never expected to marry a rich man."

"I wasn't so rich at the beginning. Do you remember how long it took before I dared ask your father for your hand? I never thought he'd let you marry someone who was not yet established."

"But it was never a problem. I was so totally in love with you that all I could think of was being with you. Besides, Papa would never have denied me anything. Now with the boys, it was another story. Papa was so strict with them. I never thought it would work out, when Edi went back to Strobnitz to help run the store. I was sure his life would be over before he had a chance to live it, and now look at him! He has a wife and a daughter and soon he'll be in Canada."

Else's words took Emil back to that conversation in the cold kitchen just a few months ago. It had come as a shock to Emil when the Nazis had taken, or rather, had been handed the Sudetenland. As far as he could see, Czechs and Germans, Jews and Gentiles had always lived side by side, especially in small towns like Krumlau that had been home for so many years. How had it happened, that his fellow doctors had meekly gone about their business, uttering not a word of protest when Emil had been stripped of his right to practice medicine?

It had seemed sensible to move to Prague where he could at least hang out his shingle. But in only six months, everything had changed. Hitler was now in Prague and the same anti-Jewish regulations had come into effect. Thank goodness, they had taken the old villa, and Elsa had worked her magic to make it a home where family and friends felt welcome. When the Fränkels had arrived from Austria with a babe in arms, there had been room enough for them.

Most of the Jews who had been forced to move had settled near the train station. District 32 of Prague had become the temporary haven of refugees from Pilsen, Marienbad, Karlsbad, and from a host of Czech towns close to the German border. There they huddled within suitcase carrying distance of the trains that they hoped would carry them to safety.

Another voice intruded upon Emil's thoughts. It was his brother-in-law Emil Fränkel, with the baby asleep in his arms.

"We'll need at least two carriages, but it shouldn't be a problem at this time of day. Otto and Marianne can squeeze in with the two sets of grandparents. That will give us a bit of time alone to talk about a few things. I'm worried about Max and Resl. How will they manage now that both daughters have left? Resl still seems pretty frail and Max has no concept of reality. All he does is pray. He really believes that God will look after everything.

"At least he has his faith. That's more than we can say. We are being persecuted for an accident of birth that means very little to either of us."

———

THERE ARE OTHER SCENES AND conversations that live in my head. Else standing in the doorway of her home in Prague, graciously receiving visitors:

Gently, Else closes the door and reaches for the tray of Brötchen, the little open-faced sandwiches that she had placed on the sideboard. She proffers the tray to her guests as she moves smoothly about the room. Sometimes she stops to listen thoughtfully, her dark head cocked to one side.

She has been stockpiling happy memories and fills the silences with tidbits from better times. Her stories are fragrant flowers grown in her garden, redolent of a world that her guests long to inhale. She invites friends, she invites family, and she invites visitors passing through town. Every Sunday afternoon in Prague, people gather at her table for "Jause." For Kaffee und Kuchen. The coffee is rich and dark, and there are sugar cubes and slender silver tongs on a tray. The tray also holds a bowl of Schlag, the wonderfully sweet whipped cream popular far beyond the confines of Vienna. Else serves Hefenteig, its fresh yeasty smell still lingering faintly, or Apfelstrudel, its tender crust still warm from the oven, or Mürbteig, its buttery crust topped with fresh fruit or a chocolate glaze.

Der Tisch biegt sich. Delicacies abound. In the early days, there are no shortages. Elsa's home is a welcoming place, and the worse things get, the more often people seek comfort in her presence. They enjoy her baking, but mostly, they come to bask in her company. They drink of her good cheer. For brief moments, it is still possible to let food and companionship sweeten the circumstances.

———

EMIL FRÄNKEL OFTEN intrudes upon my thoughts. His frustration flows like lava over the obstacles in his way:

I must do something. But do what? They keep changing the rules. "Juden raus! Jews, get out!" But where can we go? No country will have us. How can we get out? It's crazy making.

At first, moving in with Martha's sister Else and her family seemed like a good idea. I've joked often enough that it was fated, or why else would my brother-in-law and I have the same first name?

Now my jokes about the two Emils are wearing thin. Besides, humour is not my brother-in-law's strong suit. He has always left the social niceties to Elsa. She is gracious to a fault, but ever since they stripped the Herr Doktor Urbach of the right to practice medicine, our Emil is not an easy man to live with.

True, the apartment is spacious, but it was not built to accommodate eight people. Four Urbachs and four Fränkels. Frictions are inevitable. I know I should count my blessings, but it's hard, especially when Martha seems so frail. All this uncertainty is too much for her, especially following so closely upon a risky pregnancy. She tries to hide her tears from Ilserl and from me, but she's a poor actress.

———

OFTEN, IT IS MARTHA herself who takes centre stage in my thoughts. As she picks up her pen and stares at the blank page, her inner monologue seldom varies:

How can I write when my emotions are so close to the surface? I must not start crying again. It upsets Ilserl to see me in tears. She's such a good little girl. Almost an adult at seven. What a shame that her childhood has been cut so short. But what else could we have done? There have been too many decisions to make, each one more disabling than the last. How can I not weep for all that is lost?

Home in Linz is the past, and I must learn to live in the present. Prague is home now, and yet I feel homeless. I long for the familiar. For the home that Emil and I furnished together. For the nursery that we had painted after Ilserl agreed to move to her first "grown-up" bed. For the hand-embroidered linens that were part of my trousseau. For the cheerful blue and white cups that I used to fill each morning with hot milk and sugar and fresh-brewed coffee. Small things that I miss as much as the friends who used to gather at our table. Will we ever go home again? Is all this lost forever?

Here I sit, writing at a table that is not ours, under a roof that is not ours, in a city that is not ours. Only for my brother Arnold and his wife Vera can Prague be called home. They are the magnet that drew us here, and they have been incredibly kind. They are always so positive, so optimistic about everything. Perhaps it is Arnold's training as an engineer that has given him this reliance on reason. I always fall into an emotional swamp. Vera too has this calm air of being able to cope with whatever life brings. When they are around, I actually believe for a while that my world has not come to an end.

Maybe it is simply easier for Arnold and Vera to be cheerful because they have not experienced flight. My sister Elsa and her husband Emil don't want to live here either, but they had had no choice either when Hitler crossed into the Sudetenland. Things were a little easier when Edi and Gretl and Helly were here. Helly was a godsend, especially when we found out that Ilserl would not be allowed to go to school with other children.

Would things be different if I had not gotten pregnant at the worst possible time? It was just before Hitler's tumultuous welcome to Austria that the doctor confirmed my pregnancy and advised against travel. I cannot bear to remember those months after the Anschluss. All along, Emil had been certain that Austria would invite Hitler to come and fatten the nation's coffers. Emil kept saying that the good citizens of Austria would no more worry about the fate of a few million Jews than had the Germans. Greed would win the day because people always support politicians who promise to make them rich.

It's hard to feel settled while Emil continues to fret. He sings only one refrain: Somewhere, anywhere. Somewhere far from Europe.

Emil and I have spent hours discussing the options. We don't have many. We worry, especially for the children. At least as the youngest of five siblings, I had the good fortune of growing up loved by everyone. Arnold stepped into the role of the wise older brother ready to advise me at every turn. Sister Elsa has been my little mother since childhood. Smooth, sweet-talking brother Otto taught me how to deflect the discipline Mama often promised but rarely delivered. And until now, dear, soft-hearted Edi has always been there to dry my tears. Will Ilserl and baby Dorly know what it is to grow up surrounded by a loving family?

Poor Dorly! Born at a time of such great turmoil in the world. While the Austrians cheered Hitler as the new saviour, while Hitler ranted about creating an economic miracle by ridding the country of its Jews, I was in labour, giving birth to one more Jewish child. No one cares that our family is not religious. Now they lump all Jews together.

What lies ahead for Dorly? And Ilserl? She was so happy during those months when everyone was in Prague. She and Helly grew as close as sisters. Now Helly has gone to Canada and Ilserl rarely smiles. Emil will not let up on the idea that we must go to Canada too. Perhaps if we can find someone to teach Ilserl English, Canada will not seem so far away.

After the War

Beginnings are always bitter, and there is much that you will find hard and even painful.

THESE WORDS, WRITTEN IN 1939 in Arnold's own hand, cast a long shadow. In 1945, the words are poignant, prescient, and painful beyond belief.

There is no easy bridge between his last letter dated March 10, 1941 and his first letter from Prague after Victory in Europe Day, May 8, 1945. This time, it was Arnold's turn to make a new beginning. I cannot imagine how bitter, how hard, or how unbearably painful that beginning must have been. Auschwitz, where Arnold spent the final years of the war, was liberated on January 27, 1945, but it is almost six months before he takes pen in hand.

FIRST LETTER

Prague, July 10, 1945

My Dear Ones,

Dearest Edmund and Gretl, my most beloved little Helen, dear Anny and Ludwig, I embrace you and kiss you all with heart and soul as one of the unfortunately few who have stood at the precipice of death and have suffered the torments of the Under- world and yet who, at God's decree, have returned alive to the old homeland.

Often when in my loneliness, I think back to the recent years with their gruesomeness that surpasses all human measure, indeed surpasses all human imaginings, when I think back to the hun- dredfold dangers and superhuman deprivations, the countless rav- aging diseases and the hundreds of other possibilities for death, when I think of the thousands of my fallen, or rather, my shame- fully slaughtered comrades, and the millions of my co-religionists who went to ground in equally obscene ways, when I hold before my eyes the gruesome images of need and desperation that I passed through, then it seems even to me to be unfathomable that a per- son can endure all this, can withstand all this, and I can do no other than to attribute it to God's will and to God's wonder, and not just a wonder, but a chain of wonders whose links reach into one another according to God's wish and will.

But then again, when I think of my aloneness, of my dear, so inexpressibly good Vera, without whom I do not wish to live and cannot live, when I think that with each passing day, the chances dwindle for her blessed return, then desperation seizes me and I wrestle with God and ask myself and Him why, of all the many millions, it is precisely me that He chose to rescue and for what purpose I may have been selected according to His will. What task is still incumbent upon me and still hangs over my head on this earth?

My dear ones, aside from the fact of my fortunate return from those believed-to-be-dead, you will experience little joy from me.

What I can and will report to you is anything but joyful. I myself am long and far from being the old Arnold. Such years and such experiences do not pass over a person without leaving their mark. I have become tender-hearted and sad in my demeanour and in my soul, and I have aged beyond my years. Perhaps here too, time will work its healing wonders. That remains to be seen.

There are hundreds and thousands of questions I'd like to ask you, each one of you: how you spent all the years since our last written connection, how you have fared, what joys and sorrows you have experienced, how your farm and your domestic life have developed and expanded, and thousands of other questions. You must answer all of them even if I do not ask them, and preferably in the form of a thorough description of all your accomplishments and impressions during this time. I will try to do the same, although I do not know whether I will succeed, or whether all that I have experienced and suffered can even be portrayed in words.

First, I want to give you as accurate as possible but unfortunately an excessively sad accounting of the state of our immediate and extended family. However, I must acknowledge that nothing is final. Due to the precarious conditions in Germany, one or another of the missing may yet return. Still, the likelihood is slim.

Our dear, good parents are no longer alive. Sadly, it was not granted to them to witness the victory of the forces of justice and the fall of Hitler and his Reich. It is a victory that from the beginning we all were convinced would happen.

Our dear, good mother died of the devastating diarrhoea that raged in Theresienstadt and led to total loss of weight and strength. She died an easy death, and at least she died like a human being in a sickbed in the presence of Papa, Vera, and myself on October 29, 1942. A short time before, she was still able to say goodbye to Elsa who stopped for a few hours in Theresienstadt while en route to the East.

Dear Mama Resl likewise succumbed in Theresienstadt in August 1942, so that she was spared all the tortures and adversities of the later period, and above all, the inhuman obscenity of the concentration camps of the East.

It was worse for our good father. He maintained his courage in the midst of all the wretchedness and deprivation in Theresienstadt. He was full of good spirits and confidence. He remained jovial despite all the hunger and filth in which we lived, and he served as a role model for others in these surrounding for seventeen long months.

However, when we were sent to Auschwitz-Birkenau in mid-December 1943, when he saw the raw animalistic way we were treated there, he crumbled spiritually. He could not bear to see it. He refused all food; he could not swallow the dry bread and he died within three weeks of our arrival, on January 12, 1944. A few days earlier, in tears, he had taken farewell of me and of life.

A very small number of Jews had the good fortune of being allowed to stay in Theresienstadt and thus were rescued. Numbered among these are Martha Fried with Viktor and her son and Uncle Semi who lived with them. More distantly, Vera's mother who overcame her illness (internal haemorrhaging) and got well again. Vera gave her own blood so that her mother slowly got better and is still alive today. Sadly, so far, none of her three children has come back.

Papa Grünhut is missing and presumed dead. For a long time (until 1944), he kept himself in Theresienstadt where he had a very nice, influential position as head of the household division of a large barrack. Unfortunately, he did not know how to use the job to our advantage, as was common practice. Then, like most others, he too had to set out on the thorny road to the East. It is not impossible that he will still report in. It is rumoured that there are still convalescents in the Crimea, but sadly, one cannot count on it.

Of the remaining family, the following died in Theresienstadt:
Uncle Sigmund Vogel and his wife.
Uncle Heinrich Vogel.

Uncle Gustav Waldstein succumbed to acute pneumonia within three days in Unterkralowitz where he had fled from Strobnitz.

The following dear relatives and family members had to go down the awful road to Poland, to the Concentration Camps that, internally among the Germans, were called Extermination Camps, whereas for the general public, they bore the name of Work Camps:

> *Elsa with her whole family in October 1942. No news since.*
> *Martha with Emil and the two little girls in August 1944. No news.*
> *My sister-in-law Edith and her husband, also in August 1944. Last news from Stettin in 1945.*
> *My brother-in-law Eduard in February 1943. No news since.*
> *Uncle Fritz and Aunt Hilde in the fall of 1943. No news.*
> *Vally Roth with her husband and sons in September 1943.*
> *Deda Glückauf in the summer of 1943 with her husband and sons.*
> *Marenka Pick and her incredibly cute daughter Vera on the same transport as Papa, Vera, and myself.*
> *Uncle Max Waldstein with his wife and their incredibly lovely seventeen-year-old daughter.*
> *Uncle Emanuel Eisler with Aunt Bertha.*
> *Aunt Theresa of Linz.*

All of the above were with me in both Theresienstadt and in the accursed extermination camp Oswieczin (Auschwitz) with its dreaded gas chambers and with its four crematoria steadily spewing thick smoke.

And yet, wonders do occur. After five years in the infamous Buchenwald, Alfred Pick, Marenka's husband is supposed to have sent news recently. Poor Erika, a blossomingly beautiful young woman of twenty-two years, Martha and Viktor's pride and joy, went with her young husband in front of my own eyes into the gas.

Does this fact alone not scream to the heavens? Do you believe that one can stay sane in the face of such things?

Lost and gone are more distant relatives:
   Cousin Hermann Vogel and his sister Lina.
   Hermann Bloch and Emmy.
   Aunt Bertha from Strobnitz along with Erich and Walter. It is possible that the latter will still report because he was still alive in Auschwitz. Unfortunately, the end was the worst time, those last days when the wild beast of National Socialism thrashed about in its death throes, exacting that hundreds of thousands of humans be sacrificed.

These are the dreadful statistics that I have counted up for you, my dear ones, knowing that you will hardly be reading them dry-eyed.
   And now, consider that I live, that I must live in this world that I have just portrayed, surrounded by the shades of all these dead relatives and by my memories of them and of the gruesome conditions in which I was last with them, so that all thoughts and memories of that time of my deepest abasement and human degradation rise up again before me and I have nothing that I can put up in defence except for my work and one person.
   That one person, a golden person, my comfort and my joy is our brother Otto who as always is there when my need is greatest, who consoles and helps and lightens and beautifies my life as best he can. Of course, I came back sick and poor as a beggar, dependent upon the good will of people and of the Red Cross. Along came Otto at the right moment, my knight in shining armour. The reunion was so gripping and so unexpected for me that for a long time, I could not restrain my tears.

I embrace you and kiss you with all my heart
Arnold

———

SECOND LETTER

Prague, July 11, 1945

My Dear Ones,

I want to number my letters and send you another of these reports in a few days. To be on the safe side I will make a copy so that I can send it to you right away if one of the letters gets lost.

Of course, the sad list of our deceased relatives can make no claim to completeness, especially since the fate of more distant relatives remains unknown to me. In addition to this list, there is another equally sad and gruesome one, that of our good friends and acquaintances.

Many a dear person is included whose name will never again be spoken, many a dear person who will no longer exist. It would be senseless, and indeed, it would not even be possible to count them all up for you, and so I only want to name the few that you also knew.

Included among them is my dear friend and teammate Bruno Skutetzki. Along with his exquisitely beautiful young wife, he had to die so tragically in Oswieczin. He lasted for three weeks in that hell, she for only a single week. Her mother, a woman who is still stately at age fifty, is beyond herself at this loss. She stands alone and bereft in this world. I visit her every week and we usually cry together for an hour or so.

The next in line is Schiff who was your former colleague at the bank, dear Edi. His wife found her way back here after an adventurous flight. Two years ago, she was still a radiant woman. Today, she is an old hag.

And now, my dear ones, I will try to describe for you in as much detail as possible the events as they unfolded, starting with those that pertain to the family.

As you may perhaps know, after your departure Elsa and her family were not allowed to stay much longer in the apartment in Tebesin with which you were familiar, so they moved to the Kronenstrasse in Weinberge.

A little while later, our dear Mama had to come to Prague because of her ailing heart. She spent several weeks in the hospital until she was released into homecare. Under Elsa's provident ministrations and self-sacrificing attentiveness, the state of Mama's health was almost back to normal when suddenly there was a powerful relapse. Mama became completely apathetic and said farewell to us.

But my dear, good Vera would not let go. With her own medical instinct, she was the only one who did not consider Mama's life as lost. She did everything humanly possible and more. Together with a young cardiologist who really knew how to reach into Mama's soul, they slowly and almost imperceptibly brought her back up until she regained her health completely.

Interestingly enough, this so sensitive and over-strained heart survived in Theresienstadt. Doctors there shook their heads at so much will to live.

After a few months, Emil Urbach hinted that dear Mama's visit was lasting a bit too long. His words were excusable given that the Fränkels were also living in the none too spacious quarters.

Since dear Vera had meanwhile been forbidden to practice medicine, Vera and I invited Papa to leave Budweis and, with Mama, to move in with us. We fixed up Vera's former waiting room as a living room. Mama cooked and did the housework. Touch wood, it was just like in the old days.

Our dear parents spent more than a year in our circle, surrounded by what then was such a large and extended family. I think it was the nicest year of their life. Certainly it was the quietest year of their normally so hardworking and productive existence.

There was a constant coming and going of visitors, so that on Saturday afternoons, there were often not enough chairs. Uncle Fritz and Hilde, Uncle Heinrich with his wife, Walter Waldstein with his young bride, the Urbachs and the Fränkels, my in-laws, Edith and Viktor, and of course Papa Grünhut were almost daily visitors in this family circle.

Papa, Uncle Fritz, and I were the unshakable trio of optimists who never gave in. Again and again, we knew of new facts and indicators that would guarantee, or at least point to Hitler's demise. The greatest of German victories and the worst battering of our own freedoms could not disabuse us of this conviction.

I also made every effort to keep up our guests' spirits, and I pushed the good humour act to its limits. At that time, I played all kinds of instruments. Above all, I was best at the accordion. I had a wonderful instrument, a piano accordion with a keyboard, 90 bass buttons, and three octaves.

I went about studying it in a completely scholarly manner. I had someone from the conservatory as a teacher, and by dint of extraordinary hours of practice, I was making nice progress. After three to four years, I had the dexterity and could read notes well enough to play operas. This music gave me immense pleasure. It was my only source of distraction, the only one still permitted to a Jew.

But soon, that too was forbidden. I switched to the guitar, then to the Hawaiian pipe, the mandolin and finally, when all musical instruments had to be turned in, to a mouth organ.

Lacking the opportunity to do other things in those days, I discovered a talent for singing and whistling to accompany the guitar. I had a whole booklet of cheerful German and Czech songs and poems, and I entertained our many guests for hours with my productions.

To my great regret, my beautiful accordion went missing during the events of the May revolution here in Prague. Although I had forfeited so much, this particular loss pained me the most because I still cannot get a replacement for it today.

And so, we lived peacefully alongside our dear parents, until the call was issued to us to report for the transport to Theresienstadt. Our dear parents' number came up in July 1942, Vera's and mine a month later.

Now I have to reach back and chronologically describe the unfolding of events.

Contrary to expectations, nothing changed in our situation after the entry of the Germans. It remained thus for over a year. We had already begun lulling ourselves with the sweet thought that everything would remain the way it was, that we as non-German Jews would remain unshorn, when the vexations began.

The Germans followed the principle of not doing anything to us themselves. Instead, they first trained the Czechs in anti-Semitism, and in this, they succeeded very well.

For our first horrendous surprise, they picked Yom Kippur, the holiest of days, to make us turn in all radios and report the sum total of our financial worth.

Blow upon blow followed, usually at two-week intervals. Always something new, something else that was forbidden, some unexpected limitation that made our life difficult, until bit by bit, life became impossible.

Restaurants and coffee houses were forbidden, then theatres and libraries, then all parks and public grounds, even public baths and swimming anywhere.

Shopping time was limited to a few hours in the morning and in the afternoon, later to only a single hour in the afternoon when there was nothing left in the shops.

Bit by bit, we were forbidden to buy almost any groceries. First, we could not buy sugar and candies, then meat and fish, then even jam and any dried fruits like prunes or raisins, then even vegetables, milk, cheese, etc. Finally, there was nothing left except bread, flour, and potatoes.

It was forbidden for us to take a streetcar except to and from work, and even that, only standing up in the last car. Bit by bit, we were banned from all streets and city squares in the downtown area.

Later, entire areas of the city were forbidden to us. Finally, we were not allowed even to be on the street on Saturday afternoon, so we were simply under house arrest every weekend.

The worst though was the Jewish star; a mighty yellow splotch above the heart where in satirized Hebraic script stood the German word "JEW." This was the worst discrimination, for with this single move, they delivered us up to the mob at the command of the lowest of human urges.

And yet, that still wasn't the worst. Something much worse came next. Overnight, in entire sections of the city, they threw the Jews out of their homes and penned them up in ways unworthy of human beings.

Four to seven families in a single apartment. Because we lived on a main street, we alone had the unheard of luck to be spared this terrible evil.

My absolutely incomplete total has not yet included the full number of torments. Next came the endless list of bureaucratic vexations, the countless and limitless regulations concerning possessions and property of Jews and the enumeration, registration, delivery, and distribution of said possessions.

No two weeks went by without such an ordinance appearing, and these two weeks were usually filled with obtaining and filling out forms, packing and delivering the itemized objects, so that I coined the witticism "Being a Jew is a profession."

A thousand hugs and kisses from your Arnold

THIRD LETTER

July 12, 1945

My Dear Ones,

I hope that you have received both of my letters and I want to continue my description as best possible.

They used the whole powerful force of bureaucracy and red tape to strip the Jews of all their possessions, both portable and fixed. First they stripped the very rich, the ones who had houses, factories, businesses, etc. Then, with every conceivable form of spitefulness, it was our turn.

My company was not even allowed to pay me my salary directly. The money had to be processed through the bank where we were only allowed to be on the premises one predetermined hour of the week.

Then came the surrender of hundreds of items that normally, one would not even think of as possessions. In uninterrupted sequence, usually in two-week intervals, this laborious bureaucratic machinery would be set in motion. It hit us Jews all the harder because the various offices were only rarely open to us, and they created problems for us at every step of the way. It began with radios, then paintings, carpets, works of art. Next were musical instruments, trunks or suitcases, any tools or technical instruments, cars or motorized conveyances, all ski equipment, all gold and silverware. Then we had to turn in leather goods and furs, and later, even wool clothing and underwear if you had more than two sets. They did not even stop with the poor animals. All dogs and canaries had to be taken to the collection depot.

Now you must not think that we constantly had our pants full or that we promptly and correctly complied with all the regulations. On the contrary, we sabotaged whatever we possibly could, knowing that all was lost for us anyway.

On principle, we delivered up only very few and mostly useless things and we chose to give things away rather than throw them into the jaws of the Germans. We risked our necks repeatedly in those years, knowing that the Gestapo would not waste time on the fine print if one of us were caught.

However, thank God, everything always turned out well, even if we constantly had our head in the noose and we stood with one foot in crime and the other in the grave. Thus, for example, I worked in the factory for a whole year without wearing the yellow star. As I approached the factory, I would cover the star with my briefcase, and then, in the factory I would cover it with a lab coat without a star. Meanwhile, Vera practiced medicine illegally for over two years in her back room while her surgery stood empty.

You can well imagine how dangerous this was, and how many precautions we had to take, since all contact with Aryans was strictly forbidden. We even refused to give up our Sunday outings and our outdoor bathing, even if we did have to find a hidden spot. Nice game, playing hide-and-seek with the Gestapo and the police!

With food too, we in no way followed the regulations. I kept my job at Parik's until almost the end of 1940. Then I had to leave the firm, but I found another job almost immediately, albeit no longer in a managerial capacity.

I began to work as production controller in a factory that made precision tools, mainly small precision parts for military aircraft. My job was to supervise the precision of semi-finished and completed products. It was mostly a matter of a thousandth of a millimetre or less, so the responsibility was great. This was doubly true because military agents came to the factory to take possession of the finished product. Still, although the salary was rather low, the work itself was pleasant, easy, and not strenuous.

I worked here for over two years until the anti-Jewish campaign drove me out of this job as well. I had already become a source of admiration as one of the very few Jews who were still working.

And still, I found another job almost immediately. This one was in a factory in Straschnitz that made gas masks and precision instruments. I was only granted three weeks at the job, for just when we were the busiest, my name came up for the transport to Terezin.

Of course, even in the matter of the transport, we did not stand by idly and wait to be led to the slaughter. Instead, we used every conceivable means and subterfuge to put off the date of our entry. Next, despite warnings of extreme penalties, we did not report for registration, and when they forced us to do so, with Emil's help, we simply disappeared. Emil had a job in Jewish Community Services and he was able to remove our cards from the file from which the transport lists were compiled.

But in the end, we packed up kit and caboodle and awaited our deportation. For us, it was the beginning of a new world and a new life. Of course, one could only take a limited amount of baggage— I think it was 40 kg. We were supposed to leave everything else in the apartment, and this was to remain unlocked. Of course, this was another regulation that we did not obey. We each took with us about 70 kg, and we gave things away. The carpets and some of Vera's instruments, which of course should have been delivered up long ago, went to good friends for safekeeping. We gave many other things to the cleaning woman, to the caretaker of the building, etc. In the apartment itself, we only left a few things just for show.

The assembly place for the transports was a part of the fairgrounds where radios and furniture were usually displayed. The surroundings were grim, a real entry to and a foretaste of what awaited us later and actually never again left us in all the years ahead: filth, vermin, slops to eat, straw to lie upon, latrines, no opportunity to wash, and raw, bestial treatment.

I was quite able to bear all this. I had gotten used to it during World War I, and I took everything with a grain of salt. I had two bottles of cognac and some chocolate with me, and I just let things be. However, with her exaggerated love of cleanliness, my poor dear Vera absolutely could not adjust to this pigpen, and the latrine especially inflicted such violence on her that she suffered from total constipation for more than a week.

From the very first moments, Vera practiced medicine and devoted herself to every single person as if they had been private patients. In no time, she had become not only the best-known doctor but also the most beloved person in the entire transport.

And this quite extraordinary belovedness, yes, this almost deification remained her very own trademark in the years that followed. Because of her ultra-good heart and the repeated success of her medical skills, people really honoured and adored her. They showered her with gifts, as they did no one else. Vera, however, was unpretentious and modest. She simply believed that it was her duty to help every single person to the utmost of her ability.

After about a week, two thousand of us were shipped under Schutzpolizei surveillance to Terezin. At the railway station in Bauschowitz, which is about 3 km from Terezin, the S.S. received us and immediately ordered all suitcases to be left behind. We never saw them again. We took with us whatever we could manage, but it was a hot July day, and the enforced march with much too heavy gear quickly turned into a torture.

During our entry into Terezin, the streets had to be emptied of all inhabitants. Doors and windows had to be closed, so that nobody could have any contact with us until we had been "appropriately prepared."

They locked us into the old subterranean casemates from which we were only allowed to emerge after a thorough inspection of our bodies and our baggage, an inspection that stripped us of our most valuable belongings.

Even here, we cheated if we could. Dressed in the habit of a nun, Cousin Erika appeared before us and took some things for safekeeping. Thus, we were able at least to save watches, medication, and the like.

Then we were assigned lodgings. Vera was assigned to a house and I was sent to the barracks. Neither one really coincided with the meaning of the word, nor with any possibly associated terminology. Both house and barracks only looked like their namesakes from the outside. On the inside, they had been altered for mass settlement in accordance with German ingenuity and conceptualization.

Every house block had only a single entrance, usually in a back alley or a side street. All other doors and gates were locked off and nailed shut. In the courtyard, they had torn down the walls separating the individual buildings, sheds, stables, etc. Thus, from a single block of houses, they created a residential block that was numbered the way the streets are numbered. Every room inside a house from the cellar to the attic was inhabited by as many people as there was room for by laying them on the floor. Not until much *later did it occur to people to fetch straw, then bags of straw, and finally, boards. Not until two years later did the first primitive plank beds appear as substitutes for real beds.*

As many as ten to twenty people of the same sex slept, lived, and managed in a single room. Usually these were old people. The young lived in barracks where the dark, musty old rooms were filled to the last nook and cranny with bunk beds—wooden tiers filled right up. As could be expected, things went on there just like in an (undisciplined) Jewish school. The concept of a private life lost all meaning in this massive overcrowding of people. One was always surrounded by hundreds of smelly Jews, and the longing for a bit of peace and solitude was often strong.

I could write a whole book about Theresienstadt, and it certainly would not be boring. However, I will leave that to more professional pens.

What was realized in Theresienstadt was a matter of a bold and grandiose project unlike any other. It was a mass colonization of unusual dimensions, a communistic community unlike any that had ever been attempted in central Europe. Sixty thousand people who obeyed a single authority in all their activities and functions, all nourished, as it were, from one and the same kettle, a gigantic machine with but a single direction and a single will.

Everything swelled to the gigantic in this mass conscription. Included were not only the 60,000 inhabitants then living in this city, but also the hundreds of thousands of Jews from all over Europe who passed through.

The cooking was done in a dozen kitchens in the big barracks, usually for three to six thousand people at a time. The distribution of food, which took place on the basis of ration cards, lasted several hours. A single centralized warehouse stored all the food supplies, utensils, equipment, etc. An economic advisory council decided the daily menu based on the supplies in stock. Clearly, even the smallest seasonings like pepper or marjoram amounted to kilos.

The repair workshops for clothing and shoes were major enterprises with six hundred workers and thirty office clerks.

The central bakery baked 12,000 loaves of bread a day, and the most modern crematorium in Europe in which one corpse burned the other with its impressive achievement of one hundred corpses a day was by far unable to meet the daily demand, for the number of the dead each day ran from one hundred and forty to one hundred and seventy. Everything on a large scale, as you can see.

In other ways too, the city was interesting. Even the traffic in the street was more like that of a major metropolis. At certain times of the day, there were so many people together in a small space that no city in the world can point to such a multitude of traffic. The issue was particularly interesting from a technical perspective and in terms of political economy. Here, right from the very beginning and all the way through to the development of the city as a showpiece and display case to the world, everything was created by Jews. By Jewish brains and by Jewish hands.

In addition, we experienced our miracles here. Often we could not believe our eyes. What wonders were created here by the Jewish artisan, by the Jewish engineer, by the Jewish genius! Here, beyond measure, we demonstrated the nonsense of the inferiority of the Jewish race.

It was not just the Jewish bricklayer, the Jewish carpenter, the Jewish locksmith and the Jewish painter who wrought their miracles of art and craftsmanship here. It was also the Jewish chimneysweep, the Jewish drainpipe cleaner, the Jewish well digger, the porter, the railroad worker, the wagon driver. The most menial farmhand and the former estate owner did their duty, and together, they accomplished results that could not have been better.

And beyond this, Jewish manufacturing arose on an industrial scale. Even though the work had to be done without pay, dozens of workstations were created where work took place not just for the Jewish community but also for the Germans, and especially for delivery to the German troops. We excelled in every conceivable branch of production, including paper, cardboard, leather, mica, iron, metal-ware, toys, ink, products made of fur and much else that was in no way inferior to products made in comparable factories in the hinterland.

Many famous artists, especially painters and illustrators were at work in large studios. They produced hundreds of pictures that were then sold privately for millions by the gentlemen of the S.S. One of the best-known artists was a distant cousin of ours with the name Waldstein whom I got to know there. The ceramic workshops also created unique and valuable pieces of art that, like everything else, illustrated the absurdity of the shibboleth of the inferiority of the Jewish artist.

Technology also wrought its wonders that are worthy of standing next to the aforementioned. You must not lose sight of the fact that, overnight, a city of 7000 inhabitants was transformed into one of 60,000. The need for water, electricity and the like suddenly increased tenfold, and help needed to be immediately at hand. A new waterworks, an expanded electrical station, a dozen new artesian wells, a huge cemetery, later on, the aforementioned modern crematorium, garbage disposal areas, a mighty industrial plant with 4500 workers, a large agricultural enterprise, large scale pig farming, gigantic sized manure heaps and thousands of window beds, all these and more sprang forth in the shortest possible time.

From Bauschowitz to Theresienstadt, we quickly built a new stretch of railway. There is nothing to indicate the fact that from the first stroke of a pencil to the last cut of a spade, the railway was built by Jewish brains and Jewish hands. The tracks lead right to the streets in the middle of town.

One fine day in the middle of the Ringplatz at the town centre, a gigantic modern installation for shipping goods to the troops was erected. Soldiers set up huge tents and disappeared again. Within a few days, Jewish engineers in these tents created a major manufacturing complex that reflected the most splendid modern technical

AFTER THE WAR [213]

achievements. It even had an assembly line that employed a thousand workers.

Various parts were delivered from German factories, assembled here, and then packed into crates under very precise directives. Because of their manual dexterity and because they worked so very hard, women particularly shone at these tasks. People could not believe their eyes when they saw these soft, formerly so well-tended, manicured, delicate hands tackle this difficult, dirty, greasy work, or when they saw frail women drag the heavy cases. A million cases were supposed to be shipped out within three weeks, and this target was met. Overnight, the tents disappeared again and the Ringplatz reappeared.

Our Cousin Martha Fried emerged as a model worker in this enterprise, with a real flair for industrial manufacturing, a talent to which she later remained true. Of course, all who were connected with this enterprise had received certain advantages, especially in regards to food.

I could spend hours more telling you interesting things about Theresienstadt. For such descriptions, however, there is neither enough room nor enough time. I would rather go back to events that I have personally experienced.

Like every beginning, it was hard at first. Whereas the women were still left more or less in peace, or forced only to do cleaning and the like, we men had to do hard labour right from the start, usually with pick and shovel. It was especially hard for those of us who were not used to it. Such days absolutely refused to end, and the hours crept by at a snail's pace. At the same time, Hunger gnawed at our guts and grew ever stronger until it was an unending pain. Because they were ludicrously spare for someone doing hard labour, even the meals did nothing to soothe the pangs.

We (I walked hand in glove with my brother-in-law Eduard in those days) deliberated long and hard about which measures to take. Simply folding our hands in our laps and waiting for events to unfold was not in our nature. Something had to be done, and somehow, we had to get out of this precarious predicament. For lack of other options, we therefore reported for railroad building duty where the work was equally onerous, but was rewarded with double the share of lunch.

Our ploy did not succeed because there were no available spots, but at least in the process, I attracted the attention of the head of the Labour Office who asked me to work with him. This was an unheard of stroke of luck, and an advance in rank such as had never before occurred, this move to a respected office position after only a week of hard labour.

I then became division leader, the commandant of a work crew consisting of fifty men. My main responsibility was to select people for individual jobs for which we received daily written orders from the central Bureau of Labour that controlled over 30,000 workers. You can best picture the latter as a ministry that reported directly to the S.S.

My responsibilities were far from onerous. Aside from the dispatch of workers morning and afternoon, I only had a few entries to make and various lists to keep up to date. The rest of the time, I could idle away.

Aside from this influential role within the barrack, there was another great advantage connected to the position. I had a permanent overtime pass because I had to be available in case of necessity to work at any hour. Since the night hours were figured into my working time, this gave me the highest claim to premium bread. That was a huge benefit because this premium amounted to as much as an entire normal ration of bread. In other words, I got a double portion of bread.

Then, after a while, when I advanced to division leader for a hundred men, another very valuable advantage was added. I was officially authorized and registered with the S.S. and was thereby sheltered from being on the transport list.

Despite all these advantages, I gave up the job. When the opportunity presented itself, I threw myself into the social domain

*within the same Labour Office, because the job as division leader
had also had its huge drawbacks. There were jobs that were posi-
tively a pleasure and where people even got presents or food. There
were easy jobs, hard jobs, and extremely hard jobs. There were jobs
that were absolutely awful, like standing in water all day, and
there were some jobs that were life threatening. The latter was
especially the case in the so-called Small Fortress. Located about
two km from the ghetto, this old fortification dated back to the
time of St. Theresa. It had been converted into a small but all the
more gruesome concentration camp where five thousand men had
been quartered.*

*Our people worked in the garden there under the surveillance of
S.S. gardeners who were known for the sadistic way they treated
our poor boys. Countless blows, sometimes with wooden lathes or
iron bars meant that almost daily, some boys came home with
blood streaming from their wounds. Others were shipped back to
the ghetto, forever crippled.*

*On the second day after my arrival. I myself had one of my
worst experiences in the Small Fortress. The S.S. supervisor put me
to work pumping excrement. Under his shouts and threats, I had
to work the pump for one and a half hours, smoothly and without
interruption. Of course my strength often failed me, and I believed
my last hour to be nigh. However, the human body can endure the
unbelievable when the end seems near.*

*It was to such tasks and to similarly unpleasant ones that I was
supposed to, and indeed had to order my poor guiltless colleagues.
Often I had to send them out at night and in rain and storm, and I
just could not bring myself to do these things. Thus, I used the first
chance I got to do something else. When my boss was entrusted
with establishing a new Office of Labour in a newly opened barrack, he asked me to become his assistant. Since he gave me free
choice of my field of endeavour within the operation, I chose the
area of social welfare and became the operations controller. This
meant that I was responsible for supplying the workers with every*

conceivable remedy, relief, and bonus, even the ordering of clothing and shoes, and above all, improvements in food.

I had to fight for all these things in the different offices and do battle for them, sometimes even with the Germans. But I got good results, and the workers everywhere were granted their first and best advantages. We managed, for example, to get an allowance for double lunch rations for those doing hard labour, and for the others to get all the leftovers from the kitchens after the allotted rations had been distributed.

It goes without saying that in this distribution of food, I did not go hungry. Nor did Vera who was my daily guest for supper. In this respect, we had all we needed.

After a few nice months, this came to an end. Still, the dear Lord did not abandon us. As always, He helped us, sometimes on the very day that we thought it was the end, the very day that the ghosts of Danger or of Hunger stood directly before us. Once, a friend whose father was at the Office of Domestic Affairs got me a second ration card. Later, Vera and I managed to share a room with a colleague in what used to be a small vestibule of a non-commissioned officer's place. The three of us had furnished it very nicely and we lived together. This colleague was friends with everyone in the kitchen. He was able to come and go every day with so much food that all of us, finally including his mother and Vera had enough to eat. We lived idyllically in that little room where there was scarcely space for two beds, a table, and a few other pieces of furniture, which I made with my own two hands out of boards that I personally had stolen.

In time, thanks to my inventiveness and my experience of carpentry as a hobby, there were all kinds of forbidden and therefore secret and hidden luxury items like an electric stove, an electric iron, a reading light by the bed, moveable room dividers, etc. In time, we got quite used to this dog's life despite its often-unbearable discomforts.

Among these discomforts were the vermin with which we

conducted a constant battle. We young ones were able to rid ourselves readily of lice, but we had to battle uninterruptedly against
the millions of fleas and bugs that otherwise multiplied so rapidly
that it was impossible even to think of sleep. During this time, I so
thoroughly learned the idiosyncrasies of these dear little creatures—
their habits, their breeding cycles, their loves, and their customs—
that I could have made my debut as a specialist in the flea and
bug business, and I could have predicted the behaviour of every single beastie.

But here, as always, the human spirit, the capacity for thought,
the ability to keep the benefits of experience in one's brain prevailed. At least in the short run, we mastered these infestations,
even if sometimes with difficulty and at the cost of gassing entire
barracks or house blocks. Vermin preoccupied us incessantly.

Laundry, for example, was a serious problem. Some gifted
experts kept the small facility that had once served as a military
laundry operational without a break, day and night, raising its
capacity to an unbelievable 1000 kg a day. Still, what was that
compared to the needs of a town of 60,000 people?

This meant no more than 2 kg per three-month period for the
ghetto inmates, which is not even one change of underwear a month,
and it includes no bedding, etc. It was impossible to do laundry at
home. We barely had enough soap for washing our bodies.

Now I will close this report. In the meanwhile, it is already July
18 and Otto and I are going on holidays. Even though I have only
been working for six weeks, I have two weeks off and Otto has been
demobilized. We are going to Trebitsch to see Martha, the only one
of our relatives to have been saved. Otto wants to go from there to
Strobnitz, Vienna, and to Linz to check into what can be learned
everywhere.

Assuming that the experiences I have delineated and the descriptions will really be of interest to you, I will continue my reports
when we get back. For today, my dear ones, sincerest regards, hugs
and kisses from your faithful old Arnold.

———

FOURTH LETTER

Prague, August 5, 1945
New Address—XII, Manesova 32

My dear ones,

Now we are safely back from our holidays and I want to continue my description. It was very nice in Trebitsch. Martha looked after us in a touching way, as if she needed to replace both our mother and our sisters. She cooked the very finest foods, all the things that we had dreamt about and talked about while we ate the wretched watery soup as Hunger rolled about in our intestines. Here once again were schnitzel, apricot dumplings, white coffee with cake, and all the things that by unanimous consent used to occupy the place of honour in our incessant talks about food.

In other ways too, our dear relatives ensured that we felt completely at home and that we found a replacement under their roof for the homeland and for the parental home that we had lost.

We also enjoyed the pleasures of life in the country. We took long walks, we went swimming, and we wandered in the woods. I regained the feeling and the consciousness of being a free human being and not one of the debased, the hated, the ones who had been cast out. It did me good to see that my very presence could bring pleasure to my relatives.

Unfortunately, the few days passed all too quickly and I had to go back to work in Prague. Perhaps I have not yet told you that hardly a week after my arrival in Prague, I went back to work at Parik's, my old firm. I did this even though I was still a convalescent and I could have used the time to accomplish a thousand errands that remain, including going to all the different offices to cut through the red tape needed to get lodgings. However, I went on the assumption that work would be the best remedy for my pain and for my solitude, and I was not mistaken. I have a good job, and every day, I have a mountain of work that I very much enjoy.

At least filling that position in the factory gives me the feeling that my presence has some purpose.

Otto wanted to go to Vienna but only got as far as Bratislava when he had to turn around again. There is still no connection to Vienna and above all, there are no bridges over the Danube. Monday he wants to go to Strobnitz with Walter Waldstein's widow whom we accidentally met on the street the other day. So poor Walter is also dead, even though when we were together in Auschwitz, he was still a strong young man.

Now we have an apartment again. Our old one is occupied, so I had to tread the thorny path of acquiring a new one, a path that required endless patience and was entangled with hundreds of disappointments and countless difficulties. I had begun to despair, but Otto was a trusty companion at my right hand. He ran countless errands for me with military precision, tasks for which of course his British military uniform came in very handy.

The new apartment is not nearly as nice as our old one. It only has three rooms, and the furniture is modest and old, but it is quite well located and my requirements these days are not very great. The apartment (the furniture, the dishes, etc.) are gratis, of course, a replacement for our old things, which the Germans stole from us.

I live in the new apartment with Vera's mother who at age 71 is still active and energetic. She will run the household without even a maid, since this kind of work no longer exists here since the overthrow. Otto wants to stay with us for two or three weeks and then he will travel on to Paris.

My dear ones, in the last few days we have received three parcels from you, for which I must express my sincerest thanks. The first one contained mostly chocolate and sweets, the second and third ones that had Anny as sender contained cheese and honey, sugar, flour, and little tins of meat and cocoa. As you can well imagine, for me all these things are treats that I have not known for a long time, and they represent a very welcome addition to the still rather limited foods that are available here. So again, please accept my sincerest thanks for these gifts and be assured that I will never forget this loving deed.

Nor can I fail to appreciate the spiritual impulse, the consoling awareness that even if I am separated from you by an ocean, still, I have in you next of kin who are concerned for me and who care for me because I am family.

Now I want to continue my description of Theresienstadt. As time passed, we got fairly used to this degrading dog's life. With the deadening of the senses and the habituation that occurred, we did not even perceive the unpleasant circumstances as being so terrible. Later, from the perspective of Auschwitz, we looked back on Theresienstadt as paradise. In time, the conditions also improved a bit.

Above all, there was no shortage of distractions of every kind. There were numerous lectures by renowned professors, courses, concerts by first-class virtuosos, several improvised cabaret groups, even a top-notch theatre and an opera ensemble of a quality unsurpassed on any big-city stage. Even if it was with stomach growling with hunger, with underwear stiffened by dirt, and seated next to a neighbour crawling with lice, we could sit in a theatre, concert, or open-air cabaret just as we did in the best of times at home.

There was also a valuable library that enabled us to enrich our knowledge. There were even holidays of a sort, since those of us in the Bureau of Labour assigned people who had been doing hard labour for over a year to light agricultural work. Later, I advanced to a higher and more respected position as Master for Care and Control in the central Division of Labour. I had a large, bright office in the Magdeburger barrack that housed all the bureaucratic offices, a secretary, an assistant, and lots of business traffic the whole day through. I visited all the industrial enterprises and workshops, received all the requests of supervisors and workers, and played the role of the generous uncle from America who fulfills the wishes of his 5400 children to the best of his ability.

Vera was with me every day. We saw each other whenever we

had the chance, sometimes several times a day. Whenever we had something to say to each other, we just approached and talked because keeping to the exact number of hours of work was not an issue, especially at the higher ranks.

We spent very nice evenings in our own inner circle, usually with my roommate Fischer and his mother. She used to make our food more palatable with small ingredients, and sometimes she made holiday meals for us with food acquired by stealing or by spending a sinful amount of money. The black market flourished in Theresienstadt. There were people who smoked their ten to twenty cigarettes a day even though smoking was strictly forbidden. A cigarette usually cost 35 Kr and in bad times as much as 100 Kr. Although there were severe penalties for the possession of money, nevertheless, almost everyone took a chance. The often unexpected searches by our own female S.S. columns or by the gentlemen of the S.S. themselves were nightmares that haunted our being as well as our dreams.

Morality did not exist in Theresienstadt. Flirtation and the breaking of marital vows was common currency. The woman who could be had for a slice of bread and butter actually became a reality here, with the one difference that one had to substitute margarine for butter. Every woman who cared about her appearance had a man in as nourishing as possible a profession, preferably a baker, a butcher, or a worker in the central warehouse. She would justify this with the excuse that she was only doing it for the sake of her family.

I was one of the few, totally unmodern men who remained faithful to his wife. Vera and I were always together, and when Vera later moved to a room for female doctors that she shared with six colleagues, we struck a gentleman's agreement that allowed each of us to have a day to spend an undisturbed hour or two together with a wife or a girlfriend.

In November 1942, Vera got extremely sick. In the practice of her profession, she had been infected with scarlet fever. Then she got *diphtheria and jaundice on top of that, so that she had to spend eleven weeks in isolation. This was a sad and a terrible time for us both, and we couldn't even celebrate our tenth wedding anniversary except by my sending her a few little gifts and a letter that, in its sincere acknowledgement of her and in its thanks for ten so happy years, made such a deep impression on her that she wanted to keep it to the end of her life.*

I could only see her in the hospital, from behind a glass window, so we communicated by sign language as if we were deaf-mutes. However, this bad time also ended, and all was well again.

A ghoulish apparition, a perennial nightmare hovered steadily above us in the form of the transports to the East. Transports to the Unknown. Transports to Perdition. Every conceivable kind of offering was brought forth in order to safeguard against being transported away, but all safeguards were usually problematic. As a doctor, Vera shielded me, and I, in my position as Master shielded her, but this only succeeded as long as normal circumstances prevailed.

Our dear parents were assigned to a transport to the East in the fall of 1942 and twice Vera's parents were assigned to a transport. You can certainly image how awful was the thought of simply allowing our parents to be dragged off alone to their destruction. Thus, we set all the gears in motion, ran from one office to another, asked, begged, went every which way, intervened and asked our influential friends to speak up in the right places until we succeeded in exempting my parents as well as Vera's from the transport.

Thus, the fact that we missed getting passage to a safe haven at least served the one purpose: that we saved both our parents from destruction and from a dreadful lonely death in foreign parts.

Unfortunately, Elsa and her family fared worse. One day in October 1942 when a transport from Prague arrived in Theresienstadt, it was, as always, placed under strict quarantine in a barrack to which no one had access.

As luck would have it, it was my job as Head of Division to take ten men over there in the middle of the night because the complete transport was to continue on to Poland. My people were supposed to help carry the sick and the luggage to the barrack that had been readied for their departure.

Here, in the midst of this unparalleled chaos of bodies and baggage, I found our dear Elsa with Marianne. Emil had been quartered amid the sick. I promised Elsa my very best help and my most energetic efforts to get her out of the transport, even though time was short and the hurdles seemed endless. However, she did not want out. She had no idea what was meant by "the East," and she would not allow herself to be talked out of it. On the one hand, she feared that Emil would then be sent off alone, or that their luggage would get lost. As if any luggage could be saved anyway! How often in all the years have I forfeited our poor bit of belongings! How often did we stand there with only the clothes we wore! Since Elsa did not want to stay and since even Mama's illness could not persuade her, I went against her wishes and tried by every means at my disposal to get her and her family out of the transport.

It was a hard and painful piece of work, almost hopeless and beyond feasibility. I sacrificed the night and ran from office to office. In Theresienstadt, there was no limit to the working hours. During the arrival of transports, offices were open day and night. Sleep only became a possibility once the transport had left.

And so, I succeeded in the difficult task. All that was needed to free Elsa was the signature of a doctor. Because I did not dare awaken him in the middle of the night, I got the signature first thing in the morning, and I ran at full tilt to the departure barrack. The departing transport was at a full roll, and our dear, good Elsa was gone. Gone forever and ever.

There I stood in the barrack courtyard, the liberating, life-promising piece of paper in my hand, and I howled like a beaten dog. Never in my life will I forget this so dreadful, so bitter hour, nor will the wound left by this experience ever heal completely.

Otto Urbach was not with them. At that time, he was staying at a large farm in Lipa where hundreds of young Jews were doing agricultural work under the supervision of the S.S. Later, he came to Theresienstadt. He was a strong, handsome, and high-spirited young man, but he has not come back to the homeland either.

With Vera and me as well, it was a tragic chain of events that brought us into the transport to Poland. We had been in Theresienstadt for sixteen months and we had seen many dozens of transports leaving during that time. One day in the middle of December 1943, the gruesome call befell us too. As I have already told you, we had been protected against being assigned to a transport, but this time they needed two hundred doctors in the East, and they selected the youngest ones. Dear Vera belonged in this category, and I belonged to Vera, for the governing rule was not to tear apart the immediate family.

The central Office of Labour immediately set all gears in motion in order to exempt me and by automatic extension, to exempt Vera as well. And now, just imagine, my dear ones, their efforts were crowned with results, but the decision came one small half hour too late. When the clerk arrived at the train station with the exemption order, we were already sitting in the sealed freight car, and the train slowly rolled away to the Hell of Oswieczin.

Another letter will follow in two or three weeks. Best regards and kisses from your faithful Arnold

———

THERE WERE FIVE POST-WAR letters in the box, all from Arnold. There must have been more letters, but only these five were in the box when I opened it. I translated the first four quite quickly, but for a long time, the fifth letter lay untouched. Somehow, I continued to put off translating that last letter for a very long time, as if fearing to end my connection to family and to a past that had become my daily companion.

FIFTH LETTER

Sept. 11, 1945

My Dear Ones,

I received your letter dated August 1 on August 25, in about three weeks, which represents a very rapid delivery. Its contents moved me deeply, and I thank you very much for your kind words.

Dear Gretl, I did not know that you could write such nice letters. I can instinctively tell from them that your words come from the heart and that they are sincerely intended.

Your concern for my inner as well as my bodily well-being is touching and in every way reassuring for me. Even if, thank God, I have recovered enough so that I am once again standing on my own two feet, even if I've been provided with adequate food and clothing, it is still a precious source of comfort to me and to my still raw inner wounds to know that I have total support from people who are close to me through the bonds of blood, who believe in me and will never abandon me.

I was deeply touched when I read of the profound impression that my factual reports had made upon you.

The awareness of all the horror that we had become accustomed to with the passage of years has suddenly descended upon you. Only now does that awareness step out of the shadows of the unconscious into the harsh light of reality. However, you can now take consolation from the fact that all this belongs to a gruesome but at least a vanquished past. Although we shudder to remember this past with all its horrendous experiences, its feelings and its nightmare visions, we are nonetheless trying to the best of our ability to obliterate them totally from our memory, the quicker the better. The future will make all this seem to be an evil spectre from the past, a grisly hallucination of wretchedness as we follow the eternal rule of life with its irresistibly powerful vitality that turns us always toward the future.

What is impossible to forget, however, what cannot be extinguished from our thoughts and our hearts, is the awareness and the longing for all those dear ones who stood so close to us, those who were ripped away by that gruesome time and were swept into the abyss. They were torn away from our side with no regard for the fact that our hearts bleed and will bleed so long as we shall live.

I thank you very much for your well-intended invitation to come to you, but this is out of the question. My place is here in the homeland. I have my job here, and numerous attachments, as well as my memories. Furthermore, I no longer feel young enough to start a whole new life. These days, I usually follow the path of least resistance.

I am sorry to have to report to you that of the eleven packages you sent, only the five for which I had previously acknowledged receipt have thus far arrived. Since then, there has been a long pause.

Dear Gretl, I will gladly give you the requested measurements, but I notice that I am well supplied in the suit department and that I even have enough underwear thanks to Otto's help. Besides, I have learned to wear underwear somewhat longer than used to be the custom.

On the other hand, I would be very grateful if you could get me some warm, knitted things for the winter: sweaters, vests and the like, shawls, gloves, and above all, spats. I will hardly be able to get these things here since there is not even wool to be worked yet, let alone wares made from wool.

With food, things are not so bad today. As a worker, I get a supplemental ration card and an additional one on medical orders as a repatriate (former prisoner). Of course, it is not a matter of kilos but of decagrams, and certain things like meat, fat, fruit, and sweets are still very scarce.

About my reports, I would still like to tell you the following. I have already sent you four reports in three letters, and I have reached all the way to the end of Theresienstadt and to the transport to Auschwitz. Now, however, my strength fails me, or rather my ability to render in graphic form those events and experiences.

Words seem too weak and too petty to depict all that I lived to see and to witness. My thoughts entangle themselves. I would like to express everything simultaneously, and of course, that is impossible. I must therefore now put a period at the end of my sentence, or perhaps a pause. Maybe the time will come when I can depict everything in peace.

About the demise of your mother, dear Gretl, sadly I cannot provide the exact details that you have requested. My memory has unfortunately suffered a lot, and sometimes, the memories do not surface until months later. I only know that dear Mama Resl felt mentally better in Theresienstadt. She showed promise of a complete recovery of her mind, but her body broke down as was the case with all of the elderly, and her weakened state hastened her martyrdom.

The description of your life and of the building up of the farm was of unusual interest, although I hope and expect that you, dear Edi will still write to me in much greater detail about it.

Now, I want to tell you that Otto flew to Paris on August 3. He has since written that because of the inflationary prices there, he is not even thinking about reopening the factory. For now, he has gone to England for two or three weeks.

Before that, he went to Strobnitz for the third time, and using the shipping agent Fröstl who now lives in Number 62, he personally shipped out the best pieces of your furniture to my half-empty apartment. The big buffet, three large chests, your table and sofa now grace my new apartment where I reside with Mama Schick, and where the furniture constantly reminds me of my dear brother Edi and his good wife Gretl.

Now, be well, my precious and dear ones. Write soon and often and lots.

Hugs and kisses from your faithful Arnold.
For your birthday, dear Edi, my sincerest and very best wishes.

Finding Home

ONCE AGAIN, ABRUPTLY, THE LETTERS ENDED.

What happened to Arnold? Why were there no more letters from him in the box? True, he had declined my father's invitation to resettle with us in Canada, but why was there no more correspondence? I was nine in 1945, old enough to have remembered the arrival of further letters.

Otto immigrated to Canada a short time after the war, and he lived with us in Hamilton for some months. Then, he entered a business partnership with Ludwig, purchasing a small clothing store with him on Boulevard Saint-Laurent in Montreal. Unfortunately, the partnership came to a sad end and created bad blood between Otto and my father. The years of working side by side with Ludwig on the farm had led my father to respect his brother-in-law deeply. My father probably sided with Ludwig, and the resulting rupture between the two brothers never quite healed. In 1991, thirty-three years after my father's death, we were notified of Otto's death.

The mystery of Arnold could not be easily solved. Rightly or wrongly, I had put aside the post-war letters, unwilling to experience again the emotions that ripped through me when I first read them. Above all, I had not wanted my mother to re-experience the grief of her own dreadful loss.

And then, my mother's health declined. She did not linger long. On September 30, 1999, as we sat stroking her hands—her beloved granddaughter on one side, I on the other—her breathing became ever more shallow until it stopped.

There was no one left to ask.

———

MONTHS LATER, IN THE spring of 2000, my friend Rick phoned me from Toronto. *"What are you doing in September? How about meeting me in Prague for a 'roots' trip?"* It was the second time that, unknowingly, Rick was to change the course of my life.

The first time had been in November 1992, on a lazy Sunday morning as we sipped coffee in my kitchen in Vancouver. Rick and I share so much history. His mother Mimi was once my Aunt Anny's best friend. When Mimi and Robert bought their first house, it was just a few streets away from our home in Hamilton. I was twelve years old when Rick was born, and proud that Mimi and Robert trusted me as his first babysitter.

As adults, Rick and I have always been able to talk. Somewhere along the line, he began referring to me as his older sister, an honorific title that means much to me. As an only child, I have always yearned for siblings and for an extended family. Anny and Ludwig were all that I had. Unfortunately, Anny and my mother continued to play the game of good sister/bad sister that they had learned as children, thereby making my closeness to Anny an issue of divided loyalties. On the farm, there had always been jealousy and dissension between the two women, with my father and Ludwig alternately playing the role of peacemaker. When my father and then Ludwig died, my mother began to clutch me ever tighter while allowing the unresolved rivalry with her sister to fester.

Rick does have his brother Fred, and their family dynamics are very different. Their father Robert was born in Prague, and he was only seventeen in 1939 when his well-to-do parents heard that there was a Gestapo official who accepted bribes. Unwilling to risk arrest themselves, Robert's parents sent their only son on a mission to Gestapo headquarters. Riding in the back of the family's chauffeur-driven Daimler, Robert held in his lap a briefcase stuffed with Czech Kronen. The rumour had been correct, and he returned with exit visas in the now empty briefcase.

Robert never quite forgave his parents for making him the guinea pig. Family tensions were only exacerbated when Robert dropped out of university to marry Mimi, a struggling immigrant some ten years his senior. Neither her intelligence nor her charm could ever thaw the ice of her in-laws.

Now, Rick struggled to understand his father just as I was striving to connect with my mother. At some level, they were unreachable. As we refilled our coffee cups, Rick wondered aloud whether our general sense of disconnection with the world might have something to do with our backgrounds. Despite having many friends, neither of us feels that we belong. We are always on the outside looking in, and we are both prone to a real but nameless discomfort.

Still, I was taken aback by Rick's question: *"Helen, do you think that what our parents experienced in Europe has affected us?"*

In retrospect, Rick's question seems naïve. What is astounding, however, is that neither of us had ever asked ourselves that question. Our parents' silence about certain years of their life had been so total and their reluctance to talk about the past so manifest that it simply had not occurred to either of us that we'd been shaped by matters of which we knew very little.

Rick's question reminded me of an announcement in a Jewish newspaper passed to me by a neighbour. She had said, *"I know that you're not religious, but sometimes this paper has interesting articles."* And indeed, the words *Second Generation Holocaust Survivor* had caught my eye.

It was a concept I'd never thought about. In my world, there were "survivors," but I had seen no reason to draw a line connecting these emaciated-looking people with haunted eyes and tattooed numbers on their arms to my parents. Indeed, both Mimi and my mother had always insisted that because we came to Canada, we had escaped "it," as the Holocaust was called in the early post-war years before it was given a name. Indeed, I never heard either my parents or Mimi use any word but "it" for the experience of Dachau, Auschwitz, Treblinka, and all the other concentration camps.

Still, at a gut level, I felt that much had been passed on to us, if only in the form of unspoken fears, nameless enemies, and shadowy threats to our very existence. I searched through the pile of papers in the recycling box and found the notice about the conference to begin Sunday at 11 a.m. It was now 10:30.

In a flash, Rick and I had our coats on, were out the door and across town just as the keynote speaker was introduced. Her name, Helen Epstein, with its echoing tones of my pre-marital Helen Waldstein, spoke to me. So did her words and those of many workshop participants we met that afternoon. We spoke of our common experiences: the larger than life shadows cast by the silence imposed upon the past; the importance of being a *good* child who does not upset parents by asking, let alone doing the wrong thing; the need from an early age to parent our parents, and protect them in a world whose language and customs they never quite mastered.

One of the people I met that afternoon was a rather unprepossessing chap with the crumbs of lunch still clinging to his greyish beard. He introduced himself as Yitzhak, a rabbi who was starting a local group of "second generation survivors." So much had resonated for me at the conference that I agreed to attend at least one meeting. And so began my journey of return.

———

YITZHAK WAS THEN RABBI of a small Jewish community in Vancouver called Or Shalom. He explained that the Hebrew words are typically translated as "the light of peace" but that the word *Shalom* also means wholeness. Perhaps peace and wholeness are the same, for as I began to integrate the bits of my life into a coherent whole, I felt wrapped in a greater peace than I had ever known.

Out of curiosity, one Saturday morning I went to the living room of the rented house where Or Shalom held its weekly service. The service itself seemed, if not actually alien, then certainly odd and unfamiliar.

I had attended Sunday school in the United Church of Canada. I attended because my parents had wanted me to have some knowledge of religion, because our next-door neighbours were willing to take me to church every Sunday, and because my parents had wanted to protect me from the centuries-old hatred that had destroyed their own lives.

I brought home and treasured the pamphlets given to me at Sunday school. They showed a blond, blue-eyed Christ healing the lepers, blessing children, and riding a donkey on the way to Jerusalem. Later, when we moved from the farm to the city, I again found myself in the United Church, home to Canadian Girls in Training. I proudly wore the CGIT white blouse, dark tie, and assorted badges of achievement.

I was ten years old when my parents became members of the Jewish Reform congregation whose services they had attended for the High Holidays of Rosh Hashanah and Yom Kippur. Much as he loved my mother, my father was reluctant to attend services. He deemed twice a year to be more than enough religion.

It was mostly an awareness of the passing years that triggered official synagogue membership. As my mother put it, *"We have to belong somewhere. If we don't belong, they won't bury us if, God forbid, 'something' should happen. I don't like the idea of worms eating my body, but it is better than the alternative."* That was as close as my mother could come to stating that given how her parents had died, cremation was out of the question.

My father always insisted that being a decent person is what matters above all. In Europe, his family had known that they were Jewish because it said so on their birth certificate, just as it does on mine. No one in my father's family had ever paid much attention to religion. They ate pork roast and sausages along with their neighbours and attended the same village school. It was a precursor of my own experience in Canada except that here it was bologna and hot dogs.

That Saturday morning at Or Shalom introduced me to another world. From those long ago High Holiday services I attended as a child, I remembered only one prayer: *Shema Ysrael, Adonai Eloheinu, Adonai Echad,* the

age-old affirmation that there is but one God. What moved me deeply at
Or Shalom was the music. On the farm, my favourite song had been "Jesus
loves me, this I know." Later, I had often sung "Rock of Ages." Now, the
Jewish melodies awakened something deep within me.

One song in particular thawed my frozen heart. "*Barchu*. Dear One.
Shechinah. Holy Name. When I call on the light of my soul, I come home."
I wept from the moment the voices of the congregation rose until after they
faded away. As the silent tears rolled down my cheeks, I knew that I had
indeed come home.

Something changed for me that day. I'm reluctant to call myself "religious" or even "spiritual." There are days when I still question the existence
of a personal God and even more days when I wrestle with the validity of
biblical passages and their traditional interpretation. Nonetheless, there has
been a major shift in how I think and feel and experience the world. At the
very least, I have peeled off a layer of the onion and reached a millimetre
closer to knowing the core of my own being.

————

WHEN I BROUGHT MY mother to Vancouver to spend her last years with me,
she too had a sense of coming home and asked to be buried in the Jewish
cemetery here.

At her funeral, sadness flowed from Jew and non-Jew, from believer and
non-believer. For me, there was something quintessentially Canadian that
emerged: the best of a world still to be brought fully to fruition.

Integrating my own world and that of my family into contemporary
Canadian awareness is another facet of coming home. My Canada is both a
world of smug citizens and a land of diverse peoples who acknowledge
their separate ways of being and perceiving. It is a land that means well, but
has done harm to many groups. Still, what characterizes my Canada is its
willingness to learn from the past.

I needed to face my own past. The time had come. I would start with a
visit to my place of birth. A year after my mother's death, I returned to
Europe.

Searching for Family Again

AFTER AGREEING TO RENDEZVOUS with Rick in Prague in mid-August, I booked a flight that would allow me some time to travel on my own. Primarily, I wanted to go back to Linz where the Fränkels had lived to see if there was more information in the archives. I also wanted to spend time with my friends Tracey and Martin, and if possible, take them up on their offer to drive with me to Strobnitz, my hometown in the Czech Republic.

In the 1960s, I had tried to enter Czechoslovakia when it was still under communist control. Although the border guards had showed no interest in my American travel companions, one look at my place of birth resulted in my passport being confiscated for over an hour. As we sat in the hot car under a blazing summer sun, the guards grilled me, asking again and again for names of "contacts," and mocking my claim not to speak Czech. When at last I was allowed to enter, it was only on condition that I accept a "tour guide" who accompanied my every step. She sat sullenly at our table while we drank watery coffee and she leaned impatiently against the cubicle when I visited the washroom. She directed us to a souvenir kiosk and watched as we spent the requisite number of dollars on a few cheaply made trinkets. When we returned to the border crossing, there were more delays. The guards removed the back seat and placed the car on a hoist to ensure that I was not smuggling Czech citizens out of the country.

This time, entering the Czech Republic was much simpler. After a leisurely breakfast in their kitchen, I followed Tracey and Martin to their car and we drove along the river and out of the city. Despite a steady drizzle, the cheerful countryside buoyed our spirits. Tidy houses with flowers cascading from painted window boxes alternated with orchards pregnant with ripening fruit and with prosperous farmland where cows grazed in rich green meadows.

The border crossing stood in sharp contrast to the bucolic Austrian scenery. Grey cement-block buildings peppered with grey-faced guards in drab, one-size-fits-all uniforms. An indifferent guard stamped my passport. The guard yawned as he lifted the flimsy wooden barrier. We drove through to a barren road lined with prostitutes in cheap glamour outfits. Some were in stiletto heels, others in thigh-high boots. All wore ultra-short skirts and tight tops despite the driving rain. Most were young. Behind them lay nothing but deserted fields and overgrown woods.

Martin sensed our discomfort. For him, the scene was not new. "It's dreadful," he said. "Human misery as an announcement of economic adversity. There are rows of prostitutes at all the border crossings into the Czech Republic. It's the only thing they have to sell."

Faces blurred as our car rushed forward. Only the relentless click-clack of the wipers broke the dismal silence. Muffled, the countryside flowed past the windows. Grey clouds hung shroud-like over endless fields of corn broken by occasional clusters of dilapidated houses whose sagging roofs pressed upon walls long since leached of colour. No flower boxes adorned these windows, and no gardens bloomed in plots where rusting equipment sank into narrow strips of weed. Hopelessness was written everywhere, and it seeped even into the sealed car.

At last, we spotted the sign: *Horní Stropnice*. Only in my memory did its former name *Strobnitz* survive. I looked at my watch. It was only 1:30 in the afternoon, although the lowering sky made it seem later. The village was dreary beyond belief. A cheerless hamlet of unrelieved grey. Ashen cement

My hometown village, Strobnitz, is shuttered and unwelcoming

blocks beneath an ashen sky. Not a single pedestrian was scurrying for cover. The inhabitants had hunkered down in their gloomy caves. Not one welcoming light shone.

Our house was easy to find. Number 36 is one slice of a long, single two-storied block of grey cement that reaches from one street to the next. A row of colourless signs announces a variety of stores and businesses on the ground floor. Upstairs on this sunless afternoon, faded chintz curtains closed off every window. Here and there, an empty window box yawned into the unbroken greyness.

Only one house was different. Number 36. Its storefront had been crudely bricked over in ugly yellowish-brown blocks. I saw it as a clumsy effort to erase the last trace of the Jews who had once lived here. The Jews who were my family.

Tini and her family came here a few years ago. They had told me that the house was right opposite the cenotaph in the centre of the village. I looked at the inscription on the stone slab erected in the midst of a flowerless strip of unmowed grass. *To the brave inhabitants of Horní Stropnice who fell in defence of the homeland.*

I paused to untangle the words and their meaning. This area had been predominantly German speaking, and its inhabitants had welcomed the Nazis who promised to reunite them with their German brothers. This meant that those who had "fallen in defence of the homeland" had therefore been killed by Allied hands.

And what about my family? My parents and grandparents had been victims of these very inhabitants whom the inscription sought to memorialize. Tini said that before our wagon reached the edge of town, neighbours had come to ransack the house. Was a favourite plate belonging to my grandmother Fanny now gracing a mantle behind one of those unmoving curtains?

Turning away, I told Tracey and Martin to stay in the car while I took just a few pictures before leaving. I stared at the house. My heart felt as numb as my cold, wet fingers fumbling with the camera. I decided to take one last photo of the entire block from the street corner. From this vantage point, my eye caught sight of a lovely white church, its dome glistening in the rain. Delighted to find beauty in this dismal place, I asked Martin to turn the car around and to follow me.

I walked over to the church, where small groups of people were huddled under black umbrellas. Because it was Saturday afternoon, I assumed that the people were a wedding party. Moving closer, I was certain that I heard German being spoken.

This surprised me as Tini had repeatedly said that my visit would be a waste of time because people in the Czech Republic no longer speak German. Tini knew this not only from her recent visit, but because she and her

family had been among the German-speakers whom the Czechs had unceremoniously booted out after the war.

I approached the nearest group and addressed my questions to a well-
dressed man in a suit.

"*You speak German?*"

"*Of course.*"

"*Are you from here?*"

"*Of course.*"

"*Oh, that's great because I don't speak Czech. I am looking for someone
who may remember my family. They had a store here. My father was Edmund
Waldstein, and his father was Josef Waldstein.*"

Silence. Lingering, uncomfortable silence. Wordlessly, the people in the
little group eyed one another. Faces blanched. Slowly, the people melted
away, as if fleeing into the church. I was left with my hand on the sleeve of
the well-dressed man. He watched the backs of his companions. He looked
for a long while at his own shoes. Finally he spoke.

"*Of course I knew them. Everyone here knew them. We knew them well.
But now there is no time to talk. I must go into the church. Come into the
church with me and we will talk later.*"

I waved Tracey and Martin forward, urging them to join me. Together,
we entered through the arched doorway.

The interior of the church was warm and welcoming. Stained glass
windows cast flashes of ruby red onto the whitewashed walls. An ornate
rococo altar, heavy with gold drew the eye to the cross. To the right, a
life-sized Madonna garbed in deep blue stretched both arms toward the
congregation. To the left, an intricately carved staircase wound its way to
the pulpit. Everywhere, candles flickered, casting their golden glow upon
burnished wooden pews.

Already a voice was intoning from the pulpit. I tried to follow, but the
thick regional dialect allowed me to catch only isolated words. *Forgiveness.
Reconciliation.* I thought these odd words for a wedding, but looked about
expectantly for a bride and groom. A hymn and then more disconnected
words followed. *Peace. Remembrance. Moderation. Restraint.* I nudged Martin. "*Do you understand?*" He nodded. Relieved that I need not struggle to

decipher the words, I allowed the space and the music to flow around me until the congregation rose to file out.

Politely I shook the hand of the priest planted in the doorway, my eyes already searching for the man in the suit. He was surrounded by people including Martin. Tracey and I waited impatiently. Finally, Martin returned to answer our questions.

Today was August 8, the second Saturday in August. Since the end of World War II, this group had assembled every year at 2 p.m. on the second Saturday of August. They gathered to remember Strobnitz, the town where they had been born and had gone to school, had married, and established new families. The town that the Czechs had forced them to leave after the war. The Czechs had made no distinction between Nazi collaborators and Sudeten-Germans. The Czechs simply drove everyone who spoke German into exile.

Tini had been forced out too. She had been given three hours to pack her bags and leave. What the Czechs did to the Sudeten-Germans was akin to what the latter had done to my family.

For many years, the Sudeten-Germans were not allowed to enter Czechoslovakia. The Communist government refused to let them in. The closest to Strobnitz that these former townsfolk could come was to a hillside in Austria. From there, on a clear day, they could see Strobnitz. Every year, they came, from Austria, from Germany, from Belgium and Holland, and from wherever they had found refuge. At two o'clock, on the second Saturday in August, they gathered on that hillside in Austria. There, they held an outdoor church service and gazed across at their hometown.

Since the fall of the Iron Curtain, the Sudeten-Germans have been allowed to return. Now, they meet in the church in Strobnitz every year at 2 p.m. on the second Saturday in August.

"How did you find us?" a voice asked. "Who told you we'd be here today?"

I shook my head in wonderment. This was beyond coincidence. What unseen hand had guided my footsteps? What chance had brought me across the ocean on the second Saturday in August? What had led me to this church at ten minutes to two? Ten minutes later, these people would have already been inside the church and I would not have known of their existence.

Not only had I come from afar, I had arrived after an interval of more than sixty years, and had uttered the name Waldstein, a name unspoken here in all that time.

Small wonder that faces had blanched. Even to myself, I seemed to be an apparition, a revenant, a ghostly incarnation of voices long silent.

Two elderly women approached. One gently tugged at my sleeve.

"My name is Lucy. We knew your grandmother. She used to call us into her kitchen on our way home from school."

"She used to give us Buchterln fresh out of the oven. She loved to bake."

"Mitzi, do you remember a thin kind of bread she gave us just before Easter?"

"Oh yes. That was good. Especially when she smeared it with goose fat. But I don't remember what she called it."

I knew immediately. It was Matzos, the unleavened bread eaten during the week of Passover. How ironic that she would remember the item of food that was perhaps the only way in which my grandparents celebrated their Judaism.

Meanwhile, the well-dressed gentleman had introduced himself. Alois Bayer. He offered to show me around. Pointing to an empty lot overgrown with weeds that lay just behind the church, he declared this to be where the house of the "lower Waldsteins" had stood. The lower Waldsteins? Who were they? I had never heard "upper" or "lower" used before my family name. Alois was eager to fill me in.

"The lower Waldsteins were your grandfather's brother and his family. Their house was at the bottom of the hill, which is why we called them the lower Waldsteins. Their son Erich and I were best buddies. The two of us were motorcycle mad. We used to spend every spare moment repairing and riding the machines we cobbled together from old parts that nobody wanted."

I stood dumbstruck. My grandfather had had a brother, right here in this village. My father had had an uncle and an aunt and cousins and had grown up with them in this very place, yet he had never spoken of them.

Now it was Alois who was eager for information.

"Do you know what happened to Erich? Is he alive? What about his brother Walter?"

Alois (right) talks to a villager in Strobnitz

His questions drove home the enormity of all that had been lost. I knew so little of my father's family, and what little I knew came from the letters. Cousins and an uncle and aunt living in the very same village! I was eager to learn more and agreed to join the group at a coffee shop in the next town.

Unlike the welcoming places I had enjoyed in Austria and Germany, the *Kaffeehaus* was nothing but a rundown roadside tavern. It was a shabby structure whose dark interior reeked of stale smoke. Seated on uncomfortable wooden chairs, we gathered around tables too small for our numbers. The menu featured only one item: *Palatschinka*. Many in our group were already digging into plates of the jam-filled pancakes. We did have a choice of beverage: beer or coffee.

Alois suggested that beer would be a better choice. Beer is plentiful and good in this part of the world that gave birth to Pilsner and Budweiser. However, the combination of lukewarm beer and cloyingly sweet Palatschinka, especially in the crowded, smoke-filled room closed up my gullet. I sat pushing the rubbery roll from side to side, listening to the din of voices in a culture where everyone talks at once. I had so much to think about, yet so much still to ask.

We agreed to meet up again with the group for dinner in Austria. Alois told us to follow him as he wove along country roads, stopping only at a border crossing manned by a single guard whom he seemed to know well, and then continuing directly to a picturesque Bavarian-style restaurant. We were back in Austria. Flowers cascaded voluminously from boxes and balconies. Rich cooking smells greeted us, along with the cheerful sounds of an accordion. There were even red-checked cloths on all the tables, as well as the usual assortment of cuckoo clocks and stag heads between the alpine scenes that covered every inch of the log walls. A welcoming place, or so it seemed initially.

At first, a number of individuals came by our table to speak to me. One man introduced himself as "the village chronicler," and asked if I would like him to send me a copy of his history of Strobnitz. I said I would be delighted. Still, I felt uneasy. Jumbled thoughts filled my mind.

Where were these people when my family was taken away? Were some of these people the looters Tini had described? I remembered her words: *"They all came, the people from the village of Strobnitz, even the people to whom your grandfather had been kind, the people to whom he had given credit when they couldn't pay their accounts. Now they came to steal whatever they could lay their hands on."*

Certainly, no one in this festive group wanted to remember the Jews and what had happened to them. I sensed a shrinking back as I continued to ask questions. These people had attended the same village school as Martha and Elsa and Arnold and Otto and my father. They had played together and had grown up side by side. Had they also been among the neighbours who came to fill their arms with towels and sheets, with pots and pans, with whatever had been left behind? Had one of these grey-haired women raided my grandmother's kitchen? Had someone stirred his morning coffee with one of our spoons? At the very least, each person here had pretended not to know.

I looked at Tracey and saw that she understood.

"*We'll go whenever you like,*" she said softly.

Alois saw us rise, and bustled over.

"*You cannot leave now. You have not even eaten yet. Did you order?*"

"*No. Our server has been busy bringing steins of beer. We haven't even seen a menu.*"

"*But where will you go? To a hotel? Everything for miles around is filled with our group. You will not find a bed anywhere. You must stay at my house. Come to the mill. I will phone my wife and tell her to expect you.*"

"*But that would be an imposition. Would you even have room for three?*"

Someone snickered.

"*We have lots of space at the mill. Besides, I want to show you some of the pictures in my photo album tomorrow. You must do this, because I cannot leave now and I want to tell you more about the past.*"

And so, we found ourselves once again following Alois' directions, along the road to a turn-off through the woods. We wove among the trees, the lights of Martin's Mini barely illuminating the long, deeply rutted path.

A dog barked. The car rumbled over a wooden bridge and rolled to a stop. A door opened and a grey-haired woman stood framed in the light. She descended the stairs and approached, still drying her hands on an apron as she walked. She opened my door and I saw a radiant face framed with grey hair swept back into a knot. A mature face, wise and welcoming.

This was Lotte. She sensed my emotional exhaustion and took us directly to our quarters, a converted mill opposite the main house. We mounted the stone stairs and entered a high-beamed living room with deep comfortable sofas lit by the warm glow of reading lamps. Open doors led to several bedrooms. In the centre was a table with a thermos and carafes and covered plates of food.

"*I thought you'd be tired and might like privacy tonight. Tomorrow at breakfast, I will welcome you properly in the main house. Then we can talk.*"

I looked again at her beautiful face and remembered the portrait of an angel on my bedroom wall back in Canada.

We slept soundly and wakened to warm sunshine and the susurrus of water running over the dam almost below our floorboards. Lotte was already in her garden, watching for us as she plucked and snipped. In the main house, our coffee awaited, along with platters of cheese and Wurst and real rye bread and butter. The aroma of a freshly baked coffeecake wafted invitingly from the sideboard. Alois was already at the round table with its crisp blue and white cloth, waiting impatiently as he leafed through photo albums and papers.

He hovered restlessly as we got acquainted with Lotte, who had her own tale to tell. Many years before, she had fled from the former Yugoslavia, eager to leave both communism and the centuries of hatred between groups barely held together by the magnetism of a single charismatic dictator. Croatia, Kosovo. Serbia. Even as we spoke, "the Allies" were bombing bridges and killing innocent civilians in an effort to oust Milosevic, the latest dictator. Lotte's own sons were being asked to kill people who had once been their neighbours, people with whom they had gone to school, people who had been their soccer mates and friends. History was being written not in abstract concepts but in blood not far away.

At last, Alois got his turn. He had found memorabilia of himself and my cousin Erich. Again he told us that they had been motorcycle buddies, and that as teens, they had spent every spare moment repairing bent wheels and discarded parts in order to create the roaring machines that were their passion. Martin and Tracey asked all the right questions while I pondered the fact that I once had had cousins named Erich and Walter and that I had not even known it.

Alois led us back out to the mill and showed us his own private motorcycle collection. He was particularly proud of one that he said was exactly like the one that had been Eric's proudest possession. I could but wonder when and how Alois acquired this machine.

Alois kept saying *"Ich war nur ein Bub. I was just a kid."*

I was terribly uncomfortable. Later, Alois confided that he had been in the *Hitlerjugend*. *"We all were,"* he said. *"It was the norm. Everyone my age was in the Hitlerjugend."*

I reflected once again upon the dangers of doing what everyone else is doing. Is it reasonable to expect a boy of thirteen to wonder what had happened to his friend rather than to rejoice at the acquisition of a new motorcycle? Is it reasonable to ask anyone to swim against the tide of mainstream opinion? Walking in his shoes, would I have had the courage to stand alone?

My thoughts made me restless. Despite my interest in every word and every detail, I was also eager to leave. Fortunately, I had a train to catch.

———

THE TRAIN I HAD PLANNED to catch would take me from Budweis to Prague. For most people, Budweis is simply the name of a popular beer. For me, it had always been just the specific place of my birth. On this Sunday afternoon, it seemed no more than a convenient place for Tracey and Martin to drop me off. I would take the train to Prague where I had agreed to meet Rick, and they would return to Linz to prepare for the working week.

My conscious mind had not registered the fact that my parents and I had taken that same train in 1938. Besides, I was still trying to digest the encounter in Strobnitz plus all that Alois had told me. My mind was elsewhere as Martin found his way through a maze of lanes with small industrial buildings, all uniformly grey and flat on this cloudy day. He parked near the railway station and we decided to use the remaining time to walk to the town square.

The town square of Budweis is enormous. It may not compare in actual size to the Place de la Concorde or to Saint Peter's square in Rome, but for a town the size of Budweis, it struck me as disproportionately large. No café tables with bright umbrellas lined its sides, and no pedestrians crossed that vast cobblestone stretch on this sunless Sunday afternoon. Suddenly, I imagined that I heard the sound of marching feet and saw the flash of polished black boots. I knew that this square had once trembled to the click of Nazi goosesteps and resonated with shouts of *"Heil Hitler!"* I wanted neither a final coffee nor a beer.

"You two go home now," I told Tracey and Martin. *"Just get my suitcase out of the car and I'll wait for the train while you head back to Linz."* Fortunately, they chose to ignore my advice.

I am not a hysterical person. I consider myself a rational adult. I do not have panic attacks. Still, the moment I set foot inside that cavernous station with its high stone walls, I froze. I could not take a single step toward the dark tunnel that led to my track. What the mind did not remember, the body knew.

I began to weep. At first softly, and then hysterically. I could not breathe, I could not speak, I could not move. Just like my father must have done 60 years earlier, Martin scooped me in his arms and carried me to the track. I remember watching Tracey get on the train to find me a compartment. From the safety of Martin's arms, I saw her put my bags up on a rack. Still, I could not move. Only after the conductor called his "All Aboard" did I feel arms lift me up the steps to the corridor where I clung to a bar at the window as the train pulled out. I clung to that bar for hours, all the way to Prague, urging that train to go faster, pushing it forward with my last ounce of strength.

———

I COULD NOT BEAR TO BE alone that first evening in Prague. Fortunately, Rick's brother Fred had already arrived so that for a few hours, I was able to pretend that we were normal tourists. We wandered through the maze of narrow streets to the old town with its celebrated clock tower where the puppet Death chases the unwary with each chime of the hour. We checked out the restaurants and cafés, we ate a good meal and talked of our families safely at home in Canada.

The next morning, Rick and his partner joined us along with his cousin and her father. For several days, we played tourist, crossing the ancient Charles Bridge that spans the Vltava River, visiting the Hradcany Castle on the hill, checking out the souvenirs and pretending that Prague for us was merely an exquisite medieval city, a beautiful not-to-be-missed spot on the tourist trail.

One of the many must-see destinations in Prague is the old Jewish quarter. Because Jews had no Civil Rights until 1848 and because for centuries they had been confined to the ghetto and not allowed to live amongst their Christian neighbours, some 20,000 bodies had to be buried, body upon body in the tiny walled cemetery.

I watched as tour buses disgorged visitors to gape at the hodgepodge of leaning stone markers. I listened as tour guides described the strange and quaint customs of the Jews. I felt like a member of an extinct species. I shuddered as several tour guides brushed away the past as natural resentment because *"the Jews were rich."* I thought of my family who had huddled a few blocks away with only the contents of a suitcase.

It was time for me to stop playing tourist. The next day, I went in search of an address I had brought with me. Number 32 Manesova, the address on the last letter from my father's brother, Arnold.

———

NUMBER 32 MANESOVA IS an unmodernized apartment block with a heavy front door and neither nameplates nor a buzzer system. My only option was to sit on the step and wait. In due time, someone with a dog came home, and I unceremoniously inserted my foot before the door closed in my face. The man spoke neither English nor German nor French and my Czech is nil. I managed to convey the message that I was not going to leave. Eventually, he sighed, knocked on a downstairs door where he excitedly conferred with someone before stomping up the stairs to knock on another door. Soon, a woman descended and somewhat warily, approached.

She was the answer to my prayers. She had a degree from the Sorbonne as do I. French became for us the universal language it had once been for so many of the world's educated. She invited me upstairs to her apartment where I apologized for my brazen behaviour. I explained why I had seen no other option.

When I uttered the name Arnold Waldstein, she seemed to blanch. Piling coincidence upon coincidence, she told me that she knew his wife who until very recently had lived in the apartment just across the hall. Mme Waldstein had only recently been taken by her nephew to an old-age home where she had died. The apartment was now occupied by a new tenant.

From deep in the recesses of memory came the sound of my parents discussing the new woman in Arnold's life. Arnold must have married her. I explained to my hostess that when the letters from Arnold stopped, all my questions about him went unanswered. Neither of my parents ever spoke another word about him.

The silence grew. An ancient grandfather clock on the wall ticked hypnotically, its pendulum swinging back and forth, back and forth. At last, my hostess spoke:

"That was actually your uncle's clock and this was actually his apartment."

I stared, dumbfounded.

"Mme Waldstein didn't want to live here anymore after her husband died. She had this big place and my husband and I were living with our children in the much smaller apartment across the hall. During the Communist days, it was impossible to get another apartment, so we simply traded. That is why her name is still in the phone book. It used to take ten years to get a new phone, so people simply kept what was in place and gave their friends the number."

As she rose to fetch the phone book, my thoughts skipped back to the letters I now knew by heart. After the war, Otto had gone back to Strobnitz and arranged for my parents' furniture to be shipped to Arnold's half-empty apartment. In his last letter, Arnold had written, *"the big buffet, three large chests, table, and sofa now grace my new apartment where they remind me constantly of my dear brother and his good wife Gretl."*

I sat edgily on the sturdy sofa of the apartment at 32 Manesova. Had I once curled up on this cushion, listening to adult conversation? I stared at the heavy furniture that filled the room, but no memories surfaced. Perhaps my hostess knew what had happened to Arnold. Perhaps she could explain why there had been no more letters. I told her of my parents' silence.

"So you don't know the end of the story? I never met your uncle. He died before I moved into the building. Mme Waldstein told me that she was his second wife. She knew that he had suffered greatly, but it was not something we talked about."

"Did Mme Waldstein ever say anything about when or how he died? I wonder if his body was so weakened by what he went through in Auschwitz that he died soon after."

"No, they had a number of years together. Happy years, according to Mme Waldstein. It's another reason she didn't want to live in this apartment any longer after what happened."

"What do you mean? What happened?"

"Your parents never told you? You really don't know? Mme Waldstein found him."

"Found him?"

"Yes. He had come home early from work one day. She was not home yet and he decided to have a bath. Something went wrong in the pipes. Terribly wrong. Nobody knows how it happened. Gas came out. She found him dead in this very bathtub. Come, I will show you where it happened."

Gas. Auschwitz. They told people they were showers, but gas came out of the pipes. Numbly, I stared at the claw-footed tub, its enamel well worn in several spots. Several pipes ran up the wall and across the ceiling.

In silence, I followed my hostess back to the living room where she opened the glass door of a small china cabinet. There, she removed a very delicate cup and saucer and handed it to me.

"Mme Waldstein painted china as a hobby. She gave me this. I think it is now your turn to have it."

———

THE NEXT DAY, I WENT BACK alone to the Jewish quarter. This time, my destination was the rather nondescript building that constitutes the Jewish Community Centre. A security guard checked my bag and I passed through a metal detector more sensitive than those at the airport. Inside, a few aging men were drinking coffee in the small restaurant. There appeared little here to warrant such scrupulous security.

Under the watchful eye of the guard, I mounted the stairs to an office where elderly women sat hunched over typewriters. The office was a warren of small cubicles, but soon, I found the right place. A kind woman directed me to a wall of drawers holding 4 x 6 file cards.

The cards bear the names of every Jew shipped from Prague to the concentration camps. As Arnold had written, every Jew remaining in Czechoslovakia was first sent to Prague before being dispatched to a concentration camp. Once the Jews were all assembled in one place, it had been easy to move them out, like shipments of goods. Indeed, each card bears a "transport" number along with the last known address of the person.

It was here that I found the information I had not wanted to find. Here, on these green file cards, the name of every Jew had been recorded along with the date and number of the transport. It was important to keep track, to make sure that every Jew had been shipped out.

Some cards have dates of death; most do not. It was not important to keep track of when a Jew died.

The kind woman took all my file cards and made photocopies. She stamped and signed each one. *"That makes it an official record if you should ever need it."* There was no charge for this service.

My quest had been successful, yet I felt more disoriented than ever. Once more, I found myself walking through the Jewish quarter. It was early in the day, but already the area was crammed with tour buses. With a desultory eye, I wandered through the museum, gazing at artefacts that once had graced Jewish homes, Sabbath candlesticks. Hand embroidered tablecloths. Good china. Silver menorahs. Had one of these come from my family's home?

Adjacent to the museum is another ancient structure, this one empty except for the bronze plaques on its walls. The plaques are engraved with 77, 297 names. Each name is that of a Czech Jew killed in the Holocaust. I search for the handful of names that are "mine" while from a loudspeaker, a detached voice intones each name. I need not fear hearing the names repeated. It takes several days to complete the cycle.

———

I KNEW WHERE I HAD to go next. There was no choice. Theresienstadt.

Theresienstadt, or Teresin as it is called in Czech, was once a concentration camp. Not a death camp like Auschwitz, the books hasten to add. Theresienstadt was "only" a concentration camp. It had no ovens and no gas chambers. It was simply the destination to which the Jews from Prague were shipped. It is true that many Jews died there, but this was an unfortunate consequence. Conditions were deplorable, but this was not Auschwitz.

Fred and the cousins stared, as if I were mad. They had no intention of going there. Rick and his partner hesitated, and then decided they too would stay in Prague. I understood, for I too had been uncertain that I could make the pilgrimage.

Because Theresienstadt is only an hour from Prague, there are many tour buses advertising this "unique opportunity" to see a concentration camp. For me, it was out of the question to join a group of tourists.

On foot, I made my way to the public bus station and checked out the schedule. The next bus left in an hour. Impatiently I wandered the nearby streets, willing the time to pass. At a small outdoor market, I spotted leather jackets made in China and realized that I was already chilled to the bone on this warm autumn day. I translated Kronen into dollars and found a green jacket that cost only seventeen dollars. I counted out the cash and snuggled into its comforting warmth.

When the bus arrived, I selected a seat near the front so that I could read the signs rather than rely on my ability to understand the bus driver. At last, I saw ahead the signboard: Teresin. To my left loomed a huge cross. A cross? I had expected a Star of David to mark the last earthly destination of so many Jews. I double-checked with the driver, but he nodded affirmatively. This was definitely Teresin.

A young couple dismounted with me. Shyly, they asked if they could walk with me, having noted that my linguistic skills were at least better than their own. I was pleased to have company. We crossed the spacious car park filled with tour buses. Many of the visitors were eating hot dogs or licking ice cream cones. Souvenir kiosks rimmed the car park.

We paid admission, picked up maps and passed under the red brick archway into the walled fortress. Above us, in bold yellow brick letters stood the famous words: ARBEIT MACHT FREI. I pulled the leather jacket more tightly across my chest.

We consulted the map and headed for the first barrack. It was empty, except for a narrow wooden bench bearing a few rusty tools. Other barracks stood empty. The carefully swept wood floors bore no trace of those who once filled these spaces. Other barracks had the tiered bunk beds where, sardine like, humans once slept head to toe.

Teresin concentration camp, where my grandparents
along with most of my immediate family must have peered
through the window bars, hoping, longing, despairing . . .

A long underground corridor came next. We entered it through a large
stone cave with windows only at the very top. The guidebook says that the
windows permitted some circulation of air as well as allowing the inhabitants to hear the ringing of the church bells that they could not see. The
rest of the underground corridor overlooks windowless cells. Here, even
further underground, is where "uncooperative inhabitants" were kept. By
now, I was deeply grateful to the young couple who had adopted me. The
young man had taken my arm to steady me as I stumbled through the
lightless dungeon.

The guidebook stresses that this was not a place of mass killings, but that
killing, of course, was sometimes necessary. When they had to shoot people, they also buried them. Those who merited a bullet merited a grave.

Those who died "a natural death" were simply cremated. Their ashes were dumped into the river that flows peacefully through the town.

Mutely I gazed at the river that absorbed the last trace of my grandmothers Fanny and Resl.

———

MY COMPANIONS HAD HAD enough. I accompanied them to the bus stop. Alone, I walked through the town of Teresin. People were going about their business much as I imagined the townsfolk would have done during the war years. There were stores, playgrounds, and sidewalks with purposeful pedestrians. I found the very normalcy of life in Teresin as disconcerting as its history.

My footsteps took me to the museum where Jewish artifacts filled the display cases. There were yellow Star of David labels like the one Arnold so hated. There were confiscated passports and small photos of loved ones and copies of the ordinances that stripped the Jews of all human rights. Many of the exhibits tried to show the Czechs themselves as victims, but these were less convincing.

I had not imagined the scale of the camp, nor had I realized how many ordinary citizens had been needed for its daily operation. Countless willing Czech hands had reached out, ready to help execute the Nazi plan.

It was here in the museum that I found a wealth of unimagined material. I marvelled that so much had been preserved. Children's drawings collected into a book entitled *I Never Saw a Butterfly*. I had not realized that many children spent years without catching a glimpse of the outside world. I thought they had all been gassed immediately. I searched and searched for a drawing signed "Ilserl," but there was none.

I was particularly fascinated by the videotape of an old black and white film called *The Town the Nazis Gave to the Jews*. I played and replayed the tape. The film had been made to calm international protests that surfaced when the rumours of death camps became too numerous to ignore. For the film, they dressed children and adults in borrowed finery. They imported props for a theatre, a concert hall, a coffee house and for other pleasurable

Some of the skeletons in mass graves were dug up after the war
and buried with numbered headstones. Like my grandmothers
Fanny and Resl, most who perished in Teresin became ashes
dumped into the river flowing peacefully along the edge of town.

activities. Members of the International Red Cross were invited to see how
well the Jews of Theresienstadt were being treated. The members of the
International Red Cross saw no reason to look behind the scenes. The
props worked, and the Red Cross delegates reported that all was well.
Relieved that nothing need to be done for the Jews, the world went back to
sleep for a while longer.

Searching for Family
One Last Time

THE PAST MAY BE HISTORY, but my history is still open for revision. To revise is to view again, to see with fresh eyes. It is not yet over.

Nor is my quest. To learn, to understand, to come to grips with the past. With my past.

Until it is done, the past cannot be laid to rest.

And so, in 2004, I went once more to Europe, this time not really wanting to go. There was much that I still did not want to face both in Europe and in myself. It was my longing for family, no matter how distant, that drew me. American cousins with whom I share a great-grandmother on my mother's side were planning a "roots" trip to Tachau (not Dachau, as I first feared), home to my grandmother Resl's sister. I looked on a map of the Czech Republic and found Tachau to be in the northwest corner of the former Bohemia. Far from my home in Strobnitz, yet close enough to include me as a member of the clan.

Reading the email discussion of wording for the plaque that the cousins were planning to erect in Tachau awakened in me the rage that had fallen dormant since my last visit to the Czech Republic. I could not agree to the suggested wording: *In Memory of the Jews of Tachau: Our Mothers, Fathers, Sisters, Brothers Who Died under Nazi Oppression.*

Died? For me, the word was too euphemistic. Why not say *killed?* Or *murdered?* Or *slaughtered like cattle?* Or even *exterminated like vermin?* My rage knew no bounds. *"Why are we being so respectful of the feelings of the Czechs?"* I asked. *"Did they not jump at the chance to do the Nazis' dirty work? Had they not willingly plundered and profiteered in the state sanctioned pillage?"*

Anger accompanied me all the way to Marienbad where our group was staying in a resplendently renovated hotel in a town that can only be called idyllic. Its rococo mansions sit nestled in a valley of green, its myriad parks, gazebos, and outdoor cafés beckon invitingly. Like many others, my parents had chosen Marienbad for their honeymoon.

I was excited at the prospect of meeting new relatives that evening. Our dinner was a splendid affair in a picture-perfect setting of crisp white linen, heavy silver candelabra holding trios of flickering tapers, and fresh flowers nestled among the sparkling crystal goblets. Waiters bearing trays of champagne moved smoothly among the assembled group. As each of us stepped forward to say our name, there was a spark of connection that ignited. For me, it was a moment so precious that like Goethe's Faust, I longed to halt the fleeting moment and to call out *"Verweile doch! Du bist so schön!"* At long last, instead of feeling alien and outcast, I recognized myself in the other.

Next morning a bus arrived to ferry our group the short distance to Tachau where a reception at City Hall awaited. As we entered, sweet music greeted us. The local girls' choir, little blond heads serenading the return of the Jews. I was touched by the loveliness of their angelic voices but sadly aware that this was not my music. Both the language and the melodies were indelibly Czech. Did the dapper choirmaster who bowed so obsequiously ever wonder whether the Jews of his town had had their own songs they loved to sing?

Near Marienbad, where romantic ruins from a distant past
provide a welcome escape from recent realities

I was equally unmoved by the pompously inflated platitudes of the mayor whose heavy badge of office dangled ostentatiously from a multi-coloured ribbon. The mayor was not a man given to soul searching. I feared that the plaque we had presented would soon lie buried in a dusty cup-board.

I was happier out of doors where a goat grazed on someone's lawn and a cat dozed in a sun-kissed window box. An elderly woman with an empty straw basket on her arm interrupted her journey to the market to ask why a busload of visitors had come to this small town. Her first words were Czech, but suddenly, she reverted to German.

"I was here," she tells us, *"here in this town when everything happened. I knew the family. I knew the parents and I knew the children. I remember when they all left too."*

Because I was one of the few German speakers in this American group, she took my hand and spoke directly to me.

———

TODAY I SIT AT MY COMPUTER remembering not a word of what this name-less elderly woman said. My mind remains a total blank. I only know that at some point I broke away from her and from the group, that I leaned against a rough stone wall where I wept uncontrollably.

What is it that moved me so deeply that my mind cannot hold the mem-ory? Something of this woman's humanity, something of her very ordinary averageness penetrated my defences.

I came to Tachau laden with anger at those Czechs who sold their hon-our yet now feigned victimization by both the Germans and the Commu-nists. My anger fed on the awareness that some of these self-proclaimed victims had profited greatly from their complicity. Some were now living in the very homes from which our relatives had been forced to flee.

But how can I possibly feel anger at this kind, simple, grey-haired woman, probably no better and no worse than any other? But if not at her, at whom shall I then direct my fury? Systems, institutions, and even Hitler are all too easy to blame. When does this become an excuse to absolve the individual from his or her own personal responsibility?

And yet, my bottom line has long been that it is wrong to lump together all members of any group. That is precisely what the Nazis did. That is precisely the thinking of racists everywhere. Much as we deplore the actions of certain members of any country, religion, or cultural group, it is wrong to tar everyone with the same brush.

I cannot find it in my heart to hate this woman who at the very least may have looked the other way. Somehow, she brings home to me that we are all human. I know that I am not always smart enough, wise enough, or strong enough to do the right thing. I do not know how I would have reacted in those war years. Would I have risked my life and that of my loved ones to protect a neighbour?

———

IT WAS WITH SUCH THOUGHTS pulsing through my head that I continued my journey.

In the years since my first visit, Alois Bayer, whom I had met in front of the church in Strobnitz, had several times phoned and written to me. He wanted to take me back to Strobnitz and anywhere else that I would like to go. I feared that his agenda was neither altruism nor affection for me, but I accepted the fact that his command of Czech and his business-like manner could open doors that would otherwise remain locked to me.

We did go back to Strobnitz, but even his assertiveness could not crack the passive non-compliance of the staff in the archives. There were no records to be had. Alois was deeply disappointed, and he urged me to try other avenues, including writing to former U.S. Secretary of State Madeleine Albright, whose Czech family had hidden their own Jewish connection in order to protect her.

In another town, Krumlau, we had greater success. Here I found numerous items indicating that Emil Urbach had been a leading figure in the Department of Health and the owner of a gracious home nearby.

Further records indicated that Krumlau was the site of Martha and Emil Fränkel's marriage. The certificate bears the signatures of Emil Urbach and of my grandfather, Josef Waldstein.

When we stopped for afternoon coffee, Alois told me more of his own life in the late thirties. He had remembered many more incidents about his years in the *Hitlerjugend*. He saw them as humorous, as boyish hijinks. I listened, stone-faced. Despite my efforts not to condemn, the gap between us grew. It was with relief that I waved goodbye to Alois in Budweis where I had asked him to drop me off.

I spent the evening alone and the night in a hotel opposite the train station where I had so totally lapsed into hysteria on my last visit. I had to prove to myself that I was not enslaved to childhood memories. I needed to face my demons.

———

THE NEXT DAY, I CALMLY took the train to Prague.

In Prague too, I had unfinished business. I had become so accustomed to hearing that everyone in my immediate family had been consigned to the flames that I had not given proper thought to what had happened to Arnold. I had been to Prague without once thinking to look for a grave. It was time.

Early Sunday morning, I rode the Prague subway almost to the end of the line. The underpass led to high walls and a gate. The New Jewish Cemetery. For the first time, I realized that Jewish cemeteries have a common denominator—high walls and gates to protect them from those who would deface and destroy.

A helpful volunteer in a tiny office at the entrance offered to look up my uncle's name. I quickly accepted both his help and his offer to look up all Waldsteins and to give me a printout. To my surprise, there were thirty-two Waldstein names on the list, all buried in this cemetery since its inception in 1891. To my disappointment, there were no familiar names. When I looked at the dates, I understood. There had been so many Waldsteins, but only those who died before 1939 had merited a grave.

Arnold's grave

There was only a single entry for the post-war years. Arnold and Lota Waldstein.

Grasping my printout, I walked down the long gravel path. Section. Row. Plot Number. Then I saw it. Section 23, Plot Number 14, in the very first row. A simple grey stone barely visible beneath the overgrown ivy.

Two names. Arnold Waldstein, 1897-1951. Lota Waldstein, 1912-1994.

I fell weeping to the ground. I lay there for a long time. I cried out a grief that knew no words.

I wept that my father had never crossed the ocean to embrace his brother. I wept that a life had ended so absurdly just when the shadowy hope of happiness had begun to grow. I wept for the uncle I have come to know only through his letters. A man who might have smiled at my struggles and understood. A man whose lessons in living could have taught me so much.

I wept at my own stupidity. Although I was barely fifteen in 1951, I could have urged my father to go to Europe. I could have begged him to send Arnold and Lota a return ticket to Canada. In 1951, I was still too self-absorbed for such thoughts.

What was my excuse in 1990? Why did I not think to ask what had become of Arnold's widow? How could I have remained so unaware? I remember those post-war years and my parents' disappointment that Arnold had opted to remain in Europe. I even remember the upset caused by his decision to remarry. Were my parents capable of understanding Arnold?

I wept because the sense of loss was so overwhelming. My personal loss, but also the world's loss. Six million Arnolds with no grave. What contributions large and small could they have made? Who might have found the cure for a dread disease? Who might have lit just one small candle in the dark?

Epilogue

IN WRITING THIS MEMOIR, I HAVE RARELY allowed myself to think about the Holocaust. I have been to Yad Vashem in Israel and I have visited the Holocaust Museum in Washington, D.C. I have chosen not to visit Auschwitz. Still, sometimes I think about the unthinkable.

Even with conveyor belts, it could not have been easy to move thousands upon thousands of dead bodies from the gas chambers into the ovens. I remember watching a baker in Germany push loaves into a brick oven with a long paddle. Did pushing corpses into the ovens become as routine as baking bread?

Did they wear aprons, those men who gave each corpse its final push into the oven? Did they wear gloves? Were their faces covered with masks to protect them from lingering traces of gas? Who were these men who saw, but did not speak? Were they ordinary townsfolk, eager for well-paid work? Or were they Jews whose only choice was between inhumanity and death?

I think again of my grandfather Josef who had remained cheerful in Theresienstadt, determined to help others with a reassuring hand on troubled shoulders. I imagine him struggling to hold his head high as he entered the gates of Auschwitz. I visualize the living hell that led him to his own truth: *"I cannot live with what I see."* Compassion for his fellow humans led him to stop eating even the bits of mouldy bread and watery soup. Sorrowfully but consciously, he said farewell to a beloved son and to this world.

Yet no matter how noble my grandfather's death, it did nothing to halt the German juggernaut. Until I found Arnold's letter, that death was both meaningless and anonymous. Josef was but one of six million, each one no more than a number. Like the Germans, I too had lost sight of the individuality of each of those numbers.

Is it humanly possible to imagine six million individuals? I see them like candles flickering on a giant birthday cake, all blown out with a single breath of human hatred.

Like a child with a tattered security blanket, I drag the past behind me. It threatens to trip me up, this long strip of cloth woven together so long ago. Still, I cannot lay it down. Not yet. Its usefulness will only come to an end when that past is turned into a meaningful present.

———

ON FEBRUARY 14, 2005, I said the Mourners' Kaddish for Emil.

Yitgadal ve-yitkadash sh'mei raba b'alma di v'ra khirutei.

Traditionally, the ancient Aramaic words are spoken by a son. There is no son, there are no daughters, nor are there brothers or sisters. There is no one but me.

V'amlich malchutei b'hayeikhon u v'yomeikhon u v'hayei d'khol beit yisrael.

I sought comfort in the wailing words intoned by Jews in every land for thousands of years.

Ba agala u viz'man kariv, v'imru amen.

Moments later, someone touched my arm. A gentle voice spoke.

"I saw you standing among the mourners. I saw you struggle with your grief. Have you just lost someone close to you?"

"The man to whom I owe my life."

"Your father? I am so sorry. When did he die?"

"Not my father. This man died in 1945."

Silence greeted my words. I remained lost in my inner world of lamentation. A hand softly stroked my arm until slowly, with thoughts and words still intertwined, I began to tell my story:

Today I mourn an uncle by marriage. Emil Fränkel. I need to speak his name because no one has done so. I do not remember him, for I was too young to retain conscious memory. Single-handedly, he pushed us out of Europe in 1939 and he refused to let us look back, lest we turn to pillars of grief at so many loved ones left behind.

As the nations of the world slammed shut their doors to give Hitler tacit permission to do as he pleased with the Jews of Europe, as leaders and conference delegates basked in the luxury of Evian and the warm sunshine of Bermuda, listening to Britain express fear that the Nazis might change from a policy of "extermination" to one of "extrusion," Emil scrambled to keep his family from the crowded box cars headed for the concentration camps.

It is so easy just to blame the Nazis, or even just to blame Hitler. Yet at some level, the slaughter of Emil and his family required the complicity or at least the silence of countries and individuals everywhere. The Canadian government was scrupulous about conducting polls to ensure its anti-immigration policies reflected the wishes of the people.

In Europe, ordinary people cooperated in myriad ways. Many saw it as the practical way to get ahead economically. Some cooperated because they were afraid to say "no." The Danes said "no" and because they refused to identify or surrender their own citizens, only 500 Danish Jews were transported and only 51 of them died. Over 7200 Jews were smuggled in boats to safety by Danish volunteers.[11] Yet elsewhere, Europeans were jumping on the Nazi bandwagon. Not just Germans but Czechs, Austrians, Poles, Hungarians, and even the French.

Today, everyone who lived through the war claims to have been either a freedom fighter or an angel who hid Jews in the attic. Perhaps it was indeed one of these unsung angels who helped the Fränkels elude the hunters.

While others were quickly snared in the Nazi net, it was not until March

6, 1943 that the Fränkels were shipped to their first concentration camp. Theresienstadt. Teresin, as it is now called by those who seek to destroy the memory of the German imprint upon their soul.

The records I photocopied in Prague had been carefully kept. Four sequential numbers: 60114, 60115, 60116, 60117. First Emil, then Dorothea and Ilse, and finally Martha. The parents' numbers seemed like two bookends, seeking to enclose and protect the children. Together these four people walked through the gates whose chilling inscription still stands: ARBEIT MACHT FREI.

When I visited Theresienstadt, I had to force myself to place one foot in front of the other in order to walk through the archway bearing those mocking words. Like a mantra, I kept repeating, *"Theresienstadt was a good camp, Theresienstadt was a good camp."*

Theresienstadt had no gas chambers disguised as showers. Its crematorium was only for the thousands who died of hunger, dysentery, and disease. Like my grandmothers Fanny and Resl.

Y'hei sh'mei raba m'varakh l'alam u l'almei almaya.

For more than twenty months, the Fränkels survived in Theresienstadt. I do not know how this was possible. I do not know how Martha kept insanity at bay. Though I had nothing to fear, my body shuddered when I entered the dank barracks. My eyes froze as they encountered splintered boards and unidentifiable remnants of metal instruments. I longed to run full pelt from the suffocating stillness of windowless tunnels in the underground warren.

I have read much about Theresienstadt. I have read very little about the Fränkels' next destination. Those books, I cannot bring myself to open.

On October 19, 1944, still bearing identification numbers 60114 to 60117, the Fränkels were shipped to Auschwitz.

I cannot bear to read the books. So many images are already burned into my brain. Piles of glasses and children's shoes in the barracks named "Canada," the land of plenty. Emaciated skeletons too weak to emerge from their tiered bunks as the liberators stare in stunned silence. The two line-ups, those still capable of work directed to the right, women and children, the old and the sick to the left. Emil would have been forced to watch

```
ÚSTŘEDNÍ KARTOTÉKA — TRANSPORTY.
R.č. 9207

       F r ä n k e l o v á   Dorota
                10.7.1938
Rodná data: _____
Adresa před PRAHA XII.Korunní 53
deportaci: _____

        1. transport                    2. transport
dne:        6  III. 1943        dne:     19.10. 1944

         Cv                     číslo:    E S - 1432
                        364
                    č.          do:     O s v ě t i m
I.
```

This transport card for Dorly Fränkel shows her date of birth and
last address, as well as the date on which she was shipped to
Auschwitz (Osvetim). How is it possible that Emil and Martha
kept Dorly and Ilserl alive until November, 1944?

Martha take that final walk, Dorothea in her arms and Ilserl holding her
hand. Did he let himself realize that it was their final walk? The smell of
burning flesh from the crematoria enveloped Auschwitz.

No death date is given for Martha, Dorothea, and Ilse. They would have
removed their clothing, and then gone straight into the chamber where the
Zyklon B gas entered through the nozzle in the ceiling. Death would not
have been instantaneous. The claw marks in the walls of those who tried
frantically to escape bear mute testimony to the agony of those final
moments.

For Emil, there is a place and a date of death. The place of death is
Dachau. At first, I thought it must be a mistake. Auschwitz was in the
dreaded East, in Poland. Dachau is back in Germany, not far from Munich,
the happy, beer-loving Bavarian capital. The date was February 14, 1945.

The day of roses and chocolate hearts has taken on a different meaning for me. No one has been able to tell me why Emil was shipped to Dachau. It is possible that Auschwitz simply could not handle all the numbers waiting to be gassed. It may also have run out of Jews still capable of dragging corpses to the ovens. Fear of the Russian advance led the Germans to expedite the killing in every possible way before it was too late, including transports to other concentration camps and long death marches away from the Eastern front.[12]

1945. Emil almost survived. In the end, did he succumb to exhaustion, heartbreak, and disease? Or did they have to kill him because with nothing left to lose, he defied his captors until the last?

———

THE HAND CONTINUED TO stroke my arm as tears seeped beneath my eyelids.

No one had said Kaddish for Emil Fränkel. My parents had said Kaddish for their parents and I had said Kaddish for my parents. For Emil, there had been no one left.

Not until I read the letters. And now, there is no going back. Where forward is, I am still not sure.

Yitgadal ve-yitkadash sh'mei raba...

———

SOMETIMES LIFE FEELS stranger than fiction. While visiting Cham, my mother's hometown in Germany, I met Max Weissglas, the man known there as "the only Jew in town." Seven years later, I received a phone call from his wife Melanie informing me that her beloved Max had died. I expressed my condolences and thanked her for letting me know.

Many months later, I received a puzzling envelope covered in Greek stamps. I opened it to find the following letter.

Makrygialos, 13.2.06

Dear Mrs. Helen!

I am writing to an unknown woman who was born under the same star.

I am slowly awakening from unconsciousness following the loss of my dearly beloved father Max. I know that you held him in high esteem and the reverse was also true. He often told me so. There was something very spiritual that connected my father and me, something that cannot be expressed in the best of words. He has died, but he is not dead. That gives me the strength to believe in life.

As you know, I have been living for some time in a Greek fishing village 50 km south of Thessaloniki. I chose my husband quite deliberately for being a non-German and left Germany. Since you are a highly intelligent woman, I need not explain to you the whys and wherefores.

Our daughter, now 17, is totally and from the bottom of her heart a Jew. Not in terms of belief but in terms of values and attitude. She looks a lot like her beloved grandfather and he adored her. She (Rebecca) will graduate from high school next year and we are very proud.

These have been important and unimportant lines from a German-Jewish-Greek heart.

If you like, starting this summer, we will be getting an Internet connection. In the meantime, I would love to get a handwritten letter from you.

You are embraced and thought of by
Your Sonja Weissglas-Zampas from Greece.

I was of course flattered that someone I had met so briefly had thought so highly of me. While Max had made a deep impression on me, I had not thought to be able to offer much to a man who had seen the inferno and been scorched by its flames.

Standing with Max, the man locals refer to as "the only Jew in town,"
in front of the former cemetery of the Jewish community,
an impenetrable fortress with a locked gate to prevent desecration

At the same time, I understood his daughter's need to reach out to anyone who might help her deal with the loss of a beloved parent. Still, there
was something about the letter that continued to puzzle me. Surely Max
and Melanie had other friends who knew him better, and surely he had told
me little that Melanie herself did not know.

One day, as I struggled to formulate my thoughts before setting them
down in German, a light went on. I am Sonja's only connection to her Jewish roots. Like so many others who rejected God for standing by while the
Nazis exterminated those who had sung His praises, Max had rejected all
Jewish ties after his experience in the concentration camps. He wanted
nothing more to do with religion.

Sonja had been raised with absolutely no connection to anyone or anything Jewish. Her mother Melanie is not Jewish, and all other Jews in her
hometown had vanished. The handful who survived the concentration
camps chose not to return to Germany.

Sonja had never met another Jew. I am her only thread to a vanished tradition.

Or almost. In her seventeen year-old daughter Rebecca, Sonja claims to see a Jewish soul reborn. What does Sonja know of the Jewish soul? Why did she name her daughter after the great Jewish matriarch? Why does Sonja claim that this child, born and raised fifty kilometres from Thessaloniki has a Jewish heart? What can Sonja know of these matters, and more importantly, why does she care?

Tentatively, I ask a friend. He tells me *"her soul is stirring, that in her father, she has lost an anchor, a wise one who kept her grounded."* He advises me to share my memories of her father, but to tell her also of my own struggle to find my roots.

And so it has begun, this new dialogue between strangers who have not met. Two women of different generations living on different continents who each sought refuge, the one in a Greek fishing village, the other in urban Canadian anonymity. Two women raised in the safest of places and in the safest of times, yet linked by the shadow of the past. We exchange letters and emails. She shares with me the major events in her life, and I rejoice when Rebecca is admitted to the university or when Melanie writes that she will be going to Greece to be with Sonja. At Rosh Hashanah, I describe to Sonja the sound of the Shofar, the ram's horn that seems to shake my very soul. I tell her that we dip apples in honey to symbolize a sweet New Year and I explain why we fast on Yom Kippur.

I catch myself using the "we" word and realize with a shock that I now identify as a Jew.

———

Der Apfel fällt nicht weit vom Baum. When an apple falls, it lands near the tree.

I ponder these words as I look back across the span of years. Even though I was not raised a traditional Jew, I always knew of my Jewishness. Now it is my adult children who say the same. What I did not have was not mine to give. And yet, there is much that was transmitted to me that I have passed on, often in surprising ways.

A remarkable sensitivity to minority rights has surfaced in both of my daughters. Each of them has chosen to balance the scales of injustice in her own special way. Each also shares my abiding gratitude for life and its richness. Only recently did I learn that this is a hallmark of Jewishness. From the moment of waking, our tradition teaches us to give thanks for a heart that beats, for lungs that breathe, for plumbing that works, and for all that is not ours to control.

I have learned so much since I first opened my father's box of letters, I am also putting down roots that draw ever more strongly upon the nutrients of Judaism.

In 2007, for the first time ever, I ventured to hold a Passover Seder in my own home. My parents had never held a Seder. Perhaps it would only have reminded them of all the family members absent from the table. When my daughters were little, my tradition had been to send them on a treasure hunt for Easter eggs. Now, I was inviting them to a lengthy ritual that encompassed retelling the story of our liberation from slavery in ancient Egypt.

To my great delight, they accepted the invitation for themselves and for their partners who each graciously donned a skullcap for the ceremonial evening. Despite the ultra-abbreviated compilation that replaced reading a lengthy traditional Haggadah, it was *My First Passover*, a small hardboard book purchased for my year-old twin grandsons that became prime reading for the adults in my family.

In many ways, perhaps we are all operating at the level of understanding of a year-old child. Once upon a time, especially in my teens and early twenties, I thought I knew so much. Life has been a long process of realizing how little I know, and how shallow are the roots of my strongest opinions.

My life journey feels different now. I do think that at the very least, I am moving in the right direction. Life feels effortless and sometimes it even feels joyful now that I am no longer paddling against the current.

Somehow, alongside of my Jewishness, they live on in me, those family members whose lives were so prematurely interrupted. I have inherited something of their essence along with their stories. They flow through me, and to some degree, they shape me.

Perhaps that has been the lesson learned, this opening of the channels. Perhaps now, the healing waters can flow through me to lap at new shores. I know that this year, when I looked across the table at my twin grandsons dipping slices of apple into a bowl of honey, a tear fell upon my mother's white tablecloth.

Endnotes

1. Abella and Troper, *None Is Too Many*, 102.
2. Koestler, *Promise and Fulfillment*, 55–59.
3. Dirks, *Canada's Refugee Policy*, 58.
4. Davies, *Antisemitism in Canada*, 128.
5. Shapiro and Weinberg, *Letters From Prague*, 39–40.
6. Abella and Troper, *None Is Too Many*, 17.
7. Holocaust Education and Archive Research Team. www.HolocaustResearchProject.org.
8. Wyman, *The Abandonment of the Jews*, 5.
9. Troper, Harold. "New Horizons in a New Land: Jewish Immigration to Canada." Under the Canadian Jewish Experience: Historical Perspectives. B'nai Brith Institute for International Affairs, www.bnaibrith.ca/institute/millennium/millennium01.html.
10. Shapiro and Weinberg, *Letters From Prague*, 119.
11. See the following website for more information on the Danish rescue: http://www.jewishvirtuallibrary.org/jsource/Holocaust/denmark.html.
12. For more about Auschwitz and such death marches, read *Night* by Elie Wiesel.

Selected Bibliography

Abella, Irving, and Harold Troper. *None Is Too Many: Canada and the Jews of Europe, 1933–1948*. Toronto: Lester Publishing Limited, 1983.

Berenbaum, Michael. *The World Must Know: The History of the Holocaust as Told in the United States Holocaust Memorial Museum*. Baltimore: Johns Hopkins University Press, 2006.

Cohn-Sherbok, Dan. *Anti-Semitism: A History*. Thrupp, Stroud, Gloucestershire: Sutton Publishing, 2002.

Davies, Alan T. (Ed.) *Antisemitism in Canada: History and Interpretation*. Waterloo: Wilfrid Laurier University Press, 1992.

Dirks, Gerald E. *Canada's Refugee Policy: Indifference or Opportunism?* Montreal: McGill-Queens University Press, 1977.

Foxman, Abraham H. *Never Again?: The Threat of the New Anti-Semitism*. New York: HarperCollins, 2003.

Gilbert, Martin. *The Holocaust: The Jewish Tragedy*. London: Collins, 1986.

Gilbert, Martin. *Never Again: A History of the Holocaust*. New York: Universe Publishing, 2000.

Hecht, Thomas O. *Czech Mate: A Life in Progress*. Jerusalem: Yad Vashem, 2007.

Koestler, Arthur. *Promise and Fulfillment: Palestine 1917–1949*. London: Macmillan & Co. Ltd., 1949.

Lipstadt, Deborah E. *Beyond Belief: The American Press and the Coming of the Holocaust, 1933–1945*. New York: The Free Press, 1986.

Niewyk, Donald L. (Ed.) *Fresh Wounds: Early Narratives of Holocaust Survival*. Chapel Hill: University of North Carolina Press, 1998.

Paris, Erna. *Long Shadows: Truth, Lies and History*. Toronto: Vintage Canada, 2001.

Shapiro, Raya Czerner, and Helga Czerner Weinberg. *Letters From Prague, 1939–1941*. Chicago: Academy Chicago Publishers, 1991.

Troper, Harold. *From Immigration to Integration: The Canadian Jewish Experience*, Millennium Edition. Toronto: Institute for International Affairs, B'nai Brith Canada, 2001.

Wittrich, Robert S. *Hitler and the Holocaust*. New York: Random House, 2003.

Wyden, Peter. *The Hitler Virus: The Insidious Legacy of Adolf Hitler*. New York: Arcade Publishing, 2001.

Wyman, David S. *The Abandonment of the Jews: America and the Holocaust, 1941–1945*. New York: Pantheon Books, 1984.

Since receiving her Ph.D in French literature, **Helen Waldstein Wilkes** spent thirty years teaching at every level in Canada and in the U.S. Her research interests include cross-cultural understanding, language acquisition and neurolinguistics. Now retired and living in Vancouver, she is actively examining her own cultural inheritance and its impact.

3 3132 03191 1367